CU

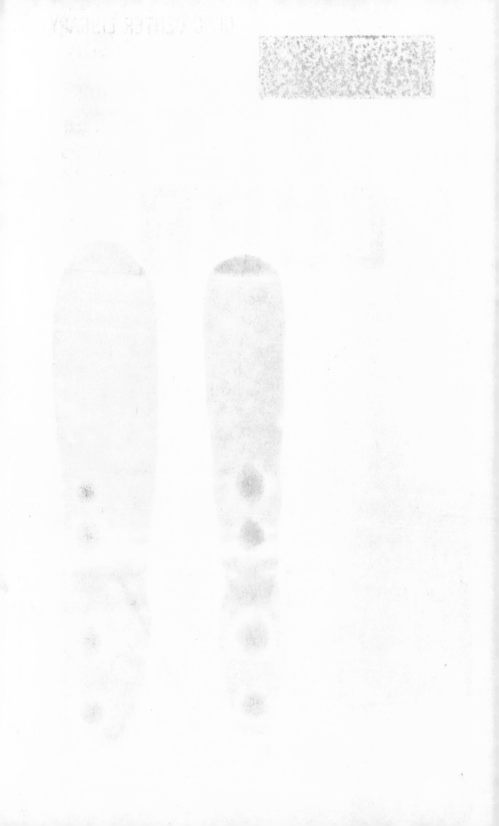

CUBA

THE UNFINISHED REVOLUTION

ENRIQUE G. ENCINOSA

EAKIN PRESS ★ AUSTIN, TEXAS

FIRST EDITION

Copyright © 1988
By Enrique G. Encinosa

Published in the United States of America
By Eakin Press, P.O. Box 23069, Austin, Texas 78735

ALL RIGHTS RESERVED. No part of this book may be reproduced in any form without written permission from the publisher, except for brief passages included in a review appearing in a newspaper or magazine.

ISBN 0-89015-657-3

Library of Congress Cataloging-in-Publication Data

Encinosa, Enrique G., 1949–
        Cuba, the unfinished revolution / by Enrique G. Encinosa.
            p.   cm.
        Includes index.
        ISBN 089015-657-3 : $12.95
            1. Cuba — Politics and government — 1959–   . 2. Counterrevolutions Cuba —
History — 20th century. 3. Government, Resistance to — Cuba — History — 20th century.
4. Cubans — United States — Interviews. 5. Counterrevolutionists — Cuba — Interviews.
6. Refugees, Political — Cuba — Interviews. 7. Refugees, Political — United States — Interviews.
    I. Title.
F1788.E53   1988
972.91'064 — dc19   88-16469
                                                                                      CIP

This book is dedicated to those who have died in battle, faced the firing squads, or drowned in the raging seas. It is also for those who are still alive but have suffered the pain of prison, the anguish of separation, the agony of repression, and who dared to dream and fight for the freedom of a nation.

POLITA GRAU — *Wearing the uniform of women prisoners in rebellion, she smiles for the camera shortly before her release, 1978.*

Contents

Preface

I did not wish to write a book that would be a mere analysis of Fidel Castro's betrayal of the still unfinished Cuban Revolution. A variety of books have analyzed different aspects of the process, from the economic to the political. I did want to write a book that would portray the individual suffering of the people, the courage of those who dared to rebel, the emotional bonds that link Cubans in exile to Cubans still suffering totalitarianism inside the Island. Hence was born the idea of interviewing almost two dozen Cubans whose personal experiences, when combined, can give the reader a vision of the magnitude of the rebellion against the system from the early stages to the present-day struggle. In this sense, the book is unique, for it attempts to give, through the eyes of the participants, a total scope of the revolution still being fought.

Some of the people interviewed are well-known, public figures in the Cuban exile communities; others are known but to a few who have fought alongside them. All of those interviewed spent hours recording their stories on tape, revising the drafts that I produced, striving for accuracy to the slightest detail. As an author, it was not only a challenge to translate hours of memories into coherent, interesting stories but also a thrill to meet in the flesh people of such valor and integrity.

A special note of thanks must be given not only to the ones whose personal experiences appear in these pages but also to others who helped me make contacts, who assisted in research, who helped in the production. Honorable mention is due to Pedro Solares, whose computer skills made my work easier. A special thanks is due to Miguel Jimenez, an Escambray veteran who helped with contacts and advice and who spent days driving me around the streets of New York. I am also grateful to Orlando Gutierrez, who assisted in locating and convincing people to grant interviews. The warmest thanks is due to my wife and two children, who patiently put up with me while I spent hundreds of hours over a nine-month period working on this manuscript.

Introduction

Fulgencio Batista dominated Cuban politics from the thirties to the fifties, moving in and out of power as he wished. A former army sergeant who became a central figure in the "Sergeants' Revolt" which led to the Revolution of 1933, Batista seized power for the last time on March 10, 1952, when he overthrew the government of Carlos Prio in a bloodless coup. Organized opposition to Batista's government began almost at once.

From the mid-fifties to the end of 1958, opposition to the Batista government was carried out by different factions, all of which had a similar strategy of clandestine attacks in the urban centers and guerrilla warfare in the hill regions of Cuba. These included the 26 of July Movement, led by Fidel Castro; the Revolutionary Directorate, led by Jose Antonio Echeverria; the Second Front of Escambray, led by Eloy Gutierrez Menoyo and Dr. Armando Fleites; and the Organizacion Autentica, led by deposed President Prio.

Conditions in Cuba were ripe for revolution. Batista's government was corrupt, and although his army had some efficient, well-trained junior officers, his generals were more concerned with graft than with persecuting the guerrillas. The Cuban Revolution, as fought by all factions, promised an end to fiscal and political corruption, the reestablishment of the Constitution of 1940, free elections, and guarantees of human rights.

Pressured by decreasing support from the U.S. government and by increased guerrilla offensives and underground resistance inside Cuba, Batista fled the Island on the morning of January 1, 1959. In the days that followed, an attempt to form a provisional government using political figures crumbled, and Fidel Castro emerged as the dominant, most charismatic figure of the Cuban Revolution.

Leading a ragged army of bearded, scruffy guerrillas, Castro marched on Havana, politically outmaneuvering and neutralizing those who would oppose him. Although he was loudly promising individual freedoms, democratic elections, and justice for all Cubans, violations of human rights and the basis of a totalitarian society began to build almost as soon as Castro took power.

In the first weeks of the revolution in power, hundreds of supporters of the Batista government were executed. When a revolutionary tribunal in Santiago de Cuba acquitted a large group of air force pilots, gunners and mechanics, Castro personally ordered a new trial, demanding that the men be found guilty. Some 200 men, not allowed to attend the second trial, were condemned to prison terms ranging from ten to thirty years, without a right of appeal.

Cuba in 1959 was gripped by collective hysteria. Some trials were televised, mobs were encouraged to demonstrate publicly, demanding more executions, while magazines devoted many pages to real and fictional accounts of the recent struggle. Some executions were filmed and shown on television. The people of Cuba, the great majority of which supported Castro in that first year, were caught up in a state of frenzy, emotionally justifying whatever was requested as being an edict of the people's revolution. Castro, a mesmerizing speaker, knew how to play with the feelings of the masses, using them as a weapon to wield his power, to consolidate himself as the new strongman in Cuban history.

Within weeks after the takeover, Castro began moving Cuba to the sphere of Soviet influence. Human rights began to disappear; real or potential political enemies were neutralized or eliminated. Mass media, under the guise of protecting the revolution against reactionary elements, were "nationalized," one by one, until only the government media was left to carry one message: the indoctrination of the masses to a new political system. Literacy campaigns were organized just as hundreds of authors' works became prohibited reading by the New Order. At the municipal level, Communists were given key positions which they quickly consolidated by firing subordinates and appointing loyal party members to replace them. The Rebel Army was restructured, and a powerful, repressive State Security machinery was created, as well as a national militia. Soviet agents, diplomats, and technicians began to arrive in Cuba by the thousands to supervise the structuring of the new system, which most of the Cuban people did not understand.

With the beginning of centralized power came the beginning of rebellion. The first organized anti-Castro group was "La Rosa Blanca" (The White Rose) — a small, clandestine group led by former congressman Rafael Diaz-Balart, who had been a Batista supporter and Castro's former brother-in-law.

Castro soon suffered dissent from within his own ranks. The first high-ranking revolutionary to oppose the regime was a young comandante, Pedro Luis Diaz Lanz, the chief of the Rebel Air Force. Diaz Lanz left Cuba in June of 1959, accusing Castro of permitting Communist infiltration into the new revolutionary government. The desertion of Diaz Lanz had a potent impact on the Rebel Armed Forces. Many of the bearded guerrillas were middle-class Catholics who resented the Communists and who had supported Batista for years, until the last days of the struggle. Castro began facing opposition from his own ranks. While Castro was prime minister, one of his early critics in the structure of power was Manuel Urrutia, the judge Castro himself had appointed president of Cuba. Urrutia was to hold office until the promised elections were carried out, but his criticism of Communist influence in the new system brought him into direct confrontation with Castro only months after the defection of Diaz Lanz.

In a staged, theatrical performance, Castro resigned as prime minister on July 16, 1959. In a televised appearance to explain his resignation, he accused Urrutia of treason and corruption. Hysterical mobs were organized to demand the resignation of Urrutia as Castro spoke. The deposed president remained in effective house arrest until he managed to escape to exile months later. By July 26, Castro was again prime minister, had appointed another president, and had rid himself of another critic. In a clever display of demagoguery, Castro had once again manipulated the masses to help himself consolidate power.

By October, the new dictator faced yet another crisis. Comandante Huber Matos, a veteran of the guerrilla war and commander of the rebel forces in Camaguey Province, resigned in protest of the Communist leanings of the government. Castro ordered the arrest of Matos and twenty-eight of his officers. Matos, now exiled in Miami, was to spend twenty years as a prisoner of Castro.

With every passing week, a new purge occurred. Of the six top men in Castro's cabinet at the beginning of 1959, only one remained eighteen months later.

By the beginning of 1960, the first large outburst of resistance began to occur as clandestine movements were organized throughout Cuba and guerrilla uprisings came into being in every single province in Cuba. The new clandestine and guerrilla organizations were created and led by former anti-Batista fighters. The MRP (People's Revolutionary Movement) was led by Manuel Ray, who had been minister of public works of the revolutionary government. The MRR (Movement of Revolutionary Recuperation) was led by Sotus, Sanjenis, and Artime, all former officers of the Rebel Army. The 30 of November Movement was led by David Salvador, a labor leader who had fought against Batista in the underground. Created from the ranks of the MRR, the DRE (Revolutionary Student Directorate) recruited college students, many of whom had fought against Batista. Scrounging weapons from the days of the struggle against Batista, these experienced fighters began a campaign of sabotages, bombings, and attacks that started a civil war throughout the Island.

As dozens of new clandestine organizations were being formed in the cities and towns, guerrilla warfare broke out in all six provinces, particularly in the Escambray Mountains of Las Villas, Cuba's central province. The guerrilla war in the Escambray is the least studied and analyzed of all the stages of the war against Fidel Castro. From its beginning in 1960 until October 1, 1966, when the last guerrilla was captured, the struggle in the Escambray was the most brutal and heroic confrontation of the present Cuban struggle. Hundreds of men on both sides died in battle over a six-year period.

As with resistance units in the cities, the Escambray fighters also came from the ranks of the Rebel Army and the II Front of Escambray, which had fought against Batista. Besides the fighting in the Escambray, guerrilla groups flourished in other provinces.

By its own admission, the Castro government published some interesting statistics in 1970, summing up the war against guerrilla units which had battled the system. According to these numbers, Cuba had during this period of time 179 anti-Castro guerrilla units, with 3,591 men opposing the militia forces. The cost of destroying these guerrilla units had been between 500 and 800 million pesos, costing the Castro armed forces some 500 men killed in combat and an unspecified number of wounded.

While heavy fighting was occurring in the hills, the underground resistance swelled. A number of groups established contact with the CIA. The U.S. government, worried about the Soviets establishing a Communist base within ninety miles of American shores, began assisting some of the resistance groups. The MRR and the DRE were heavily financed by the CIA, while the 30 of November Movement and the MRP were not. The CIA tried to control the group's internal politics at times, rather than simply support all organizations fighting Castro.

With the increased fighting inside Cuba, an exodus began as the middle class fled the Island by the thousands. As Castro nationalized banks and businesses in Cuba, destroying the basis of private enterprise, thousands of refugees began to arrive in Miami. The CIA began recruiting and training thousands of exiles for infiltration and commando missions, as well as for an invasion force which would be trained in the jungle bases of Nicaragua and Guatemala.

With or without assistance from the CIA, the resistance continued to fight. Major sabotages occurred at the electric and telephone companies. Explosions rocked Havana and other cities on a daily basis, while State Security rounded up thousands of suspects and hundreds of Cubans died by firing squad.

In the United States, the Kennedy administration inherited the master plan for the invasion of Cuba originally conceived during the Eisenhower years. The original plan intended for some 1,500 exiles to invade Las Villas Province from the south, landing near the city of Trinidad, to gain control of the area and link with the guerrilla forces in the Escambray Mountains. Before the invasion landed, air strikes would destroy Castro's air force on the ground. As the invasion attacked Las Villas, a smaller force of a couple of hundred men would land at the foot of the Sierra Maestra Mountains in the east and join a guerrilla force that would receive weapons by an air drop. The underground would then receive coded messages, and the resistance units would spring into action. Teams would attack all the police stations in Havana while dozens of sabotages and small operations would be carried out on a national level.

The original plan was never carried out. The invasion site was changed to Bay of Pigs, a swamp area easy to defend only with proper air cover, too far from the Escambray for an easy link-up. Most of the air strikes were canceled at the last minute; those that were carried out did some damage, but enough Sea Fury fighters and a T-33 jet plane were left to destroy the slow-moving, World War II Mitchell bombers that the CIA provided the invasion force. As the assault brigade battled the militia forces on that April 17, 1961, Castro's fighter planes flew over them, sinking their supply and communications ships, blowing the slow-moving bombers out of the sky. While the brigade, trapped at the Bay of Pigs, begged for air cover from the Americans, Castro's planes strafed them, pinning them down as troops massed for an assault against them. In Washington, Kennedy, afraid of the political implications, refused to provide air cover, sealing the fate of the doomed invaders.

The smaller invasion force that was supposed to land in Oriente Province was unable to land, for they found a large contingent of militia forces waiting for them. The unarmed men of the DRE who waited in the Sierra Maestra for an air drop were captured still unarmed, still waiting for their supplies. The underground units that waited for orders to attack never received the coded messages, thus being neutralized. The invasion failed miserably, while State Security rounded up tens of thousands of suspects, filling every jail in Cuba and even many theaters, sports stadiums, and schools that were pressed into service as temporary detention centers.

An embarrassed John Kennedy found himself negotiating with Castro for the release of the 1,100 prisoners of the Bay of Pigs invasion. After one year of negotiations, the survivors of the invasion were traded for more than $50 million worth of consumer goods and medical supplies.

After the invasion failed, guerrilla war and clandestine operations continued throughout the Island. The CIA continued to pump millions of dollars into exile-sponsored operations. Several attempts were implemented by the agency to eliminate Castro, one of which even included the assistance of organized crime. The sovietization of Cuba continued at a quick pace. With the end of private enterprise, private schools, and independent media, Castro was able to centralize his power even more. Every source of revenue, school, and media outlet was under his control. Castro had gained absolute power.

In 1962 an international event occurred that would affect Cuban resistance fighters and exile groups for decades. The Missile Crisis of October that year pitted the two superpowers against each other as Kennedy demanded that the Soviets withdraw offensive nuclear missiles from the Island. For a few days, the world seemed on the verge of another world war. Khrushchev finally relented to the American president's bluff, but not before the Kennedy-Khrushchev Agreement became a reality. The agreement was a pact between the United States and the Soviet Union in which the Soviets guaranteed that no offensive weapons would be placed in Cuba in exchange for the guarantee that the U.S. would not sponsor attempts to topple the Castro regime and would prevent Cuban exiles from attempting the same. The United States had become the guardian of the Castro regime.

The agreement was the death blow to the resistance movements inside Cuba. Without supplies, without equipment, it became almost impossible to carry out an underground war at the level of operations that the resistance had been functioning. MRR camps in Costa Rica and Nicaragua were dismantled. Infiltration and commando teams backed by the CIA were disbanded. The 30 of November Movement kept on fighting, but their resources were limited. In August of 1964, more than 300 members of that organization were captured in a giant dragnet and executed. The movement continued to function until 1967 but without clout.

In spite of the fact that the United States had abandoned the Cuban resistance groups, opposition to the system continued inside the Island, although in a much limited manner. The nature of a maturing totalitarian regime makes underground conspiracy extremely difficult, much more so than under an authoritarian dictatorship. As Castro consolidated his power, movement became increasingly difficult throughout the Island, consumer goods were rationed, methods of private transportation decreased, news was censored, channels of communication were monitored by the system, identity cards were issued, and real or potential opponents were purged or imprisoned. As underground organizations crumbled due to lack of supplies and logistics, for many resistance fighters the only alternative to death or prison was to flee to exile, to continue the fight from a foreign shore.

Exile groups attempted some infiltration landings as well as a number of minor commando raids. Without financial support from any government, some anti-Castro organizations regrouped, stubbornly carrying on a limited war with funding from the exile communities.

In Cuba, Castro had entrenched himself in power; however, his economy was in peril due to poor planning and ideological inflexibility. The flight of the middle class had left the country without a technological backbone. In his politicized system, ideological loyalty was more important than productivity, so production in manufacturing and agriculture continued to decline steadily with each passing year. Consumer goods were rationed to the masses, but the capitalist wealthy were being replaced by a new Communist political aristocracy. As the decade of the sixties ended, Castro boasted that his revolution would create a "new man," an example of Marxist rectitude, willing to sacrifice himself for the collective welfare of the masses without a need for the material incentives prevalent in capitalistic societies.

The seventies started with the resurgence of anti-Castro activity. In the large exile communities in the United States, particularly in South Florida and the New York metropolitan area, a number of exile groups were extremely active. Abdala Movement, a large organization of young exiles, gained headlines by a series of demonstrations geared to bringing international attention to the cause of Cuban political prisoners in Castro's jails. In symbolic demonstrations they took over the United Nations and the Statue of Liberty. Alfa 66, the commando-oriented organization, became revitalized with guerrilla landings and commando raids, which did little militarily against the system but uplifted the morale of the anti-Castro cause. In the early seventies some secret organizations like the FLNC, Accion Cubana, the Cuban Nationalist Movement, and Joven Cuba were all very active in carrying out commando attacks, bombings of Cuban embassies and properties, and attacks against governments that were trading with Castro's Cuba. Accion Cubana, led by Dr. Orlando Bosch, evolved into CORU (Congress of United Revolutionary Organizations), an umbrella movement that coordinated several groups. CORU ceased to exist in 1976, when Bosch was arrested in Venezuela, accused of the bombing of a Cuban airliner in Barbados in which seventy-three people perished.

The strategy adopted by some of these groups divided the exile community. More moderate exiles felt that certain bombings, such as the Barbados incident, were terrorist activities that discredited the anti-Castro efforts by killing innocent people. Groups like the FLNC argued that their activities were not terrorist, for they were aimed at specific targets that represented the Castro regime. In reality, the activities of these groups were often directed by their limited self-sufficient budgets. Without assistance, having to procure their own weapons and logistics, exile groups were forced to carry out low-budget operations rather than large-scale raids or infiltrations. Many exiles sympathized with the bombing of Cuban embassies but were disgusted by the Barbados bombing or by the exiles who were involved in the Washington assassination of Orlando Letelier, a Chilean diplomat who had served in the Communist government of Salvador Allende.

In the exile communities, there was a role reversal. Honoring the Kennedy-Khrushchev Agreement, U.S. authorities who only a few years before had trained thousands of exiles in covert operations now were opposed to increased activities in the exile communities. More than five dozen Cubans served prison terms in U.S. penitentiaries during this period for a variety of charges ranging from possession of weapons and explosives to conspiracy to violate the Neutrality Act. A couple of hundred other exiles would find themselves subpoenaed by federal authorities to appear in grand jury investigations concerning terrorist activities, including an attempted assassination of Fidel Castro when the Cuban dictator visited the United Nations in 1979. During this period, hundreds of weapons and speedboats were confiscated by the FBI and other U.S. authorities as they attempted to neutralize the most aggressive factions of the exile community.

While in the seventies the exiles were reorganizing and attempting to carry on the struggle, inside Cuba a new form of rebellion was coming of age. As organized struggle was becoming increasingly difficult due to the repressive vigilance of State Security and the CDRs (Committees for the Defense of the Revolution), the Cuban people, unable to organize, began individual forms of rebellion against the system. Fighting against lack of material incentives, Cuban workers slowed down production. Forced to work longer hours, they sabotaged machinery. Students, rebelling against political indoctrination and scholarships based on political loyalties instead of academic achievement, began to miss classes. In the early seventies a Castro minister complained on Havana Radio that 80,000 students in Oriente Province were chronically truant from classes. Well into his second decade in power, the regime was unable to create the "new man," being forced instead to create new laws punishing absenteeism in labor centers and schools. The individual rebellion of the seventies, the absenteeism and sabotage became known as "La Huelga de los Brazos Caidos" (The Strike of the Fallen Arms), a passive resistance which required no weapons or explosives but which continued to damage the regime as effectively as any partisan unit ever did.

With a nation unwilling to cooperate or to follow the dream of the "new man," with the price of sugar falling in the world market, and with his economy in shambles due to his capricious planning, Castro found himself in need of pumping money into his faltering economy. His enormous debt to the Soviet Union he began to pay in the mid-seventies by using Cuban troops as mercenaries in Angola and other nations, serving the interests of Soviet foreign policy. To revitalize his nation internally, he decided to promote a "Dialogue" with the exile community. The "Dialogue," which Castro portrayed as a peace plan with the exiles, was only the opening of doors in Cuba to restricted tourism from the refugee community. Hundreds of thousands of the more than one million exiles would be allowed to visit Cuba and their relatives inside the Island for short vacations, paying outrageous tour rates. Radicals, those belonging to militant organizations or with a history of open resistance to the system, would not be allowed to return. The restricted tourism plan was designed to pump hundreds of millions of dollars into the Cuban economy while at the same time weakening the base of support of the exile groups.

The radical exile leaders publicly denounced the Dialogue as a way of strengthening the Castro economy with American dollars, as an immoral stand that admitted defeat to the system. On a more private tone, these same exiled leaders felt that travel to Cuba would provide a legal way of entering the Island for select infiltrators, establishing a bridge of communication to start rebuilding underground structures.

Although it did feed millions of dollars into the Cuban economy, Castro's plan backfired. Not only were some exile groups able to organize limited resistance inside Cuba once again, but most importantly, the exiles that returned for brief visits to the Island had a deep psychological effect on the Cuban people. The millions who had grown up under socialism, feeding on promises but living with rationed consumer goods, overworked and underpaid, were impressed by the prosperity of their exiled relatives. The visitors created doubts in many young people inside the Island, who compared their restricted life of austerity and political rhetoric with the economic success and political plurality of the exiles. Opposition began to express itself among the very young who had grown under the system.

The discontent would lead to a spontaneous revolt of sorts: the incidents at the Peruvian Embassy and the ensuing Mariel boatlift that followed in its wake, in 1980. When a group of Cubans asked for asylum at the Peruvian Embassy in Havana, the Castro government became enraged that the Peruvians granted asylum. As a result, Castro, in a fit of anger, removed his guards from the embassy. Within hours, by word of mouth, the people of Havana began walking through the embassy gates requesting asylum. More than 10,000 Cubans were jammed into the diplomatic compound, like sardines in a can, shoulder to shoulder.

No doubt Castro himself was surprised by the incident. He had tried to create a problem for the Peruvians, but instead the problem had mushroomed into an embarrassing situation. As his army troops surrounded the embassy, Castro declared that he would open the port of Mariel, where exiles from Miami would be allowed to come to Cuba by boat to pick up any relatives that wished to leave the country as well as the "undesirable elements" from the Peruvian embassy.

The offer placed the U.S. government in a quandary and the exile community in an emotional uproar. For the U.S., the unrestricted entrance of thousands of exiles without documentation represented a violation of immigration laws, a potential logistical problem, and a political embarrassment. The Jimmy Carter administration did not quite know how to deal with the crisis. Had Carter tightened up the U.S. borders and forced the exodus to remain inside Cuba, it is possible that the situation would have exploded internally, in riots and mass demonstrations. But Carter weakened and, although he talked loud and threatened, he allowed the Mariel boatlift to proceed.

For the exiles, the situation was emotional. Although many of them wanted the crisis to worsen, to explode into full-scale riots, many others finally had an opportunity to rescue from the totalitarian dictatorship relatives and friends not seen in years. Families that suffered years of separation had a chance to be united once more. From South Florida, a fleet of shrimp boats, sailboats, and leased fishing craft of all sizes headed toward the port of Mariel, west of Havana.

Realizing that the more opponents left the Island the more to his advantage it would be, Castro allowed to leave the 10,000 at the embassy plus thousands of others who had relatives in exile who had traveled to Cuba to pick them up. A large number of former political prisoners and their families were also allowed to leave. To discredit the exodus, to make it appear as though the flight from Cuba was composed of "anti-social scum," Castro ordered thousands of common criminals taken to the docks at Mariel Harbor and loaded upon the waiting boats.

More than 120,000 Cubans arrived in the United States in a few months. With the exception of a few thousand hard-core criminals, the bulk of the new arrivals were hard-working, decent people who were fed up with living in a totalitarian society.

Encouraged by the new arrivals and by the explosive situation that had just occurred inside Cuba, the anti-Castro groups were rejuvenated. Alfa 66, the oldest still active anti-Castro group, recruited dozens of new arrivals, returning them to the Island in infiltration teams to set up new underground networks.

As the Cuban Revolution entered the eighties, rebellion still continued inside the Island. In 1983 more than thirty men and women of the "Grupo Zapata" were arrested inside Cuba, accused of having perpetrated more than 170 acts of sabotage against the system.

Increased involvement in Angola and other areas of conflict created dissension among young men of military age, who did not wish to travel halfway across the world to risk death in a war to protect the interests of the Soviet Union. By admission of high-ranking defectors of the regime, dissent against serving as an "internationalist" in the African wars would cause in excess of 50,000 arrests over a ten-year period, as young trainees deserted from army camps, preferring arrest to death in the Angolan jungles or the Ethiopian desert.

Having received wide criticism for constant violations of human rights, Castro released a number of political prisoners. One of them, Armando Valladares, wrote a book which has become a bestseller in several languages, an indictment of life in the concentration camps of Cuba. The book was instrumental in discrediting Castro among European intellectuals, who for years paid homage to the image of the bearded dictator as a modern-day Robin Hood. Other foes of the sixties, men like Huber Matos and Eloy Gutierrez Menoyo, were released due to international pressure.

The exile groups, entering the decade of the eighties, began to diversify their strategies. Besides the standard, paramilitary organizations, the exiles developed their political clout and their public image. The Cuban American National Foundation, a nonprofit organization based in Washington D.C., was instrumental in obtaining aid for rebels fighting the Cuban troops propping the Communist regime in Angola. Their lobby effort was also significant in obtaining funding and approval for Radio Marti, a radio station sponsored by the U.S. Information Agency to broadcast uncensored information to the Cuban people, an effort of the Reagan administration.

Another significant nonmilitary organization active in battling against Castro in the eighties has been the Congress of Cuban Intellectuals. The organization has generated publicity on an international level, uniting dozens of poets, writers, and professors in creating joint indictments of human rights violations and repression in today's Cuba.

The Castro regime, after twenty-nine years in power, now faces another crisis. In recent months, several key figures of the system have left Cuba, requesting asylum in the United States. Their public statements have rocked the present structure of the Cuban government, as all arrivals speak of discontent within Castro's ranks and of conspiracies among high-ranking officers of the armed forces and even from within the State Security repressive apparatus itself.

Brig. Gen. Rafael del Pino Diaz was a young officer in the Rebel Army who fought against Batista. At the Bay of Pigs, in 1961, he piloted one of the fighter planes that strafed the invasion forces on the beaches. Decorated several times by Castro himself, del Pino served in key positions in the Cuban military and for a time was the commander of the Cuban Air Force detachment in Angola, where he flew combat missions. After twenty-eight years of faithful service, del Pino flew to Key West in a small plane, requesting political asylum for himself and his family.

In his several public interviews, the general has admitted that there is wide discontent in the Cuban military over involvement in Africa, to the point where a number of officers are conspiring against the regime. Besides his statements regarding the massive arrests of young people refusing to serve in the military, del Pino has portrayed a pathetic image of a nation in ruins. While the Cuban masses are denied the most elemental consumer goods, which are strictly rationed, Castro and his select henchmen live in luxury homes, own yachts, are able to buy all the consumer products they desire from special stores.

Another defector, Maj. Florentino Azpillaga Lombard, a veteran of State Security, has been very critical of the system. Azpillaga has said that discontent has reached such a level that a group of officers within the State Security organization itself are actively conspiring against the system. Many hard-working people in the government, he stated, are disgusted with the manner in which Castro values political loyalty above efficiency. Incompetents are given key jobs and instead of being disciplined when they fail, they are promoted because of their loyalty to Castro.

Del Pino and Azpillaga have talked about a failed revolution where the original concepts were replaced by the totalitarian rule of a minority. Both men have predicted that from within Cuba itself, from the bowels of the structure of power, there is a need for change. The Cuban Revolution is still unfinished.

1

GRAVE DE PERALTA: AN EX-COMANDANTE

The Grave de Peralta family has left its imprint on the history of Cuba. Two members of the family were generals who fought against Spain in the late nineteenth century, during Cuba's war of independence. A park in the city of Holguin carries the family name. For a century, members of the Grave de Peralta family have been influential in Cuban national politics.

Eliecer Grave de Peralta is a man in his early fifties who resides in Union City, New Jersey, where he is employed as a salesman. As a young man, he was a comandante, the highest rank in the Rebel Army fighting against Batista. After the triumph of the revolution, he quickly became disillusioned, starting once again to conspire in the underground resistance. Grave de Peralta has fought the Castro regime as a member of the resistance, as a seaborne commando, as organizer of many groups, and as one of the most radical and trustworthy exiles in the northeastern United States.

I joined the Rebel Army when I was twenty-one years old. I have always been an idealist and I was willing to fight for a revolution that would bring to Cuba a constitutional democracy, just social laws, and individual human rights. When historians examine the Cuban Revolution, they must understand that those who fought hardest against Batista were men of democratic principles. The Castro government today, through its propaganda, has attempted to portray our efforts as a Marxist-inspired process but that is simply not true. Many hundreds

1

of officers and soldiers of the Rebel Army who survived the struggle against Batista later became martyrs of the struggle against Castro, dying in combat, executed by firing squads, suffering prison, or having to flee to exile.

I entered the Rebel Army as a private at the time when our numbers were still small. Promotions in combat came fast and by the fall of 1958, I was a captain in Column Number Two, a unit headed by the popular Camilo Cienfuegos, a charismatic man with a long mane of brown hair and a full, long beard.

By the fall of 1958 we knew that we were going to win the war, although none of us expected it to be over by January of 1959. Our units had grown, and for the first time we were able to leave the hills and carry out attacks on government installations in the flatlands. At this time it was decided that the Rebel Army would launch an offensive in which two columns would move out of Oriente Province, our base of operations, cross through the flatlands, and eventually link up with guerrilla forces in Las Villas, Cuba's central province. In Las Villas, at the Escambray Mountains, we had several units operating more or less independently. The bulk of the guerrillas in Las Villas belonged to the II Front of Escambray, which was led by Eloy Gutierrez Menoyo. It was hoped that our invasion toward Las Villas would not only help us consolidate the forces of our organization, the 26 of July Movement, but that we could merge our strength with Gutierrez Menoyo's people, either in a temporary alliance or by recruiting them into our structure.

It was decided that the two columns which would carry out the offensive would be led by Che Guevara and Camilo Cienfuegos. While Camilo would move through the north coast, Che would move his troops through the south in a parallel movement. As we would move through, the bulk of the Rebel Army, led by Fidel and Raul Castro, would remain in Oriente increasing the ambushes, the attacks, and taking over key cities and towns.

At the time, many of Batista's high-ranking officers could be bribed while others, demoralized, avoided combat. Yet, in Yaguajay, in northern Camaguey, Camilo's forces engaged in a battle with an army unit led by a very tough Oriental, a captain named Lee. Lee lives in exile today, but in 1958 we were on opposite sides. He fought very well and for several days we were pinned down in a very bloody battle.

As both columns reached Las Villas at the end of December, I was called to a meeting in Manacas, a small village. The orders came directly from Fidel. In Manacas, Camilo and Che met with the two co-mandantes of the 26 of July in the region. At this meeting, Julio Chaviano and myself, both captains, were promoted to comandante, the highest rank in the Rebel Army. I was told that from small units operating throughout Las Villas two columns would be formed. Che and Camilo would stay in Las Villas, reorganizing and strengthening their units, while Chaviano and I would move through Las Villas and Matanzas provinces in the direction of Havana. Before I moved on, however, I was to participate in the attack on Santa Clara, the capital of Las Villas Province. Batista was rushing a troop train to reinforce the city. We planned to ambush the armored train and attack the city at the same time.

The battle of Santa Clara was the biggest victory of the Rebel Army and the last battle fought in the war against Batista. In a full day of fierce fighting we destroyed the train, captured hundreds of Batista's soldiers, and took over Santa Clara after some heavy house-to-house fighting. Hours after our forces took Santa Clara, Batista left the country with his family and a select group of his followers. The Cuban Revolution had triumphed.

Camilo assigned me to take over Sagua La Grande, a large town in northern Las Villas. When I arrived there with my troops, I was dismayed. Detained Batista supporters were being held in cramped quarters, without toilet facilities. I decided to move them out to a bigger place. As I started to escort the prisoners out, I was confronted by a mob.

They had gathered in front of the building, demanding the lynching of the prisoners. Several of the more hysterical ones advanced towards us, demanding loudly that we turn the prisoners over, to hang them for crimes committed against the people.

I climbed on top of the truck. I cocked my machine gun. "You are not going to hang anyone," I told them, "we fought this revolution for justice, not revenge."

Several of the mob screamed at me, enraged.

"Where were you," I asked them, "when we were fighting in the hills? Up until a couple of days ago these men ruled this town. What did you do then? You obeyed them. And now, when they cannot defend themselves, you want to hang them. No. Nobody will be killed by a mob while I am in charge."

I ordered my troops to disperse the mob. Yet the situation was not defused. Every day some townspeople would come to my headquarters to lodge a complaint against one of the prisoners. Most of the complaints were unjustified.

After a few days in Sagua La Grande, I received a telegram informing me that I had been selected to become part of the Revolutionary Tribunals. The news disgusted me. The few days at Sagua had taught me a lesson. Mob rule had replaced the concepts of justice for which we had fought. Rumors had reached me of mass slaughters of Batista supporters in different cities of Cuba. I did not want to pass judgment or condemn men to death. I did not fight a revolution to become an executioner.

I decided to travel to Havana. Arriving in the capital, I was informed that Camilo was at the Presidential Palace, where a meeting of the revolutionary cabinet was being held. I drove to the Palace, hoping to see Camilo and have myself transferred to another job.

In the hallway I bumped into Che Guevara. Che was dressed in his usual olive green uniform, wearing a black beret. One of his arms was in a cast from a wound received in the last few days of fighting.

"Grave," he asked me, "what are you doing here?"

"I received a telegram telling me that I am to join the Revolutionary Tribunals," I answered, "but I do not want to be involved in that; I am not a judge or a lawyer. I don't have the training for such a job."

Che and I had always gotten along very well, yet he seemed upset by my refusal. Turning to one of his aides, a lieutenant, he gave him the order to disarm me. I was surprised.

"No," I told him, waving back the lieutenant, "this is not right."

Camilo appeared suddenly, also dressed in olive green fatigues, with his familiar cowboy hat. He walked up to me smiling. Camilo had a radiant smile, and with his long hair and beard he looked like a prophet from the Old Testament. His popularity in Cuba was second only to Fidel's.

"What's happening?" he asked, sensing that something was wrong between Che and myself.

I repeated the story to Camilo. Frowning, he took Che aside. They talked as I waited.

"Go to La Cabana Fortress," Camilo told me, "and wait for us."

"Am I under arrest?"

"Of course not," Cienfuegos answered, "I will straighten this whole thing out. Wait for me."

At La Cabana, the old Spanish fortress across Havana Bay, I sat in an office until four o'clock in the morning, when Che and Camilo came back from their late meeting.

Much to my relief, Camilo informed me that I did not have to join the tribunals but that he would arrange a transfer to the Armed Forces Military Academy, where I would supervise the training of new officers. As I drove out of La Cabana, I was relieved that I was to remain in the Rebel Army. But the little incident with Che had also been a warning, a realization that the newly won revolution was involved in its own internal power struggles.

With each passing day, the situation soured more and more. Prime Minister Castro forced President Manuel Urrutia to resign. Communists were being appointed to key positions in government, although they had not fought against Batista and in many cases even supported the dictator.

After three months at the Academy, I was sent on maneuvers. Thinking back on it now, I realize that these maneuvers were designed to keep the malcontents of the Rebel Army busy, away from the centers of power.

In October of 1959, Comandante Huber Matos, the head of Camaguey Province, resigned his commission in protest of Communist infiltration of the system. Camilo was sent to intercede. As Camilo offered a fair deal, Fidel Castro ordered Matos and twenty-eight of his officers placed under arrest. Camilo was privately upset with Fidel, but if he had any misgivings, they did not last; Camilo disappeared mysteriously a few days later during a flight from Camaguey to Havana in a small single-engine plane. Speculation among us was that Castro, jealous of Camilo's rising popularity and angry at his friendship with Matos, had Camilo assassinated. There might be some truth to that story, for Cristino Naranjo, one of Camilo's officers who had launched his own investigation of the events, was killed a few days later as he entered a military base, shot by a guard on a case of "mistaken identity." The guard who shot Naranjo was later shot by a firing squad without much fanfare.

In Havana, I visited the offices of Comandante Diego Paneque, a fellow Rebel Army officer whom I trusted.

"My friend," he told me, "we are going to have to fight in the hills once more."

"I know," I answered, "the revolution has been betrayed."

Paneque told me that a group of officers had begun to conspire already, that weapons and men were being sent to the Escambray Mountains to prepare uprisings.

At first, my plan was to join the guerrilla forces in the Escambray. I was twenty-four and very experienced in combat. Sandalio Cardenas, a good friend and fellow officer, offered to join me. The plotters decided that Paneque and Mimo Gutierrez, who years later was killed in an air raid to Cuba, should go to the United States to help coordinate supplies and support for the resistance.

At Varadero beach, while we waited for a boat to pick up Mimo and Diego, Paneque and Mimo insisted that we should join them on the trip to the United States. Finally I agreed, expecting to return to Cuba with the first boat full of supplies.

We almost died on that trip. A storm caught us in the high seas. Giant waves pounded us. The rain was hard, coming down with such force that it's hard to describe. Our boat rolled from side to side, up and down. Drowning seemed certain. A couple of us contemplated suicide. A bullet in the head seemed a better way to die than the slow agony of drowning. It was a terrible day. Together we had faced bullets and shrapnel in many battles, but we were not used to the sheer brutality of an enraged sea. The force of that storm was overpowering, an awesome display of power that would scare the bravest of men.

A Canadian merchant vessel rescued us, fishing us out of the water. As we sat in the ship's galley, dressed in clean clothes, eating a hot meal, all of us were happy, grateful for being alive, for having survived the most harrowing experience of our lives.

Once in the United States, Paneque and I were taken to the Pentagon to be interviewed by intelligence officials. Much to my surprise, after being questioned for several hours I was offered employment in the U.S. intelligence community.

The offer was attractive; I would spend several months receiving intensive language training and military courses after which I would be commissioned as a major in the armed forces of the United States. The one catch to the offer was that I could not work with any Cuban anti-Castro group but only work in intelligence operations under auspices of the U.S. government.

"If the situation was reversed," I asked the officer who made the offer, "would you work for me without continuing to fight for your country?"

"No," the officer said, "I guess that I could not stop fighting for my country."

"My answer," I told him, "is the same as yours. I am flattered by your offer, but I am a Cuban and Cuba needs me."

Returning to Miami, I went to live in the home of Dr. Orlando Bosch. Bosch had arrived from Cuba a few weeks before, after a dangerous trip from Havana to the Escambray Mountains, where he had taken some weapons to Sinesio Walsh.

Controversy has always followed Orlando, but even his loudest critics admit that the man is totally committed to the cause of Cuba's freedom. Bosch was arrested a half dozen times between 1960 and 1968, eventually being jailed in the United States for an attack on a Polish merchant ship on its way to Cuba. Released in 1973, he organized CORU, a union of half a dozen exile organizations. CORU carried out a number of attacks against Cuban embassies and properties but dissolved after Bosch was arrested in Venezuela in 1976, accused of blowing up a Cuban airliner in Barbados, in which seventy-three people were killed.

For the next eleven years, Bosch remained in jail in Venezuela. He was tried by both civilian and military courts, where he has been acquitted four different times. He was freed only recently on a parole that is practically a house arrest. Incredible, isn't it? Here a man has been proven innocent on four different occasions yet he is not free. Why? Because Bosch is a pawn in a game of international intrigue. Fidel Castro's government has put every conceivable political pressure on the government of Venezuela so Orlando will remain in jail, neutralized, unable to continue his struggle.

When I lived with Orlando in the early sixties, I developed a deep friendship and admiration for the man. Orlando is not just a friend, he is a brother to me. Afflicted with a stomach ulcer, he was unable to be part of the teams of commandos that raided Cuba in speedboats. But nobody worked longer hours than he did, planning operations, seeking funding, buying equipment, and transporting supplies.

I returned to Cuba as planned, on three different occasions, in infiltration and supply missions. After moving to New Jersey, I continued to work with different exile groups.

One of the stories that must be told is that of Dionisio Suarez, one of the exiles with whom I have worked in the past. Dionisio was born, like me, in Holguin but he grew up in Camaguey. From the time he was a high school student, Dionisio was in the underground against Batista. When he was about eighteen, he went to the hills. A tough kid, he was wounded a couple of times and became a lieutenant in

Huber Matos's guerrilla unit. Shortly after the triumph of the revolution, Matos resigned his commission in protest of Communist infiltration of the regime. Dionisio was one of more than two dozen Rebel Army officers arrested with Matos. Condemned to a long prison term, he escaped from the Morro Castle in Havana, making his way into exile. He arrived in Miami in time to join the Bay of Pigs Invasion. Dionisio was a squad leader in the second invasion team, a force of a couple of hundred men scheduled to land in Oriente Province to start guerrilla warfare while the main force landed at Bay of Pigs, in the south central part of Cuba. The second team was unable to land as a large contingent of militia forces waited for them at the proposed landing site.

Returning to the U.S., Dionisio settled in New Jersey with his wife and two children. He worked as a car salesman but continued to be very active with the most radical exiles in the New York metropolitan area. In the mid-seventies he was jailed for refusing to testify at a grand jury investigation of exile activities. Later, after he was released, charges were filed against him as being one of the prime suspects in the killing of Orlando Letelier, a Chilean diplomat who had been a key member of the Communist government of Salvador Allende. Dionisio went into hiding and now, years later, still remains a fugitive of U.S. authorities.

Dionisio is another figure of controversy in the exile community. Some consider him too radical but, as in the case of Orlando Bosch, one cannot deny the man's commitment to his cause. Dionisio could have adapted to the American way of life, made a good living, and raised a family without problems in his life. Yet, since he was a teenager he has fought against dictatorships and communism. Whether one agrees with his tactics or not, one must admire the man. He has been wounded in battle, has suffered jail in Cuba and in the United States, has been divorced from his wife, separated from his children, his life ruined on an economic and social level, and is now forced to live in hiding.

In my years of exile in New Jersey, I worked with Dionisio often. When I last saw him, as he went into hiding, he remained committed to the cause of Cuba, the same idealist that he had always been, since the days when I first met him as a young guerrilla in the Sierra Maestra Mountains.

After all these years of struggle, like Bosch and Dionisio, I remain an idealist. I have fought long and hard and have been betrayed many times, but I still have faith in the Cuban people. Other nations that have suffered communism have surrendered quickly to the yoke of oppression. In Cuba, after three decades, sabotages still occur, conspiracies still go on, even within the system itself, and the people still rebel. Jails in Cuba are still full of dissidents and fighters. As a nation, our spirit of rebellion remains unbroken.

2

FRANCISCO CHAPPI:
HELL AT THE ISLE OF PINES

A man in his early fifties, Francisco Chappi resides in Miami, where he is employed by a cement manufacturer. In his interview, Chappi tells of the most famous trial to occur after Batista fled the country in 1959, as well as the nightmare of suffering two decades in Castro's worst concentration camps as a prisoner in rebellion.

I was not a Batista supporter. I was a first lieutenant in the Cuban Air Force, a career military man, a fighter pilot. As a young officer in the air force, I did not have control over who the president of my country was at any time.

I was critical of Batista. He had seized power in a *coup d'etat* while I was still a student. I also did not support Castro at the time between 1956 and 1958, when he led the guerrilla army to overthrow Batista. I had known about Fidel Castro since his days as a student leader in the forties. I considered Castro a political opportunist. Batista was corrupt, but Castro was a dangerous gangster with a totalitarian ego.

In the late fifties, when Castro was attempting to overthrow Batista, I was a frustrated young officer in the military. As many other junior officers, I attempted to do my job as well as I could, but my efforts were often thwarted. Some of the high-ranking officers were corrupt, accepting bribes to evade combat. Others, who had spent decades in the military, viewed the Batista-Castro struggle as just another confrontation between strong men attempting to seize or retain power. Their apathy was evident. During those years there were many opportunities to defeat Castro's Rebel Army, but the military structure was so apathetic and corrupt that they eventually allowed the rebel forces to control sizeable portions of the country.

Batista fled Cuba on the morning of January 1, 1959. In the first few hours after the collapse of the regime we were told that a provisional government would be instituted until elections were held. Being in agreement, I hoped for the best.

For a few days it seemed as though a new civil war would start between the different revolutionary organizations. Fidel Castro, who led the best organized force, consolidated himself in power in that first week of 1959, promising elections and the formation of a democratic government.

Sitting in my air force quarters, I felt apprehensive. News had reached us that Raul Castro, Fidel's brother, had slaughtered over one hundred unarmed soldiers in Santiago. A large ditch had become the common grave for dozens of Cuban soldiers who surrendered to the rebel forces.

On the morning of January 10, 1959, I was placed under arrest, as were hundreds of others in the air force. I was no longer a first lieutenant. I had become a twenty-four-year-old political prisoner.

Revolutionary trials in those early days of 1959 were often public charades. Some, like that of Sosa Blanco, were even televised. Our trial, the trial of the air force, became the most controversial of all the early trials of the revolution. The group of prisoners that I was with, political case 127 of 1959, was tried in the city of Santiago de Cuba. Our defense attorneys and prosecutors were all officers in the Rebel Army, scruffy and bearded, with shoulder-length hair.

There were forty-eight of us tried as a group in a Santiago courthouse. Some, the officers, were pilots. Others, the noncommissioned officers, were airplane mechanics or gunners. Originally, we were accused of bombing and strafing open towns. During our trial it was proven that eight civilians had been killed by stray artillery shells fired by the army, not by aerial bombings. After several days of deliberating, the bearded tribunal acquitted us of any crime or wrongdoing against the Cuban people.

Our acquittal made headlines in every newspaper in Cuba. I felt elated, hoping to be soon released to civilian life.

Castro, however, felt different. Within hours after our trial, the new dictator ordered a new one, where we would be found guilty. Depressed and angry, we were taken to Boniato Prison in Oriente Province.

Felix Pena, a major in the Rebel Army who had presided over our first trial and was instrumental in acquitting us, died mysteriously shortly thereafter. The government claimed that it was a suicide, but many of us have felt that he was murdered for having acquitted us.

We never attended our second trial for we were not allowed. This time there was no defense, only prosecution. This second time we were judged guilty. All of the officers, I among them, received thirty-year prison terms. Aerial gunners received twenty-year sentences, while mechanics, guilty of tuning engines, received two years. The same sentences were given to other air force men being tried in Las Villas Province.

In those days after we had been sentenced, we cheered ourselves by the thought that at least we were still alive. At La Cabana Fortress, in Havana, Che Guevara's firing squads were executing Cubans by the hundreds.

In those early weeks we realized that our country was facing a new kind of dictatorship unlike any that Cuba had experienced before. Castro consolidated his power very fast. Within weeks he began to move the country toward the sphere of influence of the Soviet Union. Every day his revolutionary government would produce new laws, limiting individual human freedoms, destroying the basis of private enterprise, purging those who would oppose him, even from within its own ranks.

As the sovietization of Cuba began, I was transferred to the prison at Isle of Pines. Isle of Pines is south of Cuba. The thirty-year-old prison had held Fidel Castro from 1953 to 1955, after his first failed attempt to overthrow Batista. Under Castro, Isle of Pines would become the Auschwitz of the Caribbean, a living hell for those of us who became its unwilling tenants.

The prison at Isle of Pines consisted of six round circular buildings several stories high. In the center of each building there was a courtyard. All cells faced the courtyard. The donut-shaped buildings were almost empty at the time we arrived in early 1959. Within two years the "circulars" would hold over 6,000 men, the elite of the anti-Castro leadership imprisoned by the regime.

Although at the beginning we had adequate food, those first months of imprisonment were extremely hard to survive psychologically. I was a pilot, used to flying, used to the open space above the earth. Now, I found myself caged like an animal, mistreated and harassed. I felt frustrated that I was not free in the streets to fight against the system. As time went by, I began to understand why Castro had insisted on sentencing the air force pilots to long prison terms. We had a technology that could be used against him, so by killing or jailing us he neutralized potential enemies.

As mentally stressful as those first months were, I later realized that prison was much easier on me than on many others. I was young and healthy, a single man used to military discipline. In the following years I would see old men imprisoned. I would share space in the circular with men who did not see their families for years. I would see men become insane with the mental anguish and physical torture of our daily lives. Being single, without children, healthy and young, it was easier for me to concentrate on surviving.

With each passing week, our number grew. As Castro limited freedoms and consolidated his power, rebellion began to grow.

One of the new arrivals was Jorge Sotus, a young man who had been a captain in Castro's guerrilla forces. He was the first political prisoner on the Isle of Pines who had actually fought on Castro's side against Batista. Perhaps the guards expected him to be beaten or killed by us, who only a few months before had fought against him. We welcomed him as a friend, a fellow prisoner who had fought for his convictions. Later, he escaped and made his way to exile. He died in Florida, electrocuted in a freak accident while preparing a speedboat for a commando raid.

Sotus would be the first of many hundreds of rebels who would become convicts at Isle of Pines. In early 1960 guerrilla warfare broke out in all of Cuba. Many rebel officers who had fought Batista began to fight Castro. The war in the Escambray went on for several years.

In 1960 hundreds of the captured guerrillas began to arrive at Isle of Pines. Many were peasants who could not read or write. Others were students or former guerrillas of the rebel forces who disagreed with Castro's totalitarian methods.

With every passing day our situation worsened. The guards at Isle of Pines were handpicked for their loyalty to the system and their sadistic streak. They would beat and torture prisoners on an almost daily basis.

Every morning we were awakened at 5:30 A.M. Breakfast consisted of watered coffee and a crusty piece of bread. After this lean morsel, we were taken out in trucks to work in the citrus fields. Armed guards of the elite LCB units guarded us as we worked, picking grape-fruits or oranges. We worked about five or six hours in the morning under the broiling Cuban sun, then broke for a lunch that generally consisted of a plate of boiled macaroni and a piece of hard bread. Lunch was followed by another five or six hours of work. After working ten or twelve hours, badly nourished, we were herded back to the circulars for a cold shower and a dinner of rice and peas. We worked sixty hours a week, with little food, little water, and a lot of mistreatment.

I remember many incidents. A strong wind blew off a prisoner's hat one day while we worked in the fields. The man asked the guard's permission to walk away from the group and retrieve it. The guard nodded, then shot the prisoner in the back as the man walked over to pick up the hat.

While we worked, guards would walk among us. If a prisoner slowed down, the guards would beat him, hitting him with the flat side of machetes or bayonets. A prisoner named Jose Luis was bayo-neted by a guard. The tip of the bayonet sank on his ass cheek and al-most came out through his crotch.

Often, as our workday ended, we had to run toward the trucks while the guards beat the stragglers. Many times the trucks would stop in the middle of a highway; the guards would select a few prisoners and beat them senseless while the rest of us watched.

There was a corporal we had nicknamed Good Luis. We gave him the name as a joke because he was an inhuman son of a bitch. He often forced prisoners to work nude. Working naked under the Cuban sun can be sheer torture. The skin blisters with the heat. Mosquitoes chew at the flesh and thorns prick the skin. The humiliated prisoner would then be told to kneel on the ground and eat grass for lunch. If the pris-oner refused, Good Luis would beat him senseless.

I began to worry about my own survival. Every morning I opened my eyes and wondered what torture I would witness, what beating I would receive, what new humiliation would be perpetrated on us.

The food portions became smaller and often inedible. There were maggots in the rice and more than once we found hairy pieces of ro-dents on the stew. Anything more than a few forkfuls of dried maca-roni was considered a feast. Dehydrating under the hot sun, we became weaker every day. I had several asthma attacks, lost weight, and sur-vived several beatings.

By early 1961 we were no longer taken out to work in the fields. The prison population had grown to about five to six thousand. There were too many of us for the guards to supervise in the open fields. As rebellion increased in Cuba, repression created a living hell in the Isle of Pines.

Now I understand why we were fed so poorly, for healthy men were a threat the guards did not need. The senseless beatings were administered to keep us in fear, to dominate us psychologically.

It is ironic, but there is no one in Cuba as free as the political prisoner. Although we were tortured and starved, we did what the average citizen in the street could not do: we cursed our guards, screamed aloud our true feelings about the dictatorship, fought with our bare fists against bayonets. The average Cuban in the street lives a life of total political compromise in order to survive. We managed to barely survive but lived in total defiance.

Isle of Pines was a major Communist mistake. If they had spread us through the hundred prisons and penal farms of Cuba, perhaps they could have crushed our spirit. Instead, the Model Prison at Isle of Pines became the one detention center where the most radical leaders of the anti-Castro movement were sent. The elite of the resistance movement were housed in those six circular buildings. Physically weakened, in the unity of numbers we found collective moral strength.

On the morning of April 15, 1961, we woke to the sound of artillery fire far away. The men in the upper floors of the circulars could see airplanes flying in the distance. To the north of us, at Zapata Swamp, an invasion force was landing at the Bay of Pigs.

We were overjoyed. The freedom of Cuba seemed close at hand. For several days we were full of hope, until the invasion failed as a result of the Kennedy administration failing to provide the assault brigade with proper air cover.

On the same day, April 15, trucks started arriving. Tarpaulin-covered military trucks loaded with dynamite were brought to the circulars. Soldiers with jackhammers began drilling holes in the columns and foundations of the building. Primacord wire was being attached to the explosives.

Incredible as it seems, every building was being prepared to be blown up. If the invasion succeeded, the Model Prison of Isle of Pines was to be reduced to a mass of rubble, a mass grave for 6,000 political prisoners. We sat in our circulars, behind our iron bars, watching men in olive green fatigues prepare our mass execution, unable to fight for our freedom.

At night, several of the men in our circular who knew explosives managed to disconnect some of the charges. Brave as the gesture was, it helped little, for the amount of explosives the soldiers had set was so huge that one charge alone would have triggered off all the other ones anyway. Every minute of the day we wondered if we were about to be disintegrated by the flick of a detonator switch.

After the failed Bay of Pigs Invasion, the Castro government became firmly entrenched in power. We had never believed that the United States would permit a Communist state within a hundred miles of its shores, but they did; they let Castro survive and consolidate.

Inside the prison system we had our own private war. As we resisted, the Castro government conceived a plan that was meant to destroy the unity of the political prisoner population. They called it the Rehabilitation Plan, but we merely referred to it as The Plan.

The Plan offered better food rations, more family visits, and shortened prison sentences. Promising as it seemed, it demanded that prisoners attend Marxist indoctrination classes, sign documents admitting guilt for their opposition to the regime, and even teach Marxism to other prisoners. Those joining The Plan would be issued blue uniforms, to contrast with our khaki outfits. Those who refused The Plan became known as *plantados,* the stubborn, the prisoners in rebellion.

Those who joined The Plan were given immediate preferential treatment. For the *plantados,* a living hell doubled and tripled in intensity. In order to force us to join The Plan, the guards became more sadistic than ever. Monthly family visits, parcels or letters from our families were discontinued. We were roused from our beds in the middle of the night, beaten in the courtyard with rifle butts and machetes. Sick *plantados* were denied medical care, fed bowls of rice crawling with worms, locked up in solitary confinement for rebelling.

Men locked in solitary spent weeks and months inside small rooms with little or no light. They were not allowed to shower, expected to shit into a small hole in the floor without being provided toilet paper. They often slept in their own urine, on the floor, without pillows or blankets.

Some of the *plantados* would spend years wearing only underwear, rather than join The Plan and wear a uniform which meant a moral submission. Rather than admit defeat to the enemy, many *plantados* died in the attempt to retain the last shreds of human dignity. Even animals deserved better treatment than what the *plantados* were subjected to at the Isle of Pines.

Under such harsh treatment, thousands of prisoners cracked and joined The Plan. I never blamed them. Many of those men who joined the rehabilitation program were veterans of many months of beatings, mistreatment, and malnutrition. Men who had received no news from their relatives for many months were being offered to see their loved ones once again. The offers were tempting and the alternatives were only guarantees of further beatings and starvation.

Most who did join The Plan saw it as a charade, a game to be played in order to secure an early release. Others saw The Plan as a means of transferring out of the Model Prison to a penal farm in the mainland, where escape would be possible.

One of my best friends was Lino Lopez Quintana. He had been a captain in the Rebel Army fighting against Batista. An idealist of deep moral convictions, he had opposed Castro's sovietization of Cuba. Arrested in an underground conspiracy, Lino became one of my cellmates at the Isle of Pines. He and I made plans to escape, but were unable to carry them out.

Lino was always hoping for an opportunity to escape. His wish came true when he was transferred to a penal farm in the mainland from which he eventually managed to flee. Sadly, his brief freedom ended when he was killed by Castro's troops while trying to sneak into asylum at the United States naval base at Guantanamo. I was saddened by his death, for he was a brave man and a good friend.

As the regime increased its pressure, we fought back in every way we could. A young engineering student named Pedro Luis Boitel became instrumental in organizing resistance among the prison population.

Boitel had fought in the urban network against Batista. Fleeing persecution, he had lived briefly in Venezuela, where he became instrumental in radio, broadcasting anti-Batista propaganda to Cuba. After the triumph of the revolution, Pedro Luis returned to Cuba, where he went back to study at the University of Havana. It was at the university where he became a critic of Castro, opposing the regime in public, refusing to yield to threats. Eventually forced underground, he fought until captured, being condemned to forty-two years imprisonment.

At the Isle of Pines, Boitel began to organize the prisoners, reinforcing among the stubborn *plantados* the seed of organized resistance. He was a medium-height youth, with curly hair and good manners, full of charisma, loaded with vitality, gifted with an iron will.

We began hunger strikes to protest our inhumane treatment.

Those of us who were religious began attending clandestine masses offered by a priest, a Franciscan named Angel Loredo. We intensified our
study groups. Since before the Bay of Pigs Invasion, political prisoners
at the Isle of Pines had formed study groups to fight the stagnation of
being incarcerated. The educated prisoners would teach others whatever they knew. As time passed we developed an impressive curricu-
lum. A *plantado* could learn English, German, French, Italian, and
even Japanese. He could study philosophy, history, religion, or math-
ematics. These intellectual exercises united us mentally, entertained
us, helped us distract our minds from the horror of daily living at the
Model Prison.

One *plantado* that I shall never forget was Roberto Martin Perez.
He was captured in 1959, in a shootout in Las Villas Province, where
he had landed with a plane full of weapons meant for the underground.
He was a young man in his early twenties, with a lot of dignity. The
guards hated him because his father had been a colonel in the National
Police before Castro. The guards took their hate for the father out on
the son, but he was tougher than they expected. Even through the
worst beatings and humiliations, he never cracked. To Martin Perez it
did not matter whether a man had supported Castro or Batista. He
worked for unity among the prisoners.

At Isle of Pines we had a guard that we had nicknamed Champion. He was a strong bull of a man who enjoyed punching out prisoners. On a certain occasion Champion beat a young prisoner badly, almost killing him. From the circular, Martin Perez screamed out:
"Why don't you fight me, Champion? I'll fight back!"

Champion was enraged. He accepted the challenge. Both men
squared off in the courtyard, while guards and prisoners watched. Roberto was a man of great physical strength, and he fears no one. Although he knew that beating Champion would only bring him more
torture from the warden, he fought with the daring of a *plantado*. He
beat the hell out of Champion, who staggered away bloody.

Seconds after the guards had intervened, Champion grabbed a
weapon with obvious intention of killing Martin Perez. Luckily, a
lieutenant of the guards, who apparently did not like Champion, intervened.

"It was your fault," he said to Champion, "you gave him the
chance to humiliate you."

That night, in spite of the hunger and the cold, we slept happier.
A fistfight, insignificant as it was, provided a moral victory to our tortured souls.

Requisas were rousting searches conducted by guards with surprising regularity. Rousted out of bed in the middle of the night, we would be marched to the courtyard to receive a beating while other guards searched our cells for contraband. Contraband would be interpreted, by their definition, as family letters, smuggled books, anything that the guards felt we should not own.

The toughest *requisa* I remember was in September of 1962. The guards announced that a *requisa* would be carried out, but without violence. Because of that announcement the prisoners would always refer to that day as *La Pacifica* (the Peaceful One). We had been on a hunger strike, thousands of us. It was a protest because for months we had not been allowed visitors or even letters from our relatives. United, we represented a challenge. The death of several thousand men by starvation would mean an international scandal for the regime. *La Pacifica* was the authorities' counterpunch.

On the morning of the *requisa* we woke to find an army at the gates of the Model Prison. Tanks, armored cars, jeeps, and trucks surrounded the penitentiary. Hundreds of LCB units and army troops armed to the teeth stood ready for combat. Cuban radio stations were announcing that a full-scale riot had taken place at the Isle of Pines Model Prison. We understood the message; if we fought back with our fists, we would be slaughtered and the massacre would be justified as the squelching of a riot.

We were placed naked on a side of the courtyard, where guards with machine guns held us at bay. Squads of guards began moving through the circulars. Cell to cell, floor by floor, they emptied out every square inch of the circular.

Sleeping pallets were thrown from the sixth floor to the courtyard below. Books, clothing, shoes, underwear — everything we had, including spoons and toothbrushes, was thrown into a gigantic pile. We were sent back to empty cells, naked. Our possessions were taken away by trucks. We were not issued any clothing or sleeping pallets for several days.

La Pacifica was one of many unforgettable days at Isle of Pines.

Life at the Model Prison became a nightmare routine, a bad dream that stretched for years. Prisoners were maimed and beaten, others went insane or committed suicide. A guard we called *Perro Prieto* (Black Dog) shot a prisoner at the rock quarry. Eloy Gutierrez Menoyo, a one-time top leader of the struggle against Batista, was given a brutal beating in which all his ribs were broken. Sick men were denied treatment or only given light medication to mend serious injuries.

It is impossible to describe in full detail the horror of the Cuban concentration camps. At La Cabana Fortress in Havana, Cuban political prisoners had the blood drained from their bodies before they faced the firing squad. The plasma was then shipped to North Vietnam, as a donation of the Castro regime to Hanoi.

I survived asthma, parasites, and dysentery, as well as several beatings. In 1964 I was made to run between two lines of armed guards who whipped me with clubs and the flat side of machetes. I spent two years without being allowed to receive a letter or a visitor. I ate food that was not fit for human consumption. I continued to refuse to join The Plan.

By 1967, Castro had come up with a new whim. The Isle of Pines was to become the Isle of Youth, a gigantic indoctrination center for young Marxists, children living away from the parental influence of the family unit. To us, it meant the end of the Model Prison. The circulars would be closed and the prisoners would be sent to the dozens of other penal facilities in Cuba.

In 1967 I left the Isle of Pines with the last group of prisoners to be transferred out of the Model Prison. After eight years of hell, I did not know what the future held, but I knew it could not be worse than the suffering I had already endured.

I was sent to Sandino 3, on the western tip of Cuba, in Pinar del Rio Province. Food was still horrible and beatings were still frequent, but not nearly as sadistic as they had been at Isle of Pines.

At Sandino 3, the ground was soft dirt with a high content of sand. It was easy to dig, so we planned escapes by tunneling. The problem with escaping from prison in Cuba is that once a man escapes from within the walls that hold him, he faces another giant prison which is the country itself. National identity cards, food ration cards, and travel permits are needed to move throughout the Island. Lacking documents, food, and money, the escaped convict was usually quickly caught by the saturation of roadblocks that followed every escape.

There were, however, some who did escape. In August of 1969, while Sandino 3 was being lashed by a tropical hurricane, ten men escaped. One of them, Fernando del Toro, was captured several days later. Facing interrogation and torture, del Toro killed himself by cutting his own jugular rather than squeal on his friends.

Locked up as we were, the prison system had, and still has, an efficient grapevine. In spite of the censorship and repression, a network of relatives and friends smuggled news and messages back and forth among the prison community. Through the grapevine I learned of the death of Carmelo Cuadra and the brilliant engineering student Pedro Luis Boitel, allowed to starve to death in May of 1972. The grapevine also brought us the news of the Boniato Prison Massacre in 1975, when several *plantados* were machine-gunned in cold blood. We also learned of a new system of torture being used to break the men at Boniato Prison: the drawer cells and the *tapiados,* or boarded-up rooms.

The drawer cells were boxes the size of telephone booths, where prisoners were locked up for months. Men had to sleep squatting or standing, spending days without being able to walk. Bowel movements were done through a small hole in the floor. After weeks in these drawer cells, the prisoners came out stumbling, hardly able to walk, bearded and filthy, covered with sweat, grime, and their own waste. The *tapiados* were locked up in boarded-up cells, so dark that a man could not see his own hand in front of his face. Sleeping and eating in their own defecations, men lost all sense of time. Minutes, hours, days, and weeks all became one long night of blindness. Many of those who suffered this punishment became vision-impaired or lost their sight altogether.

After Sandino 3, I was transferred to Cinco y Medio and eventually to Pinar del Rio Prison, where I spent several years. Trying to convince us die-hard *plantados* to join The Plan, the authorities offered us monthly passes to visit our relatives, but we continued to refuse. Indeed, the only times I ever left prison during all my years in Cuban jails were in 1976, when I was allowed, with an armed escort, to visit my ailing father and later to attend his funeral.

By the mid-seventies, Castro's regime was beginning to receive some international criticism for violation of human rights. With the economy in shambles and the nation in a state of bankruptcy, Castro began to promote a "Dialogue" with Cuban exiles.

Inside the prisons of Cuba we viewed the Dialogue as an attempt to divide the exile community in the same way that The Plan had attempted to divide the political prisoners. Castro claimed that he would allow thousands of exiles to visit their relatives in Cuba in a "family reunification." The semantics merely meant that he needed money quickly and he would allow anguished, homesick exiles to pay outrageous fees to visit relatives in weeklong trips, pumping millions of dollars into his faltering economy. A few exile groups and individuals in the exile community let themselves be used by the Dialogue. Some, no doubt, were well-intentioned people who wanted the release of certain prisoners or a few meager concessions. Others were opportunists, looking to make blood money from an emotional situation, while others were obvious agents of the Castro government, carrying out orders.

Although all the political prisoners in Cuba realized that Castro's new political charade could benefit them, shorten their sentences, and even provide a bridge to travel out of the country, we remained united. We would accept an open door if the door was opened, but never would we compromise to help it open.

I became one of the hundreds of lucky ones. I left Cuba on September 14, 1979, after spending twenty years, six months, and sixteen days in Castro's dungeons. I survived hell and spent the best years of my youth caged like an animal, but I hold no ill will, for I have learned that hate is a cancer that drives men insane. But I am also conscious that communism is the most insane and inhuman political and philosophical system. As this interview is being done there are still *plantados* suffering in Boniato, El Principe, and other jails. There are still Cubans being arrested, human rights being violated, bloody *requisas* being carried out.

The story of cruelty and sadism in Cuban political detention centers does not end with my narrative, for mine is just one memory, one little story among many thousands.

3

HIRAM GONZALEZ:
THE ESCAPE ARTIST

He is a medium-sized man with a warm smile and smooth skin with few wrinkles. His hair is ash blond, curly.

At the age of fifty-one he is a successful building contractor in Miami. Among anti-Castro groups, Hiram Gonzalez is a well-known figure of legendary proportions. What follows is only a short account of his days as the most hunted man in Cuba.

I became a revolutionary while I was still a teenager. I did not become a revolutionary out of a sense of adventure but out of conviction. Batista had taken power in an illegal manner, overthrowing an elected government. His government was fiscally and morally corrupt, and a revolution was necessary. Filled with idealism, I joined the underground network of the 26 of July Movement, led by Fidel Castro.

The first time that I was arrested was in 1958. I went to a clandestine meeting where I was to meet Pedro Aponte, a labor leader who was active in the resistance.

As I approached the apartment, I saw that the front door was opened wide. I walked slowly and peered inside. A large man was inside the living room. He was smiling, as though he was enjoying himself. He beckoned me with his hand to come in quietly, as though he were playing a practical joke on someone, perhaps on Pedro.

Being inexperienced, I was duped by the man's affable manners.

As I walked in, he nailed me with a vicious punch, dropping me hard. He was a big, beefy man and I was a rawhide little featherweight. Although he was bigger than me, he was not about to play games. A big revolver appeared in one of his hands.

"Where is Pedro?" I asked.

"He was killed right here," the man answered.

I looked around. There were no traces of blood or a struggle. I suspected that the man was bluffing.

"If he was killed," I said, "then you cleaned up the place very fast. I don't see any blood around here."

He hit me again. White spots danced before my eyes. The barrel of the revolver moved closer to my face. I felt the metal jamming against my teeth, then sliding over my tongue. Through my haze, I saw a thumb cock back the hammer. The man began cursing at me. I did not move nor did I argue. With the barrel of a cocked .45 in my mouth, I was willing to agree with almost anything this man said.

I was taken to a police car waiting outside. Richard Heredia, a young university student about my age, had also been arrested. As I approached the vehicle my captor hit me again, a brutal blow to the side of the ear. It ruptured my eardrum. I went down on my knees, dazed. Looking up I said: "Hey, man, you punch pretty hard."

Taken to the Bureau of Investigations, the arresting officers kicked me in the kidneys as I walked up the stairs. I was placed on a chair in a hallway, waiting for my turn at interrogation.

I sat in that hallway, wondering what would happen now. A policeman walked down the hallway in my direction. As he passed me, he slapped me, then kept on going. A second one walked by and hit me, my head bouncing against the wall. Soon it became evident that every cop walking down the hall was going to use me as his personal punching bag. I began to lose count of how many times I was punched, kicked, or slapped in that hallway.

Eventually I was placed in a jail cell to await interrogation. The wait, no doubt, was meant to scare me, to intimidate me to the point of confession. While waiting, I was able to think and plan ahead. I decided to play innocent, no matter how rough the interrogation became, for I knew that would be my only chance of survival. A confession could mean death by torture or a bullet in the back of the head.

The interrogation began at six in the morning. A major named Medina was in charge of the questioning.

"Why did you go to that apartment?" he asked.

"Looking for a woman. I had a date."

"But you had very little money when we arrested you. You need money for a date."

"I work on credit," I answered, "besides, I wanted to make plans for the weekend."

Medina handed me a piece of paper and a pencil. "I want you to write about yourself," he said, "and write me a list of all the 26 of July Movement members that you know. I'll give you one half hour."

I was left alone, staring at the paper. Picking up the pencil I began to write a narrative about how I had been arrested by mistake when I was looking for a date. I admitted not being a Batista supporter, but denied belonging to the resistance.

Medina and other policemen came into the room. I was sitting across from him. Two burly cops stood on either side of me. The captain picked up the paper and started reading it. His face became flushed.

"What is this shit?" he said.

"The truth. I told you the truth. I don't know anything about the 26 of July Movement. I am not a brave man. I don't have the balls to fight against the government."

One of the cops hit me on the right side. I went down. Something hurt like hell. I knew I had a broken rib. I opened my mouth but could not talk. I was gasping for breath. Medina hit me in the face and I sat there, stunned, hearing a voice saying: "We are going to tear his head off."

The following day I underwent a second interrogation. Four policemen kicked and punched me in a closed room. I did not resist or try to fight back. The best way to survive a beating is to relax the body, to roll with the kicks and punches. I was bounced from wall to wall like a rubber ball. One cop grabbed me in a choke-hold, squeezing until I passed out. I opened my eyes and the squeezing started once more. Everything went blank and I passed out a second time. The choke was loosened. Air pumped into my lungs. I opened my eyes. The squeezing started again, and everything went black for the third time.

I was beaten on a daily basis. Six days, six beatings. Seven days, seven beatings. On the eighth day I was released.

I walked out of the Bureau building with a ruptured eardrum, a broken rib, and a body covered with bruises and welts. I was sore, but I was alive and I had kept my mouth shut in spite of the beatings. I was no longer a teenager playing revolution. I had graduated to a higher level.

That night, as I was being treated, my ribs taped tightly, I realized that I could not remain in Havana. I was burnt-out as far as the underground was concerned, for Batista's police would have me under surveillance.

That weekend I traveled east, to the Sierra Maestra Mountains. In October of 1958 I joined the guerrilla forces of Comandante Huber Matos. I left the clandestine life in exchange for the open warfare of the hills.

I saw three months of heavy fighting in Oriente and Camaguey provinces. Batista's government was crumbling quickly and our troops were on the offensive. We ambushed military patrols, derailed trains, blew up bridges and, in the last weeks of '58, we left our mountain hideouts to take control of cities and villages.

The war ended with the coming of the new year. Batista fled in the night and our troops raced toward Havana. We were a bearded, ragged lot. We dressed in olive green uniforms adorned with beads and religious symbols. On our heads we wore black berets, cowboy hats, bandanas, and captured army helmets. We had shoulder-length hair, handlebar mustaches, ragged beards, and an assortment of weapons that included machetes and bandoliers of bullets crisscrossing our chests.

As we moved toward Havana, our guerrilla columns were mobbed everywhere we went. Old women hugged us, young girls kissed us and gave us flowers to adorn our jeeps and hats. When we stopped, townspeople brought us containers of hot food, gifts. Little children asked us for autographs.

It was a time of joy, of incredible happiness. I was twenty years old, a lieutenant in the army of liberation. I felt on top of the world, a free man in a free country. I walked with a strut and a smile.

I was assigned to Camaguey Province, where I became the editor of *Cuba Nueva* (New Cuba), a magazine published by the Rebel Army in our province.

In those first months of '59, things happened quickly. Looking back on it now, I realize how fast the country was moving toward communism, how fast Fidel Castro was selling out the democratic principles of the Cuban Revolution. At the time, however, it seemed as though an internal struggle and political backstabbing was occurring at the highest levels. I, among many others, felt that Raul Castro, Fidel's youngest brother, was the one influenced by the Communists. We trusted Fidel, feeling that he was surrounded by bad influences which were harming the Cuban Revolution.

In June of 1959, I wrote an editorial in *Cuba Nueva* which read: "As our leader Fidel Castro has stated, our revolution is as green as the palm trees of our country. We can neither go to the American Embassy to receive orders from the Yankee ambassador, nor can we go to Moscow to receive orders from the Soviets who crushed the dream of freedom of the Hungarian people."

A few days later I received a visit from Osmani Cienfuegos. Osmani was then director of the Ministry of Culture. We had a brief conversation in which I was told that "this is not the moment to write such editorials." I did not argue much, but I began to see Osmani as one of those who wanted Cuba under the sphere of Soviet influence.

Shortly after Osmani's visit, I resigned my army commission. Packing away my olive green uniform, I left the flatlands of Camaguey, heading for Havana. Once again a civilian, I enrolled at the University of Havana and went to work as a labor organizer in a graphic arts publishing union.

The revolution that Castro had claimed to be "as green as the palm trees" was quickly turning like a watermelon — green on the outside and red on the inside.

By October of '59 the Rebel Army faced its first serious crisis. My old commander, Huber Matos, wrote a public letter denouncing Communist infiltration into the new government. Matos, a former schoolteacher, resigned as provincial commander of Camaguey. In a fit of rage, Castro accused Matos of treason. The former schoolteacher and twenty-eight of his officers, all of whom had been my friends in the war against Batista, were arrested. Matos would spend the next twenty years of his life in a Cuban prison.

The Matos affair was a milestone for me. It began to open my eyes to the sad reality of what was happening. A few days later I had a talk with Pedro Aponte, the labor leader who had fought alongside me in the resistance and in whose house I had been captured by Batista's police. Pedro told me the new government did not want labor strikes in the factories, for now the government would mediate in our behalf against management. The idea seemed preposterous to me, for I had always believed in the right of labor to organize and strike when needed. I became suspicious of the increased government control over every facet of Cuban life.

When the First Congress of the Confederation of Cuban Workers (CTC) came, in the winter of 1959, unity was imposed by the revolutionary government on behalf of the Communists. A number of labor leaders were extremely upset, but Castro still enjoyed immense popularity and in that first year anything that Castro wanted, Castro got, without opposition or complaints.

At the beginning of 1960, Pedro Aponte called me. He arranged for a meeting with David Salvador, secretary general of the CTC, who had asked to see me in private. I had not seen David for months, but I considered him a very good friend, a fearless freedom fighter who had fought against Batista in the underground. When we met, he had just returned from a trip to France representing the new regime.

The meeting took place in an apartment in Havana. Aponte took me there, leaving David and I alone. We sat across from each other, engaging in a few pleasantries until he decided to move the conversation to a more serious level.

"What do you think of the revolution now?" he asked, point-blank.

"I think the Communists are trying very hard to seize power," I answered.

"And Fidel? What is your opinion of him?"

"He is badly influenced," I answered, "he is not aware of all the bad things that are happening."

"What would you say if I told you that Fidel is a Communist?"

I stared at David. He seemed serious.

"I can't believe that, David."

"Believe it, Hiram. The revolution has been sold out. I have been at those private meetings. I have heard Fidel talk. The country is being sold out."

I'll never forget that moment with David. I sat there stunned. I felt hollow and lonely. Everything that I had fought for was being betrayed, sold, given away. I began sweating. I thought about all my friends who had been killed fighting against Batista . . . they had died for a dream, for a principle. And now the dream was out of reach once more. I had fought against one dictator to replace it with another. I felt used, angry, and confused.

"Are you sure?" I asked.

"Yes," he said, "I'm sure."

"So what do we do now?" I asked, knowing what the answer would be.

"We fight," he answered, and we both nodded, knowing what it meant.

We met again a week later. David was beginning to organize a new movement, a resistance organization with roots in the Cuban labor movement. It was to be a revolutionary organization, not a counter-revolutionary group. We saw ourselves as the real representatives of the Cuban Revolution, trying to rescue the democratic ideals of our original struggle.

The organization was to be named the 30 of November Movement. The name had special significance, for on the 30 of November of 1956, an uprising had taken place in the city of Santiago de Cuba against Batista. The uprising had failed, but it had marked the beginning of an open struggle against the dictatorship. By naming our group in honor of that struggle, we were publicly asserting ourselves as revolutionaries continuing an unfinished revolution. With such a name, Castro's propaganda machinery would have a tough time convincing anyone that we were pro-Batista henchmen or fascist-oriented.

In that second meeting, David outlined that he had structured the base for a clandestine network. Key contacts had already been established in several labor federations and student centers. Trusted men were being assigned to head different sectors on a national level: one man would be in charge of supplies, another of propaganda, while others would fill out spots in logistics, intelligence, communications, military, and finance. Every national coordinator would supervise provincial sector leaders who, in turn, would command local units through a system of couriers and liaisons. Like all clandestine organizations, it would work on a need-to-know basis. Although David expected several thousand men and women to become involved in the underground, no member would ever know more than half a dozen others to insure the safety of the internal structure.

As he talked, I sighed. I was twenty-two years old and about to start fighting my second war. This time I'd be fighting men who had been on my side before, people with whom I had shared meals, hardships, and suffering only a couple of years before. This time, I also knew, the war would be against communism, a much harder foe than Batista ever was. As David Salvador talked I began to wonder whether I would survive this second war.

"Where do you want me to work?" I asked him.

"I want you to be the national military commander of the network."

I swallowed hard, very hard. The military commander of the movement is the most dangerous of all jobs in any underground unit. Accepting the job was tantamount to signing my own death warrant.

My life expectancy would be a few weeks or, at best, a few months. It was a job for a Kamikaze.

"David," I said, "you are giving me a hot potato."

He nodded. "I need you there. I need someone I can trust."

"I'll do it," I said, knowing that I was letting my heart rule my common sense.

In February of 1960 we began to function as an organization. I recruited several top, experienced underground fighters to set up my network. Two of those men were Edgardo Valle and Alberto Perez, affectionately referred to as "The Diabolics." Both in their early twenties, they were experts at the manufacture of explosive devices. I sent the two of them on a tour of Cuba. In each of the six provinces of the Island, they trained teams in the use of explosives and sabotage. They traveled the Island, using assumed names, and trained those operatives that the newly appointed regional coordinators had handpicked for training.

Upon their return to Havana, I decided to keep "The Diabolics" as a team, so I began to make arrangements to set up another clandestine bomb factory in Havana, besides the other two at work at the time.

Since the 30 of November Movement was an independent group not financed by the CIA, it was very difficult for us to obtain explosives. So we improvised.

At the time, in 1960, it was still easy to obtain certain chemicals. Red minium, which is used in the manufacturing of paints, when mixed with aluminum dust at a nine-to-one ratio, becomes a very effective explosive mix. Placed inside a can, with a detonator, it makes a bomb strong enough to open up a hole in a cement block wall.

I had my men visit every hardware store and building supply house in Havana, buying up red minium and aluminum dust. We stored more than a ton of chemicals in the basement of a church.

Within a few weeks I had three bomb factories manufacturing some 300 explosive devices a week. Every day we distributed dozens of these homemade bombs through couriers to the teams in the different villages and suburbs of Havana Province.

We were not terrorists, for our bombs were not aimed at killing or mutilating innocent victims. We had as a purpose the destruction of the national economy, the disruption of the government structure, the demoralization of the system.

Bombs exploded in the Cuban Electric Company, producing a

total blackout of the city of Havana. Explosions destroyed machinery at the Havana Aqueduct, at the telephone company, and in dozens of government offices throughout the country. Industrial machinery exploded in factories, and warehouses burned to the ground.

Many of the young men who had fought against Batista joined in the 30 of November Movement. One of our members was Richard Heredia, the young university student who had been arrested with me during the days of the revolution against Batista.

On one occasion I went with my second-in-command, Luis Nibo, to an apartment where we were setting up a bomb factory. We had explosives stored in an apartment on top of a grocery store. Dressed in civilian clothing, we walked past two militiamen on patrol. We were only a few feet from the militiamen when Nibo's pistol fell on the sidewalk. For one brief moment we all stood frozen, looking at each other. Nibo bent over, picked up the weapon, and placed it back on his belt.

"It's a weapon," he told the militiamen, "but I have a permit to use it."

The militiamen shrugged. They seemed satisfied with our nonchalance. Nibo and I entered the building.

"We have a problem here," I told Luis, "if those idiots think about this incident for a little while, they might decide to search this building."

"I know," he answered, "we are going to have to move the explosives out."

"And," I added, "we are going to have to convince those patrolmen that we are on their side."

"Follow me," Nibo said as he walked down the stairway.

Luis had been a captain in the Rebel Army. He still had an identity card that he carried with him for emergencies. With a long-legged stride he approached the two patrolling militiamen.

"Come here you sons of bitches," he said, flashing his card, "both of you are under arrest."

The militiamen looked stunned.

"Why?" one of them asked.

"Why? Because I dropped a weapon and you two idiots did not even stop me or question me. No wonder this country is crawling with imperialist CIA agents. You did not follow procedure."

"I'm sorry, captain."

"Sorry? I'm going to throw you imbeciles in jail for a few days. That will teach you to follow procedure."

"Please, captain, let us go. It will not happen again."

"Come on, captain," I said in my best persuasive tone, "let them go. They are a couple of inexperienced boys."

"The hell with them, I'm throwing them in jail."

We stood on that street corner and argued for several minutes. Luis finally relented, allowing the militiamen to go on their way.

The following morning Luis and I returned, closed up the house, and moved the explosives.

The organization grew at the speed of light. Within months, twenty-eight out of the top thirty-three labor leaders in Cuba had joined the 30 of November Movement. We had an underground network that extended through hundreds of factories and student centers. As a matter of fact, we were growing so fast that it was becoming hard to maintain control of the clandestine structure. At its peak, the 30 of November would have over 8,000 men and women active in the war against the regime.

I was everywhere, doing everything at once. I began to coordinate plans for uprisings in the Escambray Mountains, increase the sabotages in the cities, and promote more unrest in the Island.

My own family became involved. My brother Tony was an engineer working in the control department at the recently nationalized Shell refinery. Castro's government had been taking over American properties in Cuba, and the Shell refinery had been one of their biggest prizes. Protected by heavy security, it seemed impossible to sabotage.

Although Tony had never been involved in political activities, I did my best to convince him that he could carry out the biggest sabotage in Cuba. Blowing up the controls at the refinery, I argued, would create a fire that would rage for days, would cause millions of dollars in damages, and would strike a psychological blow that would demoralize the regime and prove the power of the underground. Tony agreed, realizing that he would have to escape Cuba on the same day the bombing would take place.

We manufactured a bomb with C-3 plastic explosives. The plan called for Tony to place the device near the barometers at the control room on a Sunday morning. Then, since travel between the United States and Cuba was still unrestricted, Tony would flee the country by taking a five o'clock flight to Miami. The bomb would explode at nine in the evening, lighting up the Cuban sky.

I was worried about the plan. The plastic explosive we were using had a peculiar naphthaline odor. There was a good chance that the bomb would be found before it exploded. If the bomb was discovered, dozens of cops would be dispatched to pick up every employee of the control department for questioning. I feared that Tony might be arrested before he had time to board an airplane to freedom.

I arranged for a squad of underground fighters to be stationed at the airport. They were to remain there until Tony's plane left for Florida. If at any time it appeared as though Tony was to be arrested, they would attack the security forces, rescue him, and take him to a safe hideout.

Perhaps, to some, it might seem callous that I had placed my own brother in such a dangerous situation, but I had to do it. All good Cubans are my brothers, and better men than Tony and I were dying in Cuba every day.

On that Sunday afternoon I arrived at my parents' house to bid farewell to my brother. Tony was pale, sitting down on the edge of a bed.

"I did it."

I smiled. I was proud of my brother. For a man inexperienced at revolution, he was starting his career as a saboteur with a major coup.

That Sunday was one of the longest days of my life. The airplane, scheduled to leave at five, was delayed. Delays were not unusual, but with every passing minute our anxiety grew. It was almost eight o'-clock in the evening when the plane left the Jose Marti airport. One saboteur had left Cuba. Those of us who stayed behind waited for the final hour to pass.

At nine o'clock, the explosion destroyed the barometer at the refinery. The fire raged for eight or nine days, destroying thousands of gallons of fuel.

Winning a battle does not win a war, however. The following day I was back in the streets of Havana, planning more strikes.

Three former Rebel Army officers, Ramonin Quesada, Cesar Paez, and Fernando Valle Galindo, sponsored by the 30 of November, led guerrilla forces in the mountains of Cuba. Overwhelmed by superior forces, their small bands were crushed after fierce fighting.

In Havana, I was living under stress. I slept in different apartments, kept on the move constantly. So as not to attract attention, rather than using a car I rode in taxis. I never used telephones from private homes for fear of them being wired. It was not unusual for me to walk four blocks to make a phone call from a public telephone. When I visited a place before sitting down to talk, I would inspect the area for possible escape routes. As weeks became months, I was surprised at my own longevity, wondering every day when my luck would run out.

By the end of 1960, I had spent ten months as national military coordinator of the 30 of November Movement. The new year was approaching.

In December, Richard Heredia told me that he had found a good location for a new bomb factory. Richard had the reputation of being a very careful, discreet conspirator, so when he informed me that he had found a good site, I knew it meant that the location was very safe. The place in question was an upholstery factory with an apartment attached at San Lazaro 404, a busy Havana street. The owner of the place was Lauro Perez, a short, stocky man whom Richard had known for years.

Richard introduced us. My real name, of course, was never used. My only purpose at the time was to inspect the place, set up the operation, and then turn the whole thing over to a liaison to supervise the operation.

The site had its pluses and minuses. I did not like the fact that the escape routes were poor, but I did like the fact that bombs could be stuffed inside pillows for easy transport. I decided to go ahead with the operation. I brought the "Diabolics" to help out and a man named Rafael Pargas, whom we called "The Carpenter," for that was his daily trade.

On the night of December 30, I arrived at San Lazaro 404 by taxi. As I entered, I noticed a couple of people on the sidewalk who aroused my suspicion. I told Lauro, but the owner of the upholstery factory did not seem worried. The men down the street, he explained, were probably guarding a newly acquired government property, a house taken over from a family that had just left Cuba.

I did not buy the explanation. Edgardo Valle and Alberto Perez, the "Diabolics," were already busy setting up the equipment to manufacture a couple of dozen explosive devices to greet the new year. "The Carpenter" was late, which was unusual. Feeling edgy, I decided to walk out of the building, look for a public phone, and call Pargas to see what was causing his delay.

Edgardo Valle and I walked three blocks to a public phone. I dialed Pargas's phone number. His wife answered, but told me that Rafael had left much earlier. I began to worry.

As Edgardo and I walked back we were surrounded by half a dozen men armed with pistols. My instinct had been right. Lauro Perez had turned us in! We were being arrested by State Security.

We were taken into a room at a nearby clinic. All the time that we sat there and waited, we argued, pleading our innocence. Neither one of us was armed, so we had nothing to worry about on weapons charges. The only incriminating evidence that I had was a small piece of paper in my breast pocket which contained some coded scribbling. I managed to destroy the paper in a brief visit to the washroom.

After a few minutes in the waiting room, we were taken to the offices of State Security. While we waited to be processed, a cousin of Edgardo showed up to see us. He was Captain Furry, one of the most important men in the repressive *aparatchick*. When Furry saw Edgardo under arrest, he threw his hands up and exclaimed: "Oh, Edgardo, what a jam you have gotten yourself into this time!"

The phrase struck me as funny. For a long time afterward, I would tease Edgardo with it, using my most worried tone of voice as I talked to him: "Oh, Egdardo, what a jam you have gotten yourself into this time!"

Edgardo and I were taken to a detention cell. There, huddled up on a bunk, was Rafael Pargas, "The Carpenter." He had been picked up by State Security on the way to the meeting. I assumed that Alberto had also been arrested.

"Did you talk?"

"How the hell could I talk?" he answered. "I don't even know what your real name is."

When the inevitable interrogation came, I was taken to a room. To my surprise the interrogation turned out to be shorter than I expected. The State Security officers threatened me, of course. One pulled out a handgun and threatened to blow my brains out. Another one told me that if I did not talk I would find myself facing a firing squad. They cursed, but I had heard it all before.

"Look," I said to them, "you can shoot me or you can put me in jail. I had a rib broken and an eardrum ruptured by a beating during the struggle against Batista. I did not talk then and I am not going to talk now."

They understood. The interrogation stopped. On January 4, 1961, I was taken to La Cabana, an old Spanish fortress on Havana harbor.

At La Cabana I joined many friends who now lived behind bars, a number of them awaiting sentencing. My own trial was swift, a sham of justice, a game played out. I expected to face a firing squad, but I was lucky. My sentence was thirty years' imprisonment. It was lenient considering the fact that State Security was not aware, at the time of my trial, that I was the national military coordinator of the 30 of November Movement.

From the very second that I entered the walls of La Cabana, my only thought was to escape, to keep on fighting. I spent hours planning escapes that had to be discarded, but I never gave up.

The worst experience of living in the large prison galleys at La Cabana was the daily horror of the executions. Every day, dozens of men would be tried. Those condemned to death would be taken to a nearby chapel to await the hour of their death. Every night after midnight a small open truck would stop next to the chapel. The squad would lead the prisoner out and the truck would disappear from sight, behind a stone wall. Seconds later we would hear screams, commands, and the crackling sound of gunfire. The truck would then return to pick up another man.

It was agony to sit in our galley at night, staring through iron bars, watching those men leave the chapel one by one. Some waved and cheered at us, while others walked in silence.

Hundreds were killed in La Cabana during 1961. No death, however, was as painful as the death of Bienvenido Infante.

Bienvenido and I had grown up together in the same neighborhood. We had played together as children, attended school together, partied together as teenagers. Bienvenido was a picturesque character, always well dressed, forever smiling. A romantic soul, he was one of the most popular young men in the neighborhood. He was a good friend, the kind of buddy one could always count on.

He was in the military section of the 30 of November Movement, along with his then teenaged brother Roberto. One of his contacts was Radames Cruzata, an officer in the repressive State Security Force.

Every morning Radames was given a list of people to be arrested. Cruzata would stop off for breakfast and call Bienvenido from a phone booth, telling him who the political suspects were for the day's roundup. While Radames drove his State Security car picking up common criminals, Roberto and Bienvenido would dash all over Havana, warning political suspects to flee minutes ahead of the arresting force. The three of them saved the lives of many freedom fighters in those days.

Bienvenido was arrested for being reckless. He was preparing an operation to blow up the transformers at the Cuban Telephone Company. Although we had warned him about trusting Juan Antonio Rodriguez, whom we had suspected of being an informant, Bienvenido decided to go ahead with the mission. Radames Cruzata and Bienvenido were arrested while Roberto fled to the Costa Rican Embassy, where he asked for political asylum.

Arrested in February, Bienvenido slept on the bunk above me at La Cabana. When discussing the possibility of facing a firing squad he was not afraid of death, only sorry for his wife and baby boy, whom he adored.

"If I die," he said, "I'll never see him grow up, Hiram. That's what hurts."

When the death sentence was imposed, he accepted his fate without flinching. Bienvenido looked at another prisoner who had been bemoaning his own fate.

"Do you want to trade places?" he asked smiling.

As he left for the chapel, Bienvenido washed, shaved smoothly, and dressed as elegantly as he could under the circumstances. He looked like a man ready to party.

"I want to die looking good," he said as he left our galley.

There is nothing, no way to explain the feelings inside me as I saw him leave, as I waited for that final moment when he would come out of the chapel to face death. I remember every second, every moment of that night. Bienvenido walked out surrounded by the firing squad. He turned and looked toward us. His hand went up in the air. He waved at me and I waved back. Our last goodbye.

A couple of minutes later, as tears filled my eyes and rolled down my face, I heard the sound of gunfire. I had lost another friend.

After I was jailed, Luis Nibo took my place as national military coordinator of the movement. He lasted a short time, being jailed and condemned to a prison sentence. Nibo was followed by Carlos Manuel Delgado, a brave young student, who became national coordinator at the age of twenty-three. Carlos led the teams for a few weeks until he was caught up in a police dragnet.

When an officer tried to arrest him, Carlos disarmed the patrolman and fled. Surrounded by officers, he fled up a stairway. A bullet hit him in the back but he shot his way through, killing the officer who led the dragnet, a captain by the name of Salinas.

Running away, Delgado entered a building. A woman took him in, washed his wound, and allowed him to hide in her apartment. Carlos called on the phone, asking for a team to come and pick him up. Wounded and weak, he hid inside a closet to wait.

The movement dispatched a team to rescue him, but by the time they arrived, the neighborhood was sealed tightly. The police were searching the neighborhood house by house. Carlos was captured inside the apartment where he was hidden.

When they brought him to La Cabana, I was aware that Carlos was doomed for the firing squad. He had killed a captain in the shootout and the trial would be a mere formality before the execution. Trying to gain time, I suggested that Carlos should cut his wrists with a razor. As an attempted suicide, he would be sent for several days to a hospital where our people could rescue him. He refused, however, went to trial, and was executed by a firing squad.

Years later, Barbara Perez, one of our bravest women operatives, told me that after she was released from prison she went to the graveyard at Colon Cemetery, where she found a small urn with the dust that once had been Carlos Manuel Delgado.

"How can a man so awesome," she told me, "become dust and fill a box so small? Hiram, in my hands I held the ashes of Carlos Manuel Delgado."

We lost many brave men in 1961.

A woman named Guillermina Vazquez smuggled a woman's wig for me. I was planning to leave La Cabana with the civilians on visiting day, dressed in drag. Padron, a fellow prisoner, made a skirt for me from a blanket.

As I was preparing my plan, another prisoner had the same idea. The man made a good escape, but as I saw him leave I knew that it would make my own escape more difficult. I was right. Prisoners and visitors were separated after that by a wire fence ten feet high. The women and children on one side, us on the other, with a couple of guards walking up and down the length of the fence.

I did not give up, however. First, I had to figure out a way to move from one side of the fence to the other. Once among the civilians I then had to figure a way of leaving the fortress, for the visitors were issued a yellow pass upon entering that they had to surrender upon leaving. Third, I had to walk past a sentry post, looking convincingly feminine, undetected.

I began to elaborate the plan, telling the outside contacts that I needed someone to pick me up on the tenth of October, the date that I planned to escape.

On that morning prisoners and visitors were jammed tight against the fence. Israel Abreu, a fellow cellmate, began, with a pair of smuggled pliers, cutting an opening in the fence for me to squeeze through. One by one, hiding from the guard, he clipped the links.

Inside the cell I waited. I had stuffed my wig under a hat, dressed in the latest female fashion that our tailors could provide.

When enough links had been cut, Abreu sent word back that the "door" was ready for opening.

I walked out surrounded by other prisoners, shielded by their bodies, so only my covered head showed above the group.

It was swift. One moment I was standing among the prisoners staring at the civilians, and the next moment I was on the other side, among the civilians, staring at the prisoners. I heard a voice saying, "Help him God. Help him."

Marel, the girl from the 30 of November Movement that had come to pick me up, applied makeup to my face. Israel began to close up the opening on the fence, so the guards would not notice that one of us had sneaked through.

As I waited for visiting hours to end so I could attempt the second phase of my plan, I began teasing Israel and the other buddies who helped me in the escape.

"I'll miss you big boy," I said, blowing him a kiss.

"You make a good-looking blonde, Hiram," he answered as he closed up the hole.

The second part of my plan went well. A prepared diversion was staged in front of the guard who was collecting yellow passes. Four or five women began an argument in front of me. While the guard was distracted with them, Marel and I walked through the yellow pass checkout.

We continued walking. Ahead of us was a sentry post, the last hurdle to overcome. The guard saw a group of us approaching and opened the gate. Marel and I walked toward a waiting car.

I was free! They had given me thirty years and I escaped after ten months. Some guards were going to be very embarrassed when the patched hole was discovered!

That night I slept in a hideout. I was back in action! But not for long, for two days later our hideout was surrounded by two dozen heavily armed guards. I was picked up in a dragnet with a half dozen members of the movement.

I was angry. Three days of freedom and I was back behind bars. I was taken to a detention cell at State Security Headquarters in Marianao, a Havana suburb.

From the moment I walked in, I started planning a second escape. That night I started scratching out a hole in a wall, using a razor blade. I was flushing dirt down the toilet, but soon gave up on the idea, deciding that it was an impossible feat.

I soon noticed, however, a flaw in the State Security procedures. Every night a guard would come and read aloud a few names of prisoners that were going to be interrogated later. Fifteen minutes later, a second guard would enter and direct the prisoners to the interrogation rooms on the other side of the building. It seemed to me that the second guard never knew or seemed to double check how many prisoners he was picking up. I decided that if I moved in with the line, the guard would not notice an additional prisoner.

I liked the idea. By joining the line I would be walking out of the cell, my primary area of confinement. I also figured that if I stood at the front of the line, I could be out of the sight of the guard for several seconds as we walked through doors and passageways. The guard usually walked at the end of the line.

I began to set a plan in motion. I borrowed five pesos from one of my friends in the detention cells. From other prisoners I scrounged a pair of glasses, a magazine, a sweater, and a pair of military boots. I had a blue shirt on, very similar to those used by the militia, but I still needed a pair of olive green pants. The only military pants in our detention cell were worn by a soldier who had been arrested for a common crime.

I walked up to the soldier, leaned over, and stared him in the eyes.

"I am going to escape tonight," I told him, "and I need your pants. If you refuse me, I'll slit your throat. If you turn me in, I have men inside and outside who will kill you."

The soldier did not argue.

When the guard came at night and read off the names I had a moment of weakness, when I almost gave up on the escape. A friend of mine, a tough kid, Antonio Piolat, stood in front of me.

"Do it, Hiram," he said, "you have nothing to lose. Don't chicken out now."

Those words woke me up. I put on the uniform, stuffing the money, magazine, and shades in my pockets. I covered the blue shirt with the sweater, trying to look civilian.

The second guard came in. This was the moment. I walked out standing second in line. My heart was pounding inside my chest, but my mind was clear, working at full speed. The guard was at the end of the line. The order was given and we began moving down the hallways and corridors.

As we turned a corner in a hallway I saw my first and, perhaps, only chance. As the line walked one way, I stepped out, walked the other way, and stood behind a cooler. Seconds passed. I did not move. The line disappeared through a door, the armed guard following the prisoners.

I was alone in the hallway. So far so good. I walked into a small, empty room and removed my sweater, putting on the shades. I rolled up the magazine and bent it to the approximate shape of a weapon, tucking it under my shirt, hoping that it would seem as if I carried a sidearm. I only hoped my military outfit would be adequate.

I knew that I could exit the building through a nearby door leading to the parking lot. That exit, however, was heavily guarded. There was a good chance that I could be recognized as I attempted to leave. My best chance was to take the longest route, through the administration offices toward the other end of the complex.

I began walking through the maze of offices. Guards walked through the hallways, I saluted, walking as calmly as I could. I began to feel good. It took all my strength and willpower to control my fear, to calm my nerves. One last dangerous hurdle to overcome, the final sentry next to the sidewalk.

I approached the gate as coolly as I could. The sentry saw me approaching. He turned toward me. I was hoping he did not expect a password, for I had none to offer him.

"Good evening, comrade," I said as calmly as I could, "have you seen Lieutenant Martinez?"

The guard blinked. "Martinez?" he stammered, "Is he a short guy with slanted eyes?"

"That's him."

"No, he has not been in tonight."

"Well," I said, patting him on the back as I walked through the gate, "tell him that Lieutenant Gonzalez was here looking for him."

The guard nodded.

I walked away.

Every step that I took moved me a few inches away from the main gate. I was escaping! My heart was jumping inside my chest. My lips were dry. This cannot be happening, I told myself. They are going to shoot me in the back. I am going to die. I kept on walking, expecting the bullet to come from behind at any moment. I wanted to run but I kept on walking steadily, easily as though I was taking a stroll in the park . . . Left foot, right foot, left foot, I counted cadence as though I was marching. Why don't they fire?. . .I cannot believe that I have escaped once more. It seemed impossible. I expected that bullet to hit my back. I kept on walking. Twenty feet seemed like twenty miles. Twenty seconds felt like twenty centuries.

A car went by. I stopped a second car. A man was driving. A child sat on the passenger side.

"My vehicle broke down, comrade," I said in a military manner, "where are you headed?"

"To La Vibora," the man answered, mentioning a Havana neighborhood.

"That's exactly where I'm headed," I said, sliding into the passenger side.

As the vehicle moved through the Havana streets, I talked about guard duty. My newly acquired driver nodded but did not speak. It was obvious that the man was not a government supporter. I smiled, wondering what he would say if he really knew who I was. Even now, after all these years, I wonder whether my unknown driver ever came to exile. I would enjoy telling him how he helped save my life in October of 1961.

After being dropped off, I walked to Pedro Aponte's house, where his surprised and terrified family hid me for the night. The following day I obtained money, a weapon, and a new uniform. Dressed as a policeman, I began to look for a way to escape the country.

The word came through the grapevine: Hiram Gonzalez was to be shot on sight. After two escapes in one month, the State Security was not going to give me a third chance. I did not care. I was not going to be captured again. I had decided to escape from the country or die fighting.

I used some underground contacts to ask for political asylum at an embassy. At the time, embassies of different nations were crowded with underground fighters expecting diplomatic safepasses out of the country. One did not just walk to a consulate and knock on the door, however. One had to sneak in, or fight his way through.

I entered the Embassy of Uruguay, hidden in the trunk of a diplomat's car. I expected to be safe at last, but I underestimated the Castro regime. When the Uruguayan Embassy requested a diplomatic safepass exit for me, the Cuban authorities answered an emphatic negative. Hiram Gonzalez could rot inside the embassy, but Castro's government was not going to allow him to step outside the building in safety.

I felt frustrated. I was free and protected by the Uruguayan government, but imprisoned by politics inside the embassy. I could not leave. I was trapped, caged by international politics.

I left the embassy stretched out on the floor of the diplomatic vehicle. Within minutes I was walking back on the streets of Havana, looking for another way to escape the country.

The father of a man I knew from the embassy was a fisherman. The old man had volunteered to help me escape. He seemed like a tough, reliable character, but I did not know him. Afraid to trust him, I realized that I had no other choice. I was desperate.

I called Bonifacio, a student leader in the 30 of November Movement. Boni was a brave, steady kid that I trusted. I told him about my escape plan with the old man.

"I want a backup team," I told him, "you follow us. If there's trouble and if it is a setup, I'm going to either shoot my way out or die trying."

"I'll be there," he said.

The old man picked me up on time. A man he trusted but I did not know was the driver. I sat on the back seat near a door, my fist wrapped around a pistol.

As we cruised through Havana, the old man noticed a vehicle following us. He reached under the seat and pulled out a hand grenade.

"What the hell are you doing?" I asked.

"There is a car following us," he said. "I'm going to blow them to pieces."

"No," I said, "those are my men."

The old man looked angry.

"What is this?" he said angrily. "You don't trust me?"

"I do," I lied, "that is a backup to protect us."

The old man calmed down. He took me to the house of Salvador Diaz-Verson, a staunch anti-Communist, where we stayed for the night. After a few hours I asked Bonifacio to leave with the backup. While I waited for a new day, I could not sleep. Diaz-Verson had many dogs. Their barking kept me awake. I don't know how many dogs that man had, but it felt like a hundred thousand animals were howling under my window.

Bleary-eyed, we left in the morning and headed for Matanzas, the province next to Havana. To my amazement, the old man stopped at a bakery.

"What the hell are you doing?" I asked, sitting upright.

"I am going to stop here to buy a pastry for my contacts in Matanzas."

"You are crazy," I answered, "I am one of the most hunted men in Cuba. If I'm seen here I'll be killed."

"What's the matter," he says, "are you afraid?"

"I'm not afraid," I answered, "but I don't believe in taking crazy chances."

As the vehicle moved down Cuba's Central Highway, I began to worry more. The old man had tremendous valor, but a total disregard for safety, which could prove our undoing.

In Matanzas we stopped at a small farm near the seashore. The old man informed me that we were going to spend the night in the farmhouse while we made preparations to leave the country. The farm, like the house the night before, had an abundance of dogs.

I scouted the area. The farm was not safe, it could be surrounded easily.

"You sleep in the house," I told the old man, "I'll sleep in the bushes nearby. If the militia comes I want you to scream at the dogs telling them to be quiet. Once I hear that, I'll have a few minutes to escape."

For a second night, barking dogs kept me awake. I rested on a small hill overlooking the farm, with a cocked .45 within my grasp.

In the morning, the old man, his friend and I went to the beach where we planned on departing. I did not like the idea of scouting the beach in the daytime. Three men in civilian clothing on an empty beach could arouse suspicions.

"You scared?" the old man asked.

"Look," I answered in a rage, "I escaped twice and there's no third chance given. If I get captured they'll kill me in cold blood. And I'm not about to let myself be captured. So either way I'm a dead man. And I don't want to die due to overconfidence. You understand?"

The old man nodded. He still believed that I was overreacting, but he kept silent.

Later that night I waited while the two men went to get the boat for our ride to freedom. The old man had requested that I wait by the seashore, signaling each other by flashlight for the pick-up. Looking at the little strip of beach, I knew it would be easy to trap me there if a patrol came, or if an ambush was set up. I disregarded the old man, waiting for him on the bushes by the south side of the road. If troops came, I reasoned they would swarm over the beach while I observed them from behind. I was not going to take chances.

When I saw the signal, I moved across the road, ran through the beach, and swam dog-style toward the twelve-foot sloop where both men waited. I have never been a swift swimmer and the ink-dark water was frightening, but being shot by Castro's men seemed a worse alternative.

Inside the little boat I felt good. We were on our way. I looked around. I expected to see a bigger boat nearby, waiting.

"Where's the boat?" I asked.

"You are in the boat," the old man answered.

I swallowed hard. This little twelve-foot piece of floating wood was my passport to freedom or my coffin in the sea. I felt nervous. On a twelve-foot boat there is no place to run, only a way to sink.

For a while it went very well. We were about fifteen miles from the coast when we saw the frigate heading toward us. My heart sank. I felt like a sitting duck, expecting a round cannonball to come through the darkness toward us.

The frigate did not fire upon us. They assumed that we were fishermen who had strayed from the shore. Signaling us to turn back, the vessel began escorting us back to shore. For a couple of hours we worried about being arrested, but soon it was obvious that their intention was to assist us.

We arrived at the seashore after hours of rowing, exhausted, with bleeding, blistered hands. My escape had not worked out. After three days without sleep I returned to Havana, hoping to find another escape route out of Cuba. I never saw the old man again but heard that he died by firing squad.

In the city I made contact with Pepin, a Cuban who worked at the Embassy of Uruguay. Pepin was not a diplomat, nor did he have immunity, but he did drive an embassy vehicle.

I entered the Uruguayan Embassy with Pepin as my driver, bluffing our way in, driving past the sentries. Considering my other adventures, my entrance was a mild stroll, an easy ride to asylum. I entered the embassy knowing full well that I might remain locked up inside the building for years, for the regime was not anxious to see me leave the country.

Crowded inside the embassy, I slept on a mattress inside a closet.

Days, weeks, and months went by, until 1963, when a diplomatic compromise was reached and I was issued a safepass to leave the country.

Leaving Cuba did not stop me from fighting for its freedom. Some thirty years after I first started fighting, I still follow my dream, my struggle. For as long as I live, I will do what I can to give my people a democratic revolution.

4
RICARDO VAZQUEZ:
CHILD OF THE UNDERGROUND

Ricardo Vazquez began his revolutionary activities at the age of twelve, the youngest member of the 26 of July Movement. After the triumph of the Cuban Revolution in 1959, it did not take Vazquez long to realize that the ideals he had fought for were being betrayed by Castro and a group of his followers. It was then that Vazquez became one of the youngest conspirators in the 30 of November Movement, the largest and most active anti-Castro organization of the early sixties. The following interview took place at his home in Miami. Vazquez is married and works as a real estate agent.

At the age of twelve, I joined the 26 of July Movement. I was a little tall for my age so I lied; I said that I was sixteen and became the youngest member of the resistance against Batista. I reached puberty and learned to fight a war at the same time. By the time Batista fled the country, I was chronologically fifteen years old but my experiences had made me into a man. I had faced danger, seen men die, learned about betrayals, understood about political games played by factions in a revolutionary process. I was fifteen, but I was as seasoned as most men ten years older.

With Israel Abreu, a good friend, I was given the task of organizing the 26 of July Movement in Las Villas Province. I was made provincial organizer for the student sector. At the time, we believed that the movement would cease to be a revolutionary organization in

47

order to become a political party, a participant in the upcoming free elections that had been promised by Castro himself.

My work as a provincial coordinator allowed me to visit dozens of cities and villages in Las Villas Province, where I met dozens of student leaders and political organizers at all levels of power — from the smallest municipalities to regional headquarters. It was because I was doing this type of work, always on the road, that I became quickly aware that serious problems were occurring of which the Cuban masses had no knowledge. By direct orders from Havana, Communists were being assigned key jobs in different municipalities. Once a Communist was placed in a key position, he would replace his staff with loyal party members. In a few weeks, the Communists had gained total control of several municipalities in Las Villas.

I was upset. Although I was very young, I knew that communism was not an alternative to the Batista dictatorship, for to replace one dictatorship with another does not make a free nation. I resented the fact that the Communists had done very little against Batista. As a matter of fact, until the last stages of the revolution, the Communists had supported Batista. Although I was worried about Communist infiltration, I did not realize that Fidel Castro himself was a Communist. I believed, at the time, that the Communists were attempting to gain control without Fidel's knowledge.

Events began happening on a national scale. Castro, who was prime minister, forced the resignation of President Manuel Urrutia in a public confrontation that was cleverly orchestrated by Castro. Urrutia, who had been a judge with a reputation for honesty, was forced to seek asylum in an embassy. He was replaced as president by Osvaldo Dorticos, an old-line Communist from the upper middle class, a good yes-man of little personality or intellect.

I watched the Urrutia-Castro confrontation on television in Santa Clara. Urrutia was not invited to the press conference, but Fidel launched into a four-hour tirade against the president. After the broadcast finished, I knew that Urrutia was also finished, and I realized that Castro himself was part of the plot.

I had watched the program at the house of Rodolfo de las Casas, who was a comandante in the Rebel Army. De las Casas had been the head of security for President Urrutia. The broadcast drove him crazy. After the show was over, he took his machine gun and walked out to his car. I asked him where he was headed, and he said that he needed to ride around for a little while to cool off. I joined him.

We rode around the streets of Santa Clara. Although I was only sixteen, I knew what I had to do, once more.

"The Communists," I told Rodolfo, "have taken control. We must fight again."

"First," he answered, "we must study them, so that we know how to fight them."

"You think so?" I asked him.

"Yes."

I did not argue, but I felt that we must start fighting at once, before the Communists could gain more control, before their power became centralized and stronger.

The provincial directors of the 26 of July Movement in Las Villas had a meeting at which they decided to render a report to Fidel Castro complaining about the problems facing the movement, particularly the Communist infiltration taking place in our province.

A month later, Fidel showed up in Santa Clara. Without asking about the problems, he proceeded to destroy the movement in Las Villas. In the weeks that followed, dozens of good revolutionaries were fired from key positions, being replaced by people loyal to Felix Torres, an old Communist who had led a small guerrilla unit against Batista in Las Villas.

In February of 1960, the 30 of November Movement was created, a clandestine network with deep roots in the Cuban labor movement. I became one of its first members. Ironically, I was assigned the same job that I had been doing for the 26 of July Movement; I was to organize the students in Las Villas. Not yet seventeen, I was already involved in my second war.

For several months I was very active, moving throughout the province, using one job as a cover for another. I recruited students for the resistance units set up, as well as a few trusted friends from the anti-Batista days for the military department of our newly formed organization.

The problem with being a resistance organizer is that one cannot keep a low profile. I was constantly recruiting, setting up new cells. The more people I talked to, the more my chances of being caught. One of the men I recruited would later turn out to be a State Security informant.

I had known Luis Artiles for years. He lived in my neighborhood. At the end of the summer of 1960, he began informing on my activities to State Security.

Unaware, I kept working. Recruiting was becoming easier as discontent increased in the Island. In September of 1960, a young man named Orlando Blanco, a very popular person in Santa Clara, was ambushed by militia near Trinidad as he carried supplies to the guerrillas in the Escambray Mountains. His death created a lot of sentiment in the city, increasing the spirit of rebellion in our community.

In that same month, several prominent guerrilla leaders were captured by Castro's troops. Plinio Prieto, Angel del Sol, Porfirio Ramirez, Jose Palomino Colon, and Sinesio Walsh Rios would all be executed together on October 13, 1960.

Porfirio Ramirez was from Santa Clara, a handsome young man in his early twenties who had been a rebel captain in the war against Batista. He had been president of the FEU, the University Student Federation in Las Villas, and was considered one of the top student leaders in the country. When he was captured in the Escambray, his mother asked Castro for clemency. Castro promised that Porfirio would not be executed, but everything indicated that he would be shot by a firing squad.

Two public demonstrations were organized in Santa Clara to demand clemency for Ramirez. The first was organized by students but was quickly broken up by members of State Security wielding lead pipes. The second had many women dressed in widow-black dresses. The police stopped the second demonstration, not allowing them to continue their march.

Castro's promises, as all others, had been lies. Porfirio Ramirez died by firing squad. The night before his death he wrote a beautiful letter in which he stated: "I know that I will die in a few hours. I have no fear, on the contrary, never in my life have I felt more sure of myself; I know that my death will not be in vain . . ."

As the oppression increased, our determination to fight also increased. On a trip to Havana, I visited my old friend Israel Abreu, who had fought alongside me against Batista and whom I had helped organize the 26 of July Movement in Las Villas. When we sat down to talk, we realized that once again we were fighting on the same side; Israel was also active in the 30 of November Movement.

"I have been involved since the beginning," he told me, "but I did not want you to become involved. You are young, too young, and this will be a hard war."

"I have been here since the beginning also," I answered him.

After returning to Santa Clara, I realized that I was being followed frequently. The surveillance limited my movements. I made it a point to start visiting people I disliked, people that were loyal to Castro. If people that I visited were to be arrested and interrogated in the future, let there be those who were enemies. I began to make plans to disappear, to go completely underground in Havana.

By the time I arrived in Havana, I received confirmation that Luis Artiles was the infiltrator from State Security who had informed on me. I made plans to eliminate him, but they were not carried out. Artiles was expelled from the movement, but he was lucky and survived.

In Havana I was attached to the military wing of the movement, headed by Hiram Gonzalez. Hiram, a former lieutenant in the Rebel Army, was a baby-faced man with curly blond hair and a reputation for being fearless. One month after my arrival, Hiram was arrested by State Security. The night after his arrest, in a wave of bravado, we carried out a series of sabotages in Havana.

Escape plans were made for Hiram. Through our network, we asked him to fake an appendicitis attack. We expected that Hiram would be taken to Calixto Garcia Hospital, a large complex of buildings near the University of Havana. A team of us was to rescue him from the hospital, at whatever the cost.

The group consisted of Luis Nibo, a former Rebel Army captain who had replaced Hiram as military commander, Carlos Manuel Delgado, who a few months later would be captured in a shootout and executed, a couple of other men, and I. Every day for a couple of weeks we went to the hospital, spending hours roaming through the complex. Some days we dressed in military uniforms, other times as doctors. Since Hiram was about my size and weight, I dressed with two layers of clothing. The extra pants and shirt would facilitate his escape. I also carried two weapons, a nine-millimeter Browning and a Luger.

One day I was standing near an entrance, talking casually to a girl, when I noticed that I was being watched by two civilians talking to a policeman. When the girl left, Carlos Manuel Delgado walked past me.

"You have been spotted," he whispered.

Our people were all spread out in the area. Fernando del Valle, one of our men, was dressed in an army uniform, cradling a machine gun in his lap. If the two civilians and the policeman had approached us, hell would have broken loose in that hospital.

I played it cool. Moving my hand to my waist, I jiggled one of my weapons, readjusting it to a more comfortable position. I wanted them to know that I was armed and that I did not particularly care if they noticed, hoping that they would think that I was a plainclothes detective on duty or a member of State Security. The bluff worked. The policemen and the civilians moved away, and our team left the hospital a few minutes later.

Although Hiram had faked his illness, the authorities at La Cabana Fortress, where he was being held, refused to send him to the hospital. But Hiram Gonzalez did not give up. Nine months later he escaped from La Cabana dressed as a girl. One of the men who helped him escape was my good friend Israel Abreu, who was then also a political prisoner.

Three or four days after his sensational escape, Hiram was captured again, but they could not hold him long. Before the end of the month he escaped for the last time, dressed in a military uniform.

After the hospital incident, I was driving down a street in Havana when I bumped into two people who knew me from Santa Clara. Both men wore little hammer and sickle pins on their lapels. I told them that I was living with a relative. They eyed me suspiciously. Carlos Manuel Delgado, who was with me, scribbled a fake address on a piece of paper and handed it to one of the men.

"Here," Carlos said, "we are in a hurry, but you can contact us at this address."

We left in a hurry. Those two men contacted State Security in Santa Clara. A team of detectives, headed by Lt. Jose Garcia Beltran, later ambassador to Panama, was dispatched to arrest me.

Time was running out for many of us. The life expectancy of an underground fighter was only a few months. The firing squads at La Cabana were executing men every night, and the tribunals were handing out prison sentences to anyone they even thought was fighting against the system.

On February 24, 1961, I found myself without a car and in need of transporting a small box of explosives to another location. Taking a risk, I asked a stranger if he would give me a ride. The man nodded his head. Clutching my small package, I sat on the passenger side of the vehicle.

On Juan Delgado Street we were intercepted by a State Security vehicle, which cut in front of us, blocking our way. My hand reached for my weapon inside my shirt.

"Don't," the driver told me, "they'll kill us both and I have a wife and children."

Those words made me freeze. Looking up, I recognized all the State Security men surrounding us. It was the squad sent from Santa Clara to arrest me at the fake address Carlos Manuel Delgado had given the two men we had met a few days before.

At the interrogation at State Security headquarters I tried to save my driver, telling the officers that the man was innocent, that I had only hitched a ride with him, not knowing him. Much to my surprise, it so happened that the man, Anastasio Rojas, was also a member of the 30 of November Movement. A search of the car had yielded some incriminating papers and propaganda was found in the trunk of his vehicle!

Since I was only seventeen, a minor, I was not executed but condemned to thirty years' imprisonment. My driver, Anastasio Rojas, was executed.

I served nineteen years in the concentration camps as a prisoner in rebellion. I was at the Isle of Pines when the buildings were rigged with dynamite to blow us up if the Bay of Pigs Invasion succeeded. I suffered from illnesses, parasites, dysentery. I ate worms with my meals, was beaten with rifle butts and with the flat side of machetes, but through it all I have kept true to my principles. Communism is the scourge of humanity, and I am proud to have fought against it.

5
DR. ARMANDO ZALDIVAR:
THE MAN WHO DIED TWICE

Fifty-one-year-old Dr. Armando Zaldivar is a cardiologist in Southwest Miami. He lives in a two-level home with his wife and two young children.

In 1957, while living in Spain as a medical student, Zaldivar felt a commitment to the cause of Cuba's freedom. Returning to the Island, he joined the guerrillas in the Escambray Mountains fighting against Fulgencio Batista. After the triumph of the Cuban Revolution, Zaldivar finished his medical studies, serving as a lieutenant doctor in the Rebel Army assigned to Havana's Military Hospital. His disillusionment with the new regime motivated him, once again, to conspire on behalf of Cuba's freedom.

At the Military Hospital in Havana we held what we called Revolutionary Instruction Seminars, classes of political discussion, lectures by invited speakers, among them Fidel and Raul Castro as well as Che Guevara. Guevara did not mince words. Dressed in green fatigues, wearing a black beret, he faced a room full of doctors, speaking clearly while he looked at each of us with his piercing stare.

"We have to prepare ourselves," he told us, "to drive the United States out of Cuba. We are in the process of establishing a socialist revolution in this country. As doctors, you have a social responsibility to spread our ideas to the people. We must destroy the bases of our capitalist society."

In April of 1959, Raul Castro told us at one of our seminars that the promised free elections would never take place.

After listening to Guevara and Raul Castro, I realized that I had to leave the army, for I did not want to be involved in a betrayal of the Cuban people. I had fought for a revolution to restore democracy and suffrage, not to serve the interests of the Soviet Union.

Looking for a way out that would not alert the structure of power to my real feelings, I requested a scholarship to Mexico to study cardiology. Through Che Guevara I received a denial of my request for Mexico, but was offered a full scholarship to study cardiology at the Institute of Friendship of the Peoples in Moscow. I refused, then received a notification that I was to be transferred to Cayo Largo, an island near Cuba which headquartered a punishment battalion of the Rebel Army. Che Guevara had ended my options. I resigned my commission and joined the underground.

It was the beginning of the resistance movement. A good friend of mine, Rogelio Gonzalez Corso, would be the national coordinator of resistance of MRR, Movement for Revolutionary Recuperation, which would become one of the most active networks in Cuba. Rogelio was known in the underground as "Francisco." He was a quiet, softspoken man in his early twenties, an engineering student. As a conspirator he was indifferent to danger, very relaxed. Living clandestinely, he stayed often at the house of one of my cousins, hiding from State Security. The last time that I saw him he was on his way to the United States. He returned to organize the underground for the Bay of Pigs Invasion, but was captured and executed in April of 1961.

With guerrilla activities occurring in every province of Cuba, I became involved in the supply network to the Escambray Mountains. In Cienfuegos, a city in the south central part of Cuba, I met with a contact to go to see Joaquin Membibre, who had been a guerrilla captain in the war against Batista. Disillusioned with Castro, Membibre had returned to the hills, attacking an outpost in Camajuani, in one of the first skirmishes of the new war. Well known by the peasant farmers of the region, Membibre was a shrewd warrior who would survive many skirmishes, escaping eventually to the United States. He lives in Miami now.

The scout that took me to see Membibre met me in Cienfuegos in the morning. We walked for hours, yet I knew the region and realized that we were going in circles. We saw several farmers whom I figured to be among Membibre's supporters. Late in the afternoon, two men stepped out from behind a clump of trees. One, a guerrilla armed with a rifle, kept moving constantly in a wide circle around us. Membibre and I had a brief meeting in which he never stopped pacing. His eyes moved back and forth, looking around. He was thin, with a scraggly beard. He was armed with a San Cristobal carbine.

"Many have come to offer me weapons," he told me, "but I distrust the offers."

"Set your own safety," I told him, "tell me where you want me to leave them."

"Do you have any ready for delivery?"

"Some. Plus I have the contacts to provide air drops."

"No," he said as we kept moving through the bush, "no air drops. Bring me weapons by land."

"Then I can't bring as many." I gave Membibre an address at a doctor's office in Havana where he could leave me a message, then returned to the capital.

Weeks passed and I did not hear from Membibre, but through an engineer named Cabarga I made contact with another former captain in the Rebel Army, Sinesio Walsh.

Once more I traveled to the Escambray. A small cache of weapons was hidden in a bakery in Santa Clara, then transported by truck to a meeting site. Vicente Mendez and Jose Berberena, two guerrillas, met me at a farm. I gave them an M-1 carbine, five Garand rifles, a Thompson submachine gun, ammunition, and some hand grenades. Accompanying the guerrillas I traveled to their camp, where I met Sinesio Walsh, a stocky, bearded man with a noble personality. We discussed establishing a supply route, with air drops from the United States. Unlike other guerrilla leaders, Walsh was not in a hurry to do battle, preferring to organize as large a group as he possibly could before confronting the militia. It made sense, for many small groups were being crushed before they could organize properly.

Returning to Havana, I prepared a third trip back to the mountains. This time I was to return with a radio transmitter, more weapons, and a coordinator to establish the air drops.

There were four of us. Plinio Prieto was a former schoolteacher who had been a comandante in the war against Batista. He had returned clandestinely to Cuba, after being trained in Miami. His mission was to coordinate the air supply drops. The others were a radio man whose name I have forgotten, a man named Benigno, and myself. We traveled to Las Villas Province, where we went to a farm owned by an American named Pedro Copps. There we met two guerrillas who told us that they knew where to locate Walsh's units.

The six of us began walking through the brush. We were heavily loaded. We carried a heavy radio transmitter, a generator, and more than a dozen surplus weapons. We moved with care, for Copps's farm was near La Campana, a large camp of Castro's army, and we feared bumping into enemy patrols.

One of the guerrillas told us that militia lieutenant Obdulio Morales Torres, the nephew of Felix Torres, one of Castro's most loyal comandantes, had been killed in a guerrilla ambush. The region in which we were moving was heavy with militia patrols combing the hills. Still, we had no choice but to move through the brush, trying to find Walsh, before Castro's troops found either of us.

Plinio wore rubber-soled shoes which cracked after the first day in the bush. After three days, unable to locate friendly forces, we decided to transmit with our radio to signal our contacts in Miami to suspend the air drop. We ran a wire to the roof of a peasant's hut, cranked up the generator, and began sending coded signals. Our large transmitter could broadcast, but it could not receive signals, so we did not know whether our messages were being heard in Florida.

Later that night we heard a plane flying overhead. We wondered whether it was the first air drop, the one we had tried to stop. Unfortunately it was, as we later found out. The only air drop in the Escambray Mountain war dropped supplies and weapons for one hundred men at La Campana, on the outskirts of a Communist militia base.

The following day the six of us started on our way back toward Pedro Copps's farm. We were tired and anxious, having been unable to contact Walsh's guerrilla forces. While crossing the grounds of a farm cooperative, we were spotted by a military security squad. A burst of gunfire kicked up dirt near us. Although we were heavily loaded, we ran as fast as we could, firing our weapons. I emptied out the clip of my M-1 carbine, shooting blindly. The little skirmish was over in seconds, as we were soon out of range of each other's firepower. In the brief firefight Benigno became separated from us. He was captured by militia forces the next day.

I had stress fractures in my feet from the days of constant walking. Plinio's shoes were torn to shreds. We had been cut off from our contacts.

When the five of us returned to the Copps farm, we split up. The two guerrillas went back to the hills, while we planned our return to the city of Cienfuegos. I felt that walking through canefields was a slower but safer route back, but Plinio, with his torn shoes and blistered feet, preferred to take a taxi ride to the city. Plinio knew that the ride would be dangerous, but he felt pressured to return to Cienfuegos to reestablish contact with our organization. He was a brave man, but he was feeling the pressure of working against time. I could feel the tension that was building up inside of him.

We boarded two cabs, leaving all equipment and weapons at the farm. Plinio and I rode in the first vehicle, while our radio man rode in the second car.

The trip started out well. Our cabs drove right past La Campana, past lines of marching militia, but a few miles down the road, in the town of Manicaragua, a patrol jeep stopped us. I tried to bluff my way out, but when the soldiers saw Plinio's torn shoes, we were placed under arrest. While we were being detained, the second cab, with our radio man, drove past us. He would manage to return to Havana to tell the underground about our capture.

We were taken to the police station, where I saw a wanted poster with Plinio's photograph. After a short time Plinio was taken away. It was the last time that I saw him until our trial.

Later, at night, I was taken to Topes de Collantes, a hospital deep in the mountains that specialized in the treatment of tuberculosis. A fairly new hospital, it was built during the Batista regime. Now guerrilla prisoners were being held and interrogated in one of its wings.

The nightmare started when I was taken to see Felix Torres. A hard-line Communist, Torres was a small man in his early fifties with a scraggly Ho Chi Mihn beard. He has always been one of the most hated among Castro's henchmen. I was taken to Torres's home near the hospital. In the living room I was faced with several soldiers, a young woman, and an overjoyed Torres, who stroked his beard incessantly.

"I captured them," he said as he glared at me. "Undress."

"What?" I said.

"I said undress," he screamed as he stroked his beard.

"But," I said, looking at the woman in her early twenties, "your daughter is here!"

"My daughter?" screamed Torres as he hit me with a rifle butt, "That is my wife, you son of a bitch. Now undress before I kill you."

It was a moment of humiliation, stripping before the laughing little man who kept cursing at me. I undressed, then stood naked, in the living room, shivering in the cold night air.

"Look at him," one said laughing, "you can't even see his dick."

"Look at the way he trembles."

"I caught them," Torres said screaming to a phone caller, "I caught them and I am going to kill them. I am going to shoot all of them."

I was taken out naked and driven by jeep to another house. A State Security investigator came up to me.

"What weapon did you have?" he asked.

"An M-1 carbine," I answered.

"That's not him," he said as he walked away.

Later I was told that Felix Torres wanted to find out which one of the captured guerrillas had killed his nephew a few days before in an ambush.

I stood naked in a room while soldiers made coffee and typed reports. Being naked gives one a feeling of vulnerability, of total helplessness.

"What's the name of the one we killed today?" one soldier who was filling out a report asked.

"I don't know," another one answered, "write him in as killed in combat."

"What do we do with the body?"

"Who cares?"

Later I was told by one of the prisoners that no one had been killed, that the conversation was meant to intimidate me.

An officer named Chino Figueredo interrogated me after I was allowed to dress once more.

"I'm tired of you," he said after a brief conversation. "Leave. You can go. You are a small fish. We are not interested in you."

"I'll leave in the morning when there's light."

"You'll leave now."

I was pushed out of the building, where I kneeled next to the doorway. I was not in a hurry to leave, for I suspected that I was to be shot in the back as I walked down the dark road. I waited for a few minutes until a figure stood up from a nearby clump of bushes. It was a soldier with a weapon.

"I was waiting for you," he said as he pushed me back inside.

The soldier was called El Negro. He was from one of the elite army units, the LCB.

"You will be killed by the firing squad," he told me, "and you should ask for me. El Negro. I'll put a bullet right between your eyes.

No pain. Others here, they like to see people suffer. Not me. Right between the eyes. You won't feel anything."

I nodded. He convinced me. If I was going to die, I wanted El Negro to kill me as swiftly as possible.

On the third day of incarceration I was once again interrogated by Chino Figueredo. As he talked to me he played with a pellet gun, shooting me occasionally, the little metal beads raising angry welts on my skin.

"Did you treat any wounded?"

"No."

"We are tired of playing cat and mouse games. We are going to execute you."

"I want El Negro in the squad."

"El Negro? No. You want a bullet between the eyes. No. When we shoot you it will be in the stomach so you can twist in the mud. We want you to hurt, to die in pain."

In the final few minutes before I faced the firing squad, I felt very at peace with myself. I felt resigned to my fate, believing that nothing could change my destiny now.

I am twenty-six and I am going to die, I thought. I am twenty-six and I am going to die.

I remembered one of the first executions in 1959, when Castro took power. Cornelio Rojas was shot by a firing squad, and the black-and-white movie was shown a dozen times on television. The television image kept running through my head. The rifles fired and the top of the man's head was lifted off, encephallic mass splattering the wall, the body jerking like a puppet. I saw that firing squad in my mind and I saw myself jerking, my brain exploding, my body falling.

Then soldiers came to get me. My hands were tied. I began walking. I am twenty-six and I am going to die. My armpits were sweating. The back of my knees were sweating also.

The firing squad was standing in a line. I really don't know how many soldiers were there. Perhaps three, four. Perhaps half a dozen. El Negro was not there.

It was nighttime at Topes de Collantes. The spot where I stood was lit by reflector lights. I felt sweat on my body but I was calm, I was ready to die. I was breathing but aware of death, of eternity only a few seconds into the future. I am twenty-six and I am going to die.

Rifles pointed at me. Orders were being shouted, but I do not remember them. Rifles were pointed at my flesh. I am twenty-six and I am going to die. I felt very calm. It was almost over.

I don't know how to describe the feeling but I felt the fingers curling around the triggers, I felt the tension, the vibrations as they pressed back, firing. I could feel that trigger pressure to the microsecond.

There were flashes of light, clouds of white smoke. Then nothing happened. I did not feel any pain. My head did not explode. My body did not fall. I did not understand.

The soldiers ran toward me, screaming. They pushed me to the ground, kicking and hitting me. As I was being beaten I realized that I had been executed with blanks, one of the cruelest of tortures, for it could very well drive a man insane.

I was taken back to a detention cell. It felt strange to walk back into the building. I was supposed to be dead, but I wasn't. I was still alive and it felt good, very good, to be living on borrowed time.

I have never slept as soundly as I slept that night. Prisoners walked around me, voices talked and argued, but I slept in a state of total unconsciousness.

The following day, Chino Figueredo, who had interrogated me several times, told me that I would be executed that night.

"This time," he said, "it will be for real."

For this second time I felt ready. I sat in my cell, praying. I felt very at peace with myself. I had already faced the firing squad; I knew what it felt like.

El Negro came to see me.

"They tell me," he said, "that you will be executed tonight."

"Yes. What do you think?"

"I hear that you asked for me," he said. "I'll be there tonight. It will be over fast. Do not worry."

I nodded. I wanted it to end.

The second time I walked out with my hands tied in front of me. Although the night air was cool, I was sweating. Rifles pointed at me. I am twenty-six and I am going to die. For the second time in twenty-four hours I stood under the lights of reflector lamps. I waited, expecting the fingers curling on the triggers, the tongues of flame exploding from the nozzles of the rifles.

This second time there was no gunfire. After being cursed, I was pushed back inside, to join the other political prisoners.

A few days later I was taken to trial. Dozens of us were crowded in a room in the city of Santa Clara. Plinio Prieto was there, the first time that I had seen him since we had been captured together.

Our trial lasted twenty-four hours. In that time more than sixty of us were condemned to prison terms and five others were sentenced to death. I received a thirty-year sentence while Plinio, the brave schoolteacher, was one of the five condemned to death. He died the following day as I was being transported to El Principe Castle in a bus full of handcuffed guerrillas.

6
JOSE BERBERENA:
A SOLDIER'S STORY

Jose Berberena is a stocky man in his late forties, with a thick mustache and black, wavy hair. He smokes incessantly, talks without hesitation, and projects the image of a man who can be very tough or tender. Berberena, who works as a baker in East Brunswick, New Jersey, where he lives with his wife and twenty-eight-year-old son, is an emotional man who never hides his feelings. His interview, at a friend's home in Elizabeth, New Jersey, was an emotional story told by a man who fought against Castro's guerrillas, becoming later a guerrilla himself to continue fighting against Castro.

In 1957, at the age of eighteen, I joined the Cuban Army as a private. I did so because I wanted a military career. My father was also a military man, having served thirty years as a noncommissioned officer. I identified with military life, wanting to serve my country, to defend our constitution.

I also joined because I wanted to fight in the war against Fidel Castro. At the time, Castro was in the mountains of Oriente Province, leading a guerrilla war against Batista. Although I did not care for Batista, I always felt that Castro was a bigger threat, a real menace to the Cuban people. Castro fooled millions, but he never fooled me.

I underwent two months of basic training at Camp Columbia in the city of Havana. I am proud to say that I won the top recruit award in the training program. I worked like hell in that training. I could assemble a Garand rifle blindfolded and applied myself to learning everything I could about soldiering. After the basic training was completed, I was invited to a luncheon with the chief of staff and several high-ranking officers. In a ceremony I was awarded a new .45-caliber pistol, a cash bonus, and a three-day pass. Standing in that room, dressed in a starched uniform, surrounded by colonels and generals, I felt proud, confident. I had been number one among seven hundred. The sense of achievement overwhelmed me. It was one of the greatest moments of my life.

I was assigned to H Company in Victoria de las Tunas, a town in northern Oriente. For a year and a half I saw combat on an almost weekly basis. My unit was in charge of patrolling roads and escorting convoys of supplies through rebel territories. Our jeeps and trucks were constantly harassed by small ambushes and sniper fire. It was a frustrating war where I was involved in dozens of skirmishes.

I took my work seriously. Promotions came fast for good soldiers, and I had sergeant stripes on my sleeves by the time I was twenty years old. I went on patrols armed to the teeth. I carried extra clips for my Garand in my belt and knapsack. Two bandoliers of bullets crisscrossed my chest, and I usually carried eight hand grenades, besides my pistol and knife. I was a walking arsenal.

On January 1, 1959, I woke up to the news that President Batista had fled the country. Several officers and soldiers seemed alarmed.

"So Batista left," I said, "so what?"

I was naive. I did not feel allegiance to Batista, for I considered myself a soldier of the Cuban Republic, not of Batista's army. My allegiance was to the army and to the constitution, not to any president. My own father had served thirty years under several presidents, some of whom had been good and some of whom had been bad. So Batista had left Cuba, so what? I expected another politician to scramble for power to take his place. The army was intact and I assumed that the army would continue to fight against Castro and his guerrillas.

As we stood on formation in the drill field that morning, our first sergeant told us that we would be expected to surrender our weapons to the rebel forces in the next few hours, as soon as arrangements were made. I was stunned. I was angry. The army had not lost the war; the army had been betrayed by corrupt politicians and high-ranking, gutless officers. I did not want to surrender to a rabble of bearded guerrillas. About forty other men in my company wanted to continue fighting, but in most men there was only a sense of frustration, of being betrayed.

On the morning of January 2, Piti Fajardo, a comandante in the Rebel Army, showed up at our camp to negotiate the surrender. His path and mine would cross several times over the next couple of years. He would later become the highest ranking of Castro's officers to die in the mountain war at the Escambray.

Fajardo left after a forty-five-minute talk with our officers. A few minutes later, our camp was surrounded by a convoy of buses, jeeps, and trucks loaded with bearded guerrillas and with civilian supporters carrying placards. They shouted and screamed, beeping the horns of their vehicles, taunting our troops.

We were told to surrender our weapons. I cocked my Garand rifle. Ibarra, a lieutenant that I liked and respected, tried to calm me down.

"I'll surrender my rifle," I told him, "but they'll never be able to use it."

I smashed the Garand against a tree, hitting it until it broke in two pieces. I felt angry and humiliated. In my pockets I kept three hand grenades, feeling that they might be useful in the future.

We surrendered. It was a humiliating moment, a bitter day in my life. Outside the camp gates hysterical mobs screamed for us, for our imprisonment and execution.

A group of prisoners was brought in to our camp. They were part of a personal army of Senator Rolando Masferrer, political hired guns. One of them tried to escape, running through a field. About sixty of the members of the Rebel Army started firing their weapons at him, hundreds of bullets crisscrossing the field. The man fell over, dead.

Seeing the man killed in cold blood made my blood heat up. My hand went in my pocket to instinctively grip the grenade. As my fingers curled around the metal, I realized in horror that the grenade I held had come undone. For one terrifying moment I stood frozen, expecting to explode in a hundred pieces, to disintegrate in a burst of white light and hot shrapnel. But nothing happened. I withdrew my hand from my pocket. My fingers were covered with a white powder. Detonating powder. I was lucky to be alive.

On January 17 we arrived in Havana, where we were told that our company would be assigned clean-up duties at the military base until the Rebel Army decided what was to be done with us. I decided that I was not going to be a cleaning maid for the Rebel Army while they decided whether to imprison me, kill me, or discharge me. I had a young bride waiting for me in Las Villas Province, so I began looking for a way to escape the base.

Some of our officers were allowed special privileges such as leaving the base for short visits. My friend, Lieutenant Ibarra, was a man of proven courage. I asked for his help and he provided me with civilian clothing, sneaking me out of the base in the trunk of a car.

With a modest roll of cash and two hand grenades in my pocket, I headed east, riding a bus to Santa Clara. When I arrived home, I was told that my father had been arrested. I went to the local jail to see if I could arrange his release.

In our town we had a local character named Guagui, a poor idiot who had spent many years as a mental patient in psychiatric hospitals. When the Rebel Army swept through the region in their victory march, Guagui had joined the rebels. As a joke the Rebels gave Guagui an old Thompson tommy gun without bullets. It was this village idiot with a five-day beard who had pressed charges against my father.

"I had your father arrested because he abused me," he said.

"What did he do to you?"

"Well, he pushed me once."

"Why? What did you do to him?"

"Nothing," Guagui said, "absolutely nothing. I was just drinking and I pulled a knife on him. That's all. And he pushed me."

"Well," I said, "if I give you eighty pesos so you can buy some beer, will you drop the charges?"

"Sure," he said, "for that I would drop charges to the Devil."

My father was freed, but my problems were just beginning. My money was running out, my young wife was pregnant, and I was an unemployed civilian. Desperate for work, I went to seek employment at a nearby forest preserve where laborers were needed to plant trees. It was unskilled labor with little pay, but it was work. I needed to feed myself and my new family. When I filled out the work application, a foreman looked it over.

"So," he said, "you were a soldier of the dictatorship? And you have the guts to come looking for work here? Get out, there's nothing here for you."

That scene would be repeated many times that year of 1959. When my son was born, I was unemployed, living on the charity of a few friends, scrounging a few pesos doing oddjobs. My wife earned a little money doing some hairdressing, but our situation was desperate.

I had always been a proud man, a hard worker. I had earned my stripes in the army by hard work and courage. Now I was discriminated against in my own country, insulted and humiliated for the sin of having fought bravely on the losing side of a civil war.

I tried to survive. I attempted to sell mops door to door but failed, for I was not a salesman.

I remember clearly one of the worst days of my life. My son was ill with diarrhea. That small baby had a green tint to his skin. I looked at him, so small, so sick, with that strange color, and I knew that I had to do something. My wife looked at me with tears in her eyes.

"*Se nos muere,*" she said, "he is going to die on us." I went out in the streets. In my pocket I carried a .38-caliber revolver. I was desperate. In my hands I carried one of the mops that I had been attempting to sell. As I walked fast I knew that I was about to commit a crime. I would knock on a door, mop in hand, and hold up whoever answered the bell. I knew it was wrong, I knew that I would regret it, but I also knew that my son was dying and needed food and medicine. I was not going to let my son die. I was ready to burn in hell, to do whatever was needed to help that baby, my son.

I knocked on a door. A man answered. He saw the desperation in my face, the look of madness in my eyes.

"Have you gone mad?" he asked me.

"No," I stammered, "I am selling this mop."

The man shook his head sadly. "No, you are not," he said as he took out twenty pesos from his pocket. "I can see that you have a problem. Take this money and I hope it helps you."

Dumbfounded, I took the money. I extended my hand, giving him the mop.

"I'm not buying this," he said, "but I am holding it for you. Anytime that you want it, come back for it."

I nodded, turned around, and walked away.

Tears filled my eyes. God had helped me stay honest. Of all the houses, I had picked at random one where a kind soul had understood my suffering, giving me not only the few pesos I needed so badly, but a gesture of kindness that had saved my soul.

My life began to change. A doctor named Curbelo cured my son. For five months he nursed the child back to health, without wanting to charge me a dime. When I insisted on paying, he did not want to hurt my pride, so with a smile he took a five-peso bill, put it in his pocket, and said to me, "We are even, Berberena." I will never forget him as long as I live.

My wife was hired full-time as a hairdresser. Life became normal once more, as normal as things could be in a Cuba in transition toward communism.

Day by day things changed. Private industries were nationalized. Civil rights were being abolished. Cubans were being arrested by the hundreds. Priests were harassed. Newspapers were being forced to close down. Censorship was being imposed.

I had two grenades and a revolver. I wanted to fight. I attempted to make contact with the underground units being formed in the Island. In Santa Clara I began fighting once again against Castro. One night, armed with a gallon of gas and a few matches, I set a government truck on fire. It felt good.

At the beginning of 1960 I was arrested for a few days. With discontent growing in the Island, underground units were being organized. Soldiers who had belonged to the Constitutional Army were prime suspects, often being detained for interrogation and harassment.

One of my relatives, a cousin named Antonio Berberena, was executed by a firing squad. A tough man, he requested to be allowed to puff a couple of minutes on a cigar as well as to command his own firing squad.

Another one of my cousins, a man named Castellon, had established contact with the guerrilla groups that were forming in the Escambray Mountains.

"We need experienced men up there," he told me.

"Count me in."

I had two friends who were also experienced and willing to fight. One was Orlando Quintero, a former soldier, while Rigo Sarduy, a heavyset man, was a former sergeant in the Rebel Army. A year before, Rigo and I had been fighting on opposite sides; now we were depending on each other for survival. The three of us traveled to Manicaragua, a small town. In a cafeteria we met a contact who drove us in a jeep toward a meeting place. On the side of a hill, a scout on horseback waited for us. I felt like a new man as I started our trek toward the camp.

We arrived at two in the morning. A .30-caliber machine gun hidden in the bushes covered the trail. Rather than cooling the weapon with water, the guerrillas had adapted a cooling system with oil in the mechanism. It worked very well.

I was surprised to find, deep in the mountains, a small house made of cement blocks. I was told that all the materials had been brought by mule a couple of years before, during the previous war.

The leader of the guerrilla unit was Sinesio Walsh, a man in his thirties. He was a smiling, charismatic figure with fair skin and dark hair. A heavy smoker, Sinesio was an emotional man who had been a captain in the Rebel Army battling against us before.

"You are experienced?" he asked me.

"Yes, sir," I answered, "I was a sergeant in what my side called the Constitutional Army and yours called the forces of the dictatorship."

He nodded. "I don't care about the past," he said, "here we are all just Cubans fighting communism."

Food was being heated for us. I sat on the ground to eat rice and beans from a metal container. Sinesio and a few of his men sat around us, asking questions about the growing discontent in the cities.

I felt like a frog in water. I was going back to battle, to fight for my country. I was happy. I was given a Garand rifle, and it felt good to grip that wood stock in my hands.

In early 1960, when the uprisings started, men came in droves to fight but weapons were scarce. When I arrived, there were eighteen men in the camp. In a few weeks our group had grown to sixty but many were unarmed.

Sinesio Walsh was trying to organize our guerrilla unit and equip it as well as possible before launching into battle. Some of the guerrillas constantly begged Sinesio to take the offensive and set up ambushes. However, with the exception of burning a few government buses and setting roadblocks, Sinesio was content to wait for the weapons. Weapons did not come. The only shipment received by our group in the Escambray was a few weapons brought by Dr. Armando Zaldivar, a wiry doctor who quickly gained my respect. Vicente Mendez, a former captain in the Rebel Army, was sent to meet Zaldivar at a place called Veguitas. I was his companion on the journey.

Mendez would survive the Escambray, flee to exile badly wounded, and then return to Cuba several years later to attempt to start another guerrilla war against Castro. He died in combat in 1970, becoming one of the best-known martyrs of the war against Castro.

We walked to our rendezvous through thick bush and mountain ravines. Our only food was a can of sardines and some peppers. Vicente carried a San Cristobal, a Dominican-made carbine which was popular but overheated easily. I carried my dependable Garand.

Zaldivar brought us a few carbines, hand grenades, some knapsacks full of ammunition, and a few hammocks which were sorely needed, for many of us slept on the hard ground. Zaldivar told us that he would accompany us back to camp, for he had to confer with Sinesio

Walsh. I suggested that we should leave the ammunition and the hammocks behind, taking only the weapons with us. The doctor shook his head.

"No," he said, "everything goes."

"Look, doctor," I said, "it's going to be very tough moving through those hills at night with an extra sixty or seventy pounds on our backs."

"What's the heaviest bag?" he asked.

I pointed to a thick canvas knapsack, brimming with bullets. It was as heavy as a small boulder.

"I'll take that one," he said, strapping it on, "let's go."

Much to my surprise, the wiry young doctor turned out to be a seasoned warrior, moving well through the bush with that immense knapsack strapped to his back. He surprised me. We arrived at the camp at three in the morning. The doctor met with Sinesio for a couple of hours, then left camp at the crack of dawn with a scout, on his way back to Havana.

A few days later, Porfirio Ramirez and several new guerrillas joined our camp. Ramirez was a former captain in the Rebel Army as well as president of the FEU, the University Student Federation in Las Villas Province. He was a handsome young man in his early twenties, very popular and patriotic.

Our guerrilla unit had grown to over 100 men. With the increase of military patrols in the area, many of us felt that it was becoming unsafe to remain there. Vicente Mendez and Joaquin Membibre, two of the squad commanders, went to Sinesio, telling him that they had decided to leave camp with their men.

"Look, Sinesio," they told him, "you have been here too long and the militia will soon come this way. This place is hard to defend, and it does not offer good escape routes. We have a better chance operating in small groups, always on the move. We are leaving."

I was sorry to see Vicente Mendez leave. The former Rebel Army officer and I had become very good friends. The strong *campesino* was one of the bravest men I've ever met. It was an honor knowing him. Although I had really sided with him, wishing to join his group, I stayed with Sinesio out of loyalty. Quintero and Sarduy, who had joined the guerrillas with me, left with Mendez and Membibre.

At Veguitas the group was intercepted by militia forces. Quintero and Sarduy were captured. Mendez and Membibre split up their forces, moving into the bush, where they continued battling. Eventually, both men made it to exile.

Three days after the combat at Veguitas, I suggested to Sinesio that we should break up our force into several units of a dozen men. Sinesio, however, did not listen to my advice. He was waiting for a shipment of weapons, a drop that would eventually be sent to the wrong site, dropping the weapons at La Campana, near a militia base camp.

My worst fears came true. A twenty-two-man militia patrol stumbled into our camp area. A fire fight began at once. I had a Thompson tommy gun and I quickly began to fire at the blue-shirted figures below us. Our .30-caliber began firing at once, pinning the patrol briefly near a river. The militia retreated with five wounded men.

That night Sinesio finally decided to break our force into small units. I hoped that it was not too late, for I knew that thousands of militiamen would be sent to sweep our area. Porfirio Ramirez left with some men. Tierrita, a young squad leader who could smile even in the worst of times, left with another group. Sinesio, Elio Escandon, Eusebio Penalver, Cipriano, Tanga, and I left camp together that same night.

For three days we moved through the bush, without food and with little water. Surrounded, we hid in a cave that did not have an escape route. I disagreed with the choice, for I felt that in an open field our chances of escape would be better than in a hole on the side of a hill. I could see the militia coming through the undergrowth. Clean uniforms. Soviet weapons. I had only one clip left in the Thompson. Grimly, I cocked it, feeling that I was about to die in battle. To my surprise, Sinesio stood up with his hands in the air.

"Do not fire," he told the militiamen, "it's me, Sinesio Walsh. We don't have ammunition to fight, not even for two minutes. I don't care if I die, but I don't want my men slaughtered."

Sinesio had spoken with authority, in a clear voice. He began walking toward the militia, striding with a sure step, as though he was the one in command instead of a man surrendering. A lieutenant who knew him embraced him. I was stunned. As the militia surrounded us I smashed my Thompson on a boulder. Sinesio was mentally crushed. For months he had planned and prepared a large-scale uprising and it had failed. He was a brave man who had survived many battles, but at the time of his surrender he was physically run down, hungry, and sick.

Mayor Piti Fajardo, the same comandante who had arranged my battalion's surrender at Victoria de las Tunas after the fall of Batista, came to the area where we had been captured. Fajardo cursed at Sinesio, humiliating him, telling him that he would be executed. Sinesio, exhausted, did not answer. Fajardo was not saying anything we did not know already. Sinesio faced a firing squad within a month, but Fajardo did not outlive him by much. He died in a guerrilla ambush soon after.

A group of us were packed up on an open truck to take us to Topes de Collantes, a hospital in the hills that was being used as a guerrilla prison camp. When we arrived at a small town, we were paraded slowly through, so the people could see us captured. Castro's supporters chanted *"paredon, paredon"* (the wall), meaning the firing wall, death by firing squad. An old man tried to jump in the truck to strike us. I kicked him, sending him sprawling. Guards fired their rifles into the air.

Elio Escandon was sitting down on the bed of the truck. He lived in that town before becoming a guerrilla. His family lived only a few meters from where we had stopped. The old man I had kicked recognized him.

"Elio Escandon is here. He is one of them."

Elio stood up. The crowd calmed down for a moment. His ill father approached the truck with Elio's wife, who held a small baby in her arms. Escandon picked up the child, looked at him fondly, kissed him, and gave him back to the mother.

"Paredon," some screamed, *"paredon."*

I looked at the crowd and screamed, "Yes, we will die by the firing squad and our blood will be on your hands."

The truck lurched forward, on its way to our imprisonment. I would survive years of prison at the Isle of Pines and other concentration camps of Cuba.

On October 13, 1960, Sinesio Walsh was executed. Porfirio Ramirez, the student leader, also faced the firing squad, as did the schoolteacher Plinio Prieto, Angel del Sol, and a former officer of the Constitutional Army, Jose Palomino. The five men, some of whom had fought on different sides, were united in blood at the hour of their death. But as Sinesio had said, it mattered not what they had been, only what they were: Cubans fighting against communism.

7
JUAN RODRIGUEZ MESA: GUERRILLA WAR AGAINST CASTRO

He is a tall man, all muscled rawhide fiber, with long arms and wide, thick hands. Juan Rodriguez Mesa lives in a modest apartment in Union City, New Jersey, with his family. The following interview tells the story of a man who fought against Batista and against Castro as a guerrilla. Rodriguez Mesa arrived in the United States after serving almost nineteen years as a political prisoner in Castro's concentration camps.

In the fifties, when I was a young man, I fought against Batista, in the II Front of Escambray. Eloy Gutierrez Menoyo led a guerrilla force in the Escambray Mountains of central Cuba. He was an idealistic, fearless leader who later would spend twenty-two years incarcerated by Castro. I fought under his orders in the hills. Years later, I would share time with him at the Model Prison at the Isle of Pines.

After Batista fled the country, at the beginning of 1959, I went to Havana, where I was assigned the task of being chief of patrol for the Military Police. I was not happy at all, for I did not trust Castro's leadership, being very suspicious of the new regime.

One day in early 1959, I went to the office of Camilo Cienfuegos, one of Fidel's most trusted comandantes. When I entered the room, I was surprised to find that one-half of the wall was covered by a huge photograph of Jesus Menendez, a well-known Communist labor leader.

Later that day I talked to two of my fellow officers, men that I trusted. I told them what I had seen in Camilo's office. "This country is headed for communism," I told them.

"Then we will have to fight again," they answered.

In March, I requested a discharge from the army. After some difficulty, I was discharged on March 26. Frustrated, knowing full well that a new revolution would have to be fought soon, I returned to my hometown of Trinidad.

By the end of that year dozens of small groups were forming all over Cuba, planning uprisings. The Escambray Mountains near Trinidad were a hotbed of conspiracies. The *guajiros,* the peasant farmers, were an independent lot who resisted the Soviet-style state farms and the nationalization of private farms by the new regime.

I had saved some weapons and ammunition, waiting for the days of new uprisings. In early 1960 I headed for the Escambray once more. I had a Thompson tommy gun and a .45-caliber pistol. I was ready for war.

In the mountains I linked up with Benjamin Tardio, Edel Montiel, and Zacarias Lopez, all former guerrillas of the war against Batista. Those men were organizing a guerrilla unit formed of veteran guerrillas and local *campesinos.*

Soon after I arrived, the Escambray had its first martyr. A man named Pedro Rodriguez was gunned down by Castro's troops at Finca Can-Can while he prepared an uprising. Several of the survivors from his group, former soldiers of Batista's army, joined our group in the hills.

Our first fire fight took place at an area called El Naranjal, the orange grove, where we were surprised by a militia patrol. We exchanged gunfire briefly, then we broke contact, being chased from that day on by hundreds of militiamen.

From the very first weeks, Castro saturated the Escambray with thousands of soldiers. Before we could establish our supply lines, before we could consolidate ourselves, we were overwhelmed. It was the overkill principle. To capture a dozen men, he would use 5,000.

When one talks about guerrilla war in the Escambray, one must talk about the *cercos* and the *peines. Cercos* were rings of troops, while *peines* were combing operations in which thousands of troops were used.

The whole mountain region was surrounded by one gigantic ring of troops — thousands of them. Inside this ring every highway was blocked, every farm taken over by a squad of militia, every civilian moved out and relocated to refugee villages in another province. Every time a guerrilla group was spotted, whole battalions would be mobilized into the region.

For example, if a dozen guerrillas were believed to be hiding out in a pasture, the field would be surrounded by a triple ring of hundreds of militiamen. The first ring would begin to close, sometimes preceded by mortar fire. If the guerrillas broke through the first ring, they would find themselves caught between the first and the second ring; if they broke through the second ring, they faced a third. If any guerrilla broke through, they knew that in the following hours new *cercos* would be thrown in the area, looking for stragglers.

Still, dozens of guerrilla groups fought in the Escambray for several years. In spite of the *cercos*, without food, ammunition or supplies, it took Castro six years to flush out the rebels.

One of the big myths that the Castro regime perpetuated about us was that we received CIA aid, that tons of weapons were dropped by air into the hills to supply our groups. That was a lie. I do not know of a single guerrilla unit that received an air drop. Some of us who joined the guerrillas took our own weapons to the hills. *Campesino* farmers who had weapons left over from the days of the war against Batista donated them to us. Some weapons we captured from the enemy in battle. A few guns we received from the underground. A few rifles here, a few handguns there. Never enough.

With the gigantic ring of troops that surrounded the Escambray Mountains, we were caught inside the noose. It was a very tough situation. To try to break through the ring to escape to the cities would mean being a deserter to the guerrillas; to remain in the mountains meant to eventually be killed or captured. Either way was bad.

That the guerrilla war in the Escambray lasted for so many years was due to the bravery and ingenuity of the *campesinos*, who knew the area well, who were elusive and developed their own network of contacts.

I knew one guerrilla leader, Pedro Gonzalez, who would avoid the big militia offensives by traveling to a small island key a few miles to the south of Cuba. He would hide in the little island for weeks, then return to the mainland to reorganize his units as soon as things calmed down. He did this several times until he was turned in by an informant.

Another guerrilla, Chua Gonzalez, had his family dig a hole

under their house, underneath a stairway. Chua would live inside the house with his wife, Fina. Anytime the militia troops came looking for him, Chua would slip into his hiding hole. For over a year no one could catch him until he made the mistake of making his wife pregnant. Neighbors started whispering that Fina had been unfaithful to her guerrilla husband, yet, Chua's own parents did not seem upset by Fina's pregnancy. The militia soon figured out that Chua was in the neighborhood, and they tore the house apart until they captured him. Chua was taken to a concentration camp. Fina had a son who was called by all in the neighborhood "El Hijo del Hoyo" (The Son of the Hole).

Chua was one of the guerrillas of Luis Vargas, a big mulatto with huge hands that would cover an eating dish. Vargas spent years in the Escambray. He survived from 1960 until December 1, 1965, longer than anyone else ever did. An infiltrator from State Security offered to take Vargas out of the country by boat. When Luis accepted, he walked into a trap. He was executed by a firing squad. Too bad. That man was so elusive that the only way to catch him was by betrayal. Militia troops pinned him down a hundred times with triple *cercos*, but he always slipped through, week after week, month after month, year after year.

When militia troops could not catch us on the field of battle, they tried to set up traps through infiltrators. One very famous story is that of Alberto Delgado, a militia sergeant who was sent to infiltrate the guerrillas in the Escambray. Delgado was given a cover job as a farm administrator in Maisinicu, where he provided some guerrilla groups with food, boots, and medicines to gain their confidence. After becoming friendly with the units operating in the area, Delgado offered Emilio Carretero a way out of the Escambray. Delgado claimed to have contacts in Matanzas Province that could provide a boat and crew to escape to the safety of exile in the United States. For the hungry, badly armed guerrillas, a chance at escaping the hell of the Escambray *cercos* was a ticket to paradise. Dangerous as it seemed, Carretero had to risk escape. But Emilio Carretero, well-seasoned guerrilla that he was, did not trust Delgado completely. Carretero went to see Cheito Leon, a young twenty-three-year-old guerrilla leader.

"If I make it to Miami," he told Leon, "I will send you a message by radio. I will give Delgado only half the message. If you receive the full message over the airwaves, follow me with your men to Florida. If you only hear half the message, it means that I have been betrayed by Delgado and that State Security is trying to set you up also."

A few days later Emilio Carretero, Zoila Aguila, known as "The Girl of the Escambray," and fourteen guerrillas were captured in a trap set up by Alberto Delgado.

Cheito Leon, the young guerrilla, received half of the radio message. While Carretero was being killed by a firing squad, his friend in the Escambray gathered his men and headed for the farm at Maisinicu. The following day the body of Alberto Delgado, hacked by bayonets, was found by militia troops, hanging from a tree by a river bed. Carretero had been avenged.

Cheito Leon continued to fight in the Escambray. The short, dark-haired kid was a tough warrior. Surrounded in a *cerco*, he fought until he ran out of ammunition, blowing himself up with a hand grenade rather than be captured by the militia.

Another famous group of guerrillas were the Tardio Brothers. There were six of them; only one is still alive today. The Tardio Brothers were active in the Escambray from 1960 to 1962. They were a tough bunch. On one occasion, their guerrilla force was surrounded by a triple *cerco,* but they broke through in a fire fight. When they reached a river nearby, Blas Tardio realized that one of their men had been wounded and left behind. They returned, fought their way back into the *cerco,* then fought their way out again. They broke through nine rings of soldiers that day.

When Blas Tardio was wounded in the leg during a skirmish, he plucked the bullet out with the point of a knife, removed pieces of bone chip, digging with his fingers, then stitched up his own wound. He was a hard, tough man. It took thousands of troops months to capture him. Camilo, Blas, and Benjamin died facing a firing squad. Lupe Tardio was killed in combat and Toto committed suicide, hanging himself in prison. The only Tardio still alive is Genaro, who was a political prisoner and is still living in Cuba.

I was captured on September 14, 1960, on a farm near Santa Cruz. In the morning light we were surrounded by a wall of soldiers, a triple ring where their riflemen stood shoulder to shoulder.

I was taken to the hospital at Topes de Collantes, where more than sixty captured guerrillas were being held in an isolated wing. After a few days there, we were tied to each other and transported by buses to the city of Santa Clara, where the trial took place on the twelfth of October. Five men were executed two days later. The rest of us were transported by buses, tied to each other, to the Principe Castle in Havana.

Years later, when a political commissar was trying to convince me to join their phony "rehabilitation" plan, the commissar looked at me sarcastically.

"If you guerrillas were so brave," he told me, "how come you let yourselves be captured instead of dying fighting? You were cowards."

I looked at the man across from me, thinking how Fidel Castro in his youth had attacked the Moncada Barracks and then surrendered to Batista with an archbishop serving as mediator.

"Commissar," I said, "don't make such a statement in front of your prime minister."

"And why is that?"

"Because," I answered, "when he began his war against Batista he attacked an army outpost, hid in the hills for a week, and surrendered, holding on to the skirts of a Catholic priest."

The commissar left the room in anger.

It felt good to tell him off.

8

GUILLERMO PEREZ CALZADA: THE LEGEND OF OSVALDO RAMIREZ

Guillermo Perez Calzada is seventy-two years old, a beefy man with square shoulders and thick hands. He lives in a small apartment in Union City, New Jersey, an area teeming with Cuban exiles.

He grew up in Las Villas Province, where he worked as a farm laborer, eventually becoming a leader in the Sugar Workers Union. A man of deep democratic ideals, he joined the II Front of Escambray in the struggle against Fulgencio Batista. After Castro seized power, Perez Calzada became one of the first revolutionaries to conspire against the system, helping organize the guerrilla uprisings in the Escambray Mountains of central Cuba. His interview portrays not only the difficult life of a guerrilla fighter but also a personal insight of the legendary Osvaldo Ramirez, one of the most fearless freedom fighters of the Cuban struggle.

In June of 1959 we held a secret meeting at a house in Havana. One by one or in pairs, men began arriving until there were fifty-two of us.

Conspiracy at the time was still fairly easy. Castro had only been in power for six months and his repressive machinery had not yet been refined. Opposition against the system was only beginning. Besides, thirty-four of the men gathered in that house were officers of the Rebel Army, veterans of the war against Batista. Our gathering looked more like a military staff briefing than a conspiracy to overthrow the system.

In that short meeting we all were in agreement. Our revolution had been betrayed by Castro and his followers. A war was imminent. The time had come to start preparing for it once again.

Osvaldo Ramirez, a captain in the Rebel Army, was selected to coordinate guerrilla uprisings. Others, like Capt. Clodomiro Miranda, were assigned key positions in preparing the rebellion. Osvaldo Ramirez was a man that I trusted. He was of medium height, mustached, in his late thirties. He had grown up in Las Villas Province, where he had worked as a truck driver, hauling sugar cane to the mills. In the war against Batista he had become a guerrilla leader known for his fearlessness. A serious man, he had little formal education but a high sense of morality and personal dignity.

Throughout the rest of 1959, I worked under orders of Osvaldo Ramirez, who was still an officer in the Rebel Army, attached to the newly created National Revolutionary Police. Working as discreetly as possible, we began transporting small caches of weapons and supplies to the Escambray Mountains, preparing for battle. Osvaldo began recruiting for the new war, contacting former guerrillas and trusted peasants of the region.

The first martyr of the Escambray Mountains was a man named Pedro Rodriguez. He was planning a small uprising with a group of friends. A unit of militia surprised him at a farm, murdering him before he could carry out his plan.

The first combat in the Escambray took place in an area called Sitio de Juana, a hill region in Las Villas. There were eighteen of us, including Osvaldo, preparing an uprising, when we were spotted by a militia patrol. Although we wanted to avoid combat, we had no other choice but to defend ourselves. We fired upon each other. After a few seconds they retreated. It was an uneventful skirmish, but it marked the beginning of a bloody war in the mountains of Cuba.

Within weeks, the Escambray had become a battleground. Dozens of small guerrilla bands became active. Militia patrols were ambushed, roads were blocked, government installations were destroyed.

In those first few months we had so many volunteers that we had to turn them away. We had more men than weapons. With enough guns we could have armed thousands more. The only weapons that we had were a few meager supplies received through the underground or whatever we could take from the enemies we killed in ambush.

On one occasion, at a place called Las Tinajitas, thirty-eight of us were surrounded by a much larger militia force. We broke through their lines, fleeing through the bush with their troops in pursuit. They pinned us down in a hill. Behind us hundreds of militiamen were advancing slowly, while in front we had a small cliff. Below the cliff was a thick jungle and a river.

"We can die here fighting," Osvaldo said, "or we can jump."

Rifles strapped to our bodies, we jumped into the darkness. The bush below was so thick, so dense that it felt like landing on a gigantic mattress, slowly sinking through the foliage to the ground below. Bruised and tired, we prepared to cross the river before our pursuers realized where we were. Crossing that river at night was very tough. The river was very swollen, with a strong current. We lost all our knapsacks. The only things that we saved were our weapons, but these were so important to us that many would have rather drowned than lose their guns.

Soaking wet, gasping for breath but still clutching my Garand rifle, I made it to the shore. Osvaldo was walking up and down the shore, making sure that we were all safe. Osvaldo was the kind of leader who worried about his men. While the militia was still searching for us in the hill on the other side of the river, we began to move deeper into the bush.

That night we hid in the outskirts of a farm called Finca La Ceiba. By morning we were surrounded once more. We decided to disband, regrouping several days later at a prearranged site. Every time we were surrounded in a *cerco* we would dissolve, sneak through the lines of a tightening noose, then regroup at a nearby site.

At La Ceiba one of our men, a farmer from the region, was shot in the back. We skirmished and dispersed. An elite unit of LCB counterinsurgency troops caught Osvaldo Ramirez as he made his way through the noose of troops that surrounded us.

The LCB troops did not realize that they had captured the best-known guerrilla leader in Las Villas. As he was being taken by a squad to an interrogation, Osvaldo broke free. To the surprise of the soldiers, Osvaldo ran to the edge of a nearby cliff and jumped. Our jump the night before had been a calculated risk, a leap from a small hill into a mat of thick brush. What Osvaldo Ramirez did that afternoon at La Ceiba was a suicidal blind leap from a tall cliff, a recklessly daring jump where his chances of survival were one in twenty.

He was lucky: he hit a mattress of leaves, branches, and vegetation, slowing down his fall. Full of cuts and bruises, he hobbled away through the jungle while the surprised squad of troopers gawked down at him from the heights of the cliff.

While Osvaldo was busy making his escape, Emilio Carretero and I hid in the bush. We found a thick clump of lemon trees, like giant umbrellas of foliage with branches reaching the ground. We crawled underneath the foliage, hiding in a small canopy inside the umbrella.

I had my Garand rifle and Emilio was armed with a Dominican-made San Cristobal carbine, a piece of garbage that overheated after firing a few clips. Militia and LCB troops were all around us. We could hear them talking. Carretero and I did not move, did not talk. The heat inside that lemon tree became intense. Sweat matted our hair, drenched our clothing.

When the militia threw a *cerco,* a surrounding maneuver, they never abandoned the area immediately. Dozens of troopers would stay in the area for days, trying to flush out guerrillas hiding in the bush.

Carretero and I hid inside that lemon tree for eight days. At night we crawled through a pasture ground to a creek to drink water. During the day we broiled inside our green foliage hideout. We had no food. Hunger gnawed at us; we were weak. Every day we sat, hour after hour, crowded in that clump of leaves, staring at each other without talking, melting in the heat while militia troops ate and chatted a few yards away from our hideout.

When we linked up with our guerrilla force, we were surprised at how bruised Osvaldo was, how miraculous his survival seemed. I thought he would be incapacitated for weeks, but in fifteen days he was back in action, fighting once more.

In 1960 the Escambray was full of guerrilla bands. Besides our own group there were dozens of others, many of whom came under Osvaldo Ramirez's leadership as time went on. In spite of being outnumbered and outgunned, our guerrilla force grew. At our peak, Osvaldo Ramirez had 208 men under his command operating in a dozen small groups throughout the region. Keeping so many men fed was a logistical problem, but we had a couple of hunters who were very skillful at stealing stray steers from government cooperatives.

One of our most unusual allies was Captain Bombino, an officer in the army who was supposed to be hunting us down. Bombino had several friendly meetings with us, helping us in any way that he could. He would joke with Osvaldo, offering to exchange Osvaldo's M-1 carbine for a modern Belgian FN rifle. Although Osvaldo could have his choice of any weapon in our arsenal, he always preferred the M-1 carbine, feeling that it was a light weapon, very suited for bush warfare.

By the end of 1960, Castro placed a top priority on the elimina-

tion of the Escambray guerrillas. The year 1961 began with what became known as "The Great Offensive."

The Great Offensive was a massive troop mobilization. First, the
Escambray Mountains were surrounded by a gigantic ring of militia
which blocked all access roads in and out of the mountain region. Sec-
ondly, all farmers were evacuated from the area so they could not offer
us help. Thousands of families were relocated out of the Escambray to
resettlement areas in Pinar del Rio Province, hundreds of miles away.

Inside the gigantic ring, dozens of fixed outposts were established
with heavily armed platoons of LCB troops. Then, gridding off the
map, militia batallions started combing specified areas where they suspected guerrillas to be hiding out.

Once a guerrilla band was spotted, a triple *cerco* would be prepared. The three rings of troops would start closing the noose. If the
guerrilla band broke through the first *cerco*, it would find itself facing
two others, with the first one attacking from behind.

It was a hopeless situation for us.

One week after the Great Offensive began, we set up an ambush
at San Ambrosio, deep in the mountains of the Escambray. Rafael Ar-
agones, a good friend and a brave partisan, knew of a creek that ran
through a small gorge on top of a mountain. Rafael set up two squads
for a crossfire ambush, while sentries observed the trails from higher
ground.

We heard them coming from a distance, patrolling unconcerned,
believing in their numerical superiority. They heard the rumbling
noise of the water and ran toward the creek, thirsty. Their lieutenant
was talking loudly, saying how this was a perfect place to lay an ambush for the bandits, to catch them tamely while they came to drink.

The "bandits" were waiting there already. It was over in a few
seconds. Our crossfire tore them apart. Seventeen died. One, a lucky
straggler, survived as he ran away through the trail, down the moun-
tainside. For us it was a good ambush. We captured seventeen weapons. We had welcomed Castro's Great Offensive with a flourish.

But the offensive took its toll. One by one the guerrilla groups
began crumbling.

Without food or ammunition, I decided to take through the line
a seven-man guerrilla unit that I commanded. We moved carefully
through the militia-saturated territory. Every night we slept on hill-
tops so we could observe the enemy troop movements in the morning.

When we arrived near San Pedro, I saw a sight that chilled my blood. Hundreds of militiamen were stationed along the highway. Every few yards there were foxholes with sentries. At four or five in the morning, I spoke to my men.

"We have not eaten in days," I told them, "and we are low on ammunition. If we stay inside this ring we will die. We have to cross the lines, but it is dangerous. Every man must decide for himself."

Six of the men decided to stay behind. Only one, Ramon, decided to risk crossing with me. The six that stayed behind were later killed in an ambush.

Ramon and I covered ourselves with branches. We crawled in the dark through a pasture field toward the highway, toward the militia foxholes. It was a long crawl, done slowly; we wondered every second whether we would be spotted. Ramon and I communicated through hand signals, for a whisper can be heard clearly in the night. We had tied our shoes to our necks, for crossing the highway on bare feet makes less noise than with footwear.

It was the hardest moment of my life. We stayed still, waiting for the right moment. A militiaman left his foxhole, walking across to visit another one, passing directly in front of us.

Then we made our move. As the militiaman walked down the highway with his back toward us, we crossed behind him, in our bare feet. The whole movement was done in a couple of seconds, but it felt like a hundred years long. My heart was pounding in my chest.

As we moved through a ditch, Ramon slipped and fell. The sound he made attracted attention, but the militiaman moved the other way, not being sure where the noise had come from. We crawled through another pasture field, moving away from the line of foxholes behind us.

Although I broke through the ring that surrounded the Escambray, I was captured by a platoon of militia a couple of days later as I drank water from a river. I was a dehydrated mass of skin and bones. I had not eaten in thirteen days. Ahead of me were twenty years of Castro concentration camps, including some at the dreaded Model Prison of the Isle of Pines. But I survived and I am still the same, much older but full of the same ideas and convictions that made me spend over a year with Osvaldo Ramirez in the Escambray.

Osvaldo survived the Great Offensive of 1961. He remained a symbol of the rebellion of the Cuban people. Fidel Castro, frustrated at not being able to trap the elusive guerrilla, even offered Ramirez an amnesty, but Osvaldo did not accept it. For the truck driver-turned-guerrilla, there was no compromise with communism.

On April 16, 1962, his guerrilla force was surrounded at Las Aro-mas. Breaking through three rings of militia in a fire fight, Osvaldo dispersed his band, agreeing to meet at a later date in a new camp. As he walked through heavy brush, cradling his M-1 in his arms, he walked underneath a militia sentry standing on a cliff. Not being able to see anything below him but hearing a noise, the militiaman fired a single shot into the brush. Osvaldo Ramirez, the most famous of all guerrilla leaders, died instantly.

After Osvaldo's death, Tomas San Gil took command of the unit. Tomas died on March 1, 1963, killed in combat with a dozen of his men. Emilio Carretero, my good friend, followed in the leadership. After Carretero died, executed by a firing squad, came the brave Cheito Leon, who also fell fighting for Cuba's freedom.

That is the way with the Cubans. Every time one falls, another is willing to take his place. The dream never dies.

9

TONY SALGADO:
DEATH RIDE AT BAY OF PIGS

On April 17, 1961, a CIA-trained assault brigade of 1,500 Cuban exiles landed at the Bay of Pigs, on a boot-shaped swamp in the southern shores of Cuba. Hoping to establish a beachhead, coordinated with a national uprising, the invasion nevertheless failed due to poor planning and lack of air support.

Tony Salgado was a twenty-seven-year-old squad leader in the Second Battalion, Assault Brigade 2506. Today he is the fifty-three-year-old owner of an auto parts store in Miami.

Salgado arrived in Miami in 1960, leaving a wife and three children in Cuba. A member of the resistance, he had come to the U.S. to enlist in the invasion force. After six months at Base Trax in Guatemala, he returned to Cuba to the three-day war at the Bay of Pigs.

We disembarked from our transport ship before one in the morning. I was dressed in camouflage fatigues and armed with an M-1 Garand rifle with a telescopic sight. The 102 men in my battalion boarded sixteen-foot boats equipped with single engines. We moved swiftly toward Playa Larga Beach, our destination.

Before my boat arrived we began to hear scattered gunfire. We knew that our frogmen were skirmishing on the beach with militia patrols and that our airborne battalion was being dropped to the north of Playa Larga.

As we landed on the sandy shore, our battalion commander,

Hugo Sueiro, gave us the order to move up to the area's only highway, to stop the first of Castro's units attempting to reach the beachhead.

The first of Castro's troops to reach Playa Larga was a battalion of militia from the city of Cienfuegos. They had moved down a road that the paratroopers were unable to seal up. We caught them in a crossfire from our .30-caliber machine guns, killing and wounding dozens of them, but they fought back well, very bravely.

The night lit up with tracer bullets ripping back and forth in the darkness. The sound of gunfire was deafening, constant. Screaming from the wounded and cursing intermingled with the sounds of explosions. It was a brutal battle that lasted for hours. The sun came up over Playa Larga and in the light of the morning we fought on, sometimes so close that we could hear their squad leaders screaming instructions to each other.

At ten o'clock in the morning I volunteered to lead my squad in a flanking maneuver on one of their point units. My Garand rifle was useless by then, jammed beyond repair, but I had several grenades. We came in from the side, without being spotted. They were too busy paying attention to our heavy machine guns up the road. I crawled up as close as I could, then lobbed a grenade in their direction. There was a white flash followed by screams. The militiamen began running and my squad opened fire on them, wounding several.

As I began to turn toward my men, a sniper fired at me from a nearby tree. The bullet entered my chest, pierced a lung, and made an exit hole in the back. I began to open my mouth, but felt it filling up with the sticky taste of blood.

I felt light and calm. Everything was white. I felt a spinning sensation, as if I was twirling in the air, away from myself. It was a very strange feeling, a euphoria that made all anxiety vanish, lifting me upwards. I realized that I was dying, but it did not seem important at the time. In my only moment of anguish, I asked God to let me see my wife and three children one last time.

Reality came rushing back. Pain burned through me. It felt as though a hot iron had been pushed through my body.

Panfilo, a very brave soldier from my squad, came to my aid. Carlos Rivero and the Cala and Babun brothers also came to my rescue. Coughing blood, I was taken to a small cottage at Playa Larga. There were other wounded there, waiting for medical assistance.

I remembered what I had learned in my training. If shot through the belly, do not drink water; if shot through the chest, do not talk. I knew the blood in my mouth indicated that my lung had been pierced, so I said as little as possible. Yet, I told Enrique Diaz, a fellow brigade member: "Tell my wife that I have died fighting for freedom for my children, against communism."

As I waited for medical assistance, Castro's Sea Fury planes flew above the beaches, strafing and destroying the *Houston* and the *Rio Escondido,* our supply ships and communications centers. Large clouds of black smoke rose to the sky south of us, from the sea.

Our own planes could only overfly the beach for a few minutes, for they were flying from faraway bases in Central America and lacked fuel to give us proper cover. We had only slow-moving Mitchell bombers, leftovers from the Second World War, while Castro's air force still had several fast Sea Fury fighters and even a T-33 jet fighter. Our commanders on the ground begged on the radios for proper air cover, but the air cover never came.

Rodolfo Sorondo, a fellow brigade member, was the medic to assist me. He stripped my shirt off, bandaging me, plugging the holes in my chest and back so air would not enter the wounds. A brigade medical officer looked at my wounds. He looked at Sorondo and shook his head. "There is nothing we can do for this one," he said, "make him as comfortable as possible."

I was given a morphine injection. The drug relieved the pain. I rested in a stupor, drifting in and out of sleep, listening to the explosions and the sounds of gunfire that never seemed to end.

One of the times that I woke up, I found myself alone in the room. Drugged, I wondered whether I had been left alone to die in that room at Playa Larga. I had not, however, for Sorondo and others were outside, digging trenches to protect us from the fire of Castro's advancing artillery.

As the first day of battle ended, our situation seemed very dismal. Without air support, we were sitting ducks for Castro's air force. Our supply and communications ships had been destroyed. Behind us was the sea, littered with sunken and burning ships. In front of us, some 30,000 troops were being massed to overwhelm about 1,300 of us.

As nighttime began to fall, the artillery shells started pounding the beach. Mortar rounds lifted geysers of sand as we crouched in our recently dug trenches.

I was fully conscious again. After those first injections of morphine, I had decided to bear the pain rather than accept the drugs. I feared becoming dependent on the morphine and I also wanted my senses as clear as possible to face the coming events. I did not have any movement in my right arm. It dangled, useless at my side. My chest was bandaged and I was wearing pajama bottoms that someone had dressed me in during one of my unconscious moments. I was pale and weak. I looked so pathetic that I received a new nickname; I was called *El Muerto Vivo,* which means "the Living Dead," a ghoulishly appropriate name.

Throughout the night our men reorganized, scrounging for ammunition and weapons. Without supplies, Brigade 2506 seemed doomed. We needed air strikes and air drops.

Expecting to be evacuated by a supply plane scheduled to come in, I was taken to Giron Beach on the morning of April 18. At some beach cabanas I joined the other wounded brigade members. Although I was tired and in pain, I was able to walk slowly. When I entered the cabana, I recognized one of the wounded. It was a squadmate, one of the Cala brothers who had picked me up when I was wounded the day before. He had assumed command of my squad until he was shot in the leg later on that day.

A couple of our Mitchell bombers had been shot down by Castro's fighter planes. Matias Farias, one of our pilots, was at the cabanas also, waiting to hitch a ride on the transport evacuation. His B-26 had been shot down by a Sea Fury the evening before.

As the morning battle began, the supply plane came in, flying through a barrage of artillery. Unfortunately, it was unable to pick up the wounded, for Castro's Sea Furies were in the area hunting for him. All that could be done was to drop off a few boxes of pistol ammunition before taking off seconds ahead of Castro's strafing planes. Pilot Farias was the only one able to leave on the plane.

Realizing that air evacuation of the wounded was impossible without air cover, several of us decided to go to a nearby clinic near Giron Beach in search of supplies. Less than a dozen of us, half of us wounded, set out in jeeps toward our objective.

The clinic was only a small first aid station and a few huts. As we approached it, we realized that it was being held by a squad of militia. To our surprise, they retreated on the run, perhaps expecting us to be part of a larger strike force. We spent a couple of hours at the station before deciding to retreat back to the beach at Giron.

By the end of the second day of combat, we all realized that our situation was hopeless. Fighting had been fierce on all fronts. The brigade had fought heroically. Our youngest hero, sixteen-year-old Felipe

Rondon, had destroyed a tank with a bazooka at such close range that his own shrapnel killed him. Another one, Gilberto Hernandez, was blinded by shrapnel in one eye, but fought on until killed while manning a bazooka. Less than twenty of our paratroopers had held back a full battalion of regular troops, pinning them on a road. Dozens of our men had been killed. We were almost out of ammunition and even drinking water, pinned down on a strip of beach only a few miles long, outnumbered by more than thirty to one.

The word soon came down. The brigade was to disband into small groups, to hide in the huge Zapata swamp or try to link with the Escambray guerrillas, 100 miles or so to the east of Giron. A few members of the brigade set out to sea in rafts and boats. Some were captured, some died of dehydration and thirst, while others were rescued days later by friendly ships cruising the area. During the last day, the CIA informed Jose San Roman, the brigade commander, that the agency would evacuate the headquarters staff to safety. San Roman declined. "Either we all leave," he said, "or we all die here. I will not leave my men." San Roman stayed on, fighting in the swamp until captured. I consider him one of the bravest men I've ever met.

We knew that it would be impossible to break the wall of troops ahead of us. Castro had bottlenecked us in with every available unit he had, including buses full of policemen from towns in Las Villas and Matanzas provinces. There was a giant traffic jam of tanks, armored vehicles, and trucks on the road to Bay of Pigs, toward us. To puncture holes in that wall to reach the Escambray was impossible, but we were unwilling to surrender.

Rodolfo Sorondo and I said goodbye at Giron Beach. Gunfire was breaking out along the lines. He told me he was headed for the Escambray. I would have wished to join him, but it was impossible for me to make such a distance on foot. I was seriously hurt.

I sat with several wounded inside a bullet-riddled Volkswagen van that had been commandeered from some civilian. We began to move down a road, away from the gunfire of the last skirmishes fought at the Bay of Pigs. We had not traveled far when we heard the roar of an approaching plane, one of the Sea Furies on a strafing run. We ran from the van seconds ahead of the tracer bullets which tore the vehicle to shreds, setting it on fire.

I found myself alone in Zapata swamp, dressed in pajama bottoms, with a punctured lung, hungry and unarmed. I did not know where I was headed, but I knew that I did not want to surrender. I spent the rest of the day walking through the swamp. Above me, helicopters cruised on patrol, looking for us. Throughout the rest of the day I heard scattered gunfire as small skirmishes were fought in their mopping-up operation. At night I sat alone in the darkness, too tired to walk. I leaned back on a large boulder, totally exhausted.

I felt small animals moving near me in the darkness. I felt one touch me. I kicked out. Others moved closer. In the darkness, I realized what was happening. Dozens of crabs were moving toward me in the night, attracted by the smell of my blood. It was a moment of supreme horror. I could feel in the darkness dozens of little pinhead eyes staring at me. I could hear the clicking of little claws opening and closing. I was going to be eaten alive!

I stood up, lashing out with my feet. I had no movement in my right arm, but with the left I seized a branch from the wet ground. Breathing hard, I managed to climb on the boulder that I had been leaning against. I sat on the rock and began to move the branch back and forth, slowly. I knew that crabs are not courageous by nature. I knew the slight movement of the branch would keep the ugly little creatures at a distance, but I wondered how long I could stay awake, protecting myself.

It was the worst moment of my life. I sat on that rock for hours, moving that branch while the crabs circled me. My left arm cramped and I could not move the right one. My chest felt hollow and my bandages were filthy. I had not slept, showered, or shaved for days. Worst of all, the invasion had failed.

I sat on the rock and I cursed and cried. I cursed the airplanes that never showed, the poor planning of the CIA that had caused the failure. I cried with rage, thinking of my friends who had died, of a nation, my nation, doomed under a dictatorship. I felt pain, hunger, exhaustion, but worst of all, the humiliation of defeat.

If I had been in possession of a weapon I would have killed myself. Death would have been a relief, a welcome. I wished for death many times that night, but I kept moving the branch, thinking about my wife and my three children in Havana.

I survived. Somehow I did not pass out and the crabs moved away. The sun came over the swamp. I stood up, stumbled, and continued walking through the mud and brush.

I was captured early on the morning of the twentieth. I turned a bend on the trail, stumbling into a battalion of militia. Machine guns and rifles pointed at me. One militiaman screamed at me to raise my arms above my head. I raised my left arm. They screamed again. I told them that I was wounded and unable to move my other arm.

Escorted by four soldiers I was made to walk back to Giron Beach, where all prisoners were being held. I was taken to one of the cabanas there, where more than a dozen brigade members were being held.

I had the wound treated by an army doctor. He was a sadist, for he did not give or offer any anesthetic to ease my pain. He would probe, digging in with his instrument, asking me, smiling, if it hurt. It hurt like fire and I was scared, but I kept looking at him and answering: "No it does not hurt."

The following day, sometime after noon, we were told that we would be transported to Havana. We stood in a single file, giving our names, ranks, and serial numbers to a sergeant with a notepad.

Osmani Cienfuegos stood by the door to the room when I was a couple of feet from the sergeant. Cienfuegos was Castro's minister of public works, a man with a reputation for sarcasm and cruelty.

"How many are there?" he asked.

"One hundred and sixty plus nineteen wounded," the officer said.

"Put them all together. Let the healthy offer the wounded their seats," he answered.

There were no seats, however, for healthy or wounded. We were to be transported to Havana in a sealed eighteen-wheeler tractor trailer truck.

We were packed into the truck like cattle, pressed shoulder to shoulder, jammed in. I sat down next to Oscar Rodriguez, then leaned back against the wooden wall of the trailer. Moments later, the doors closed and I heard the metallic sound of latches locking.

It was dark inside the truck. As we began moving, prisoners were falling, bumping into each other. It was hot, very hot, until it became an oven. Sweat began to pour off our bodies, soaking all of us, as though we had been hosed from head to toe. With every passing mile it became harder to breathe. Men began banging on the walls, screaming. One man vomited. Then another, and another, until it was impossible to keep count. Men around me were hyperventilating. One began praying aloud, and then others. The sound of prayer mixed with the sound of vomiting and screams of rage and anguish. The floor became slick with vomit and sweat.

Condensation from our bodies formed on the ceiling of the truck, then dripped down in cold drops over us. Some men used their belt buckles to try to make holes in the wood and metal walls around us. After what seemed like hours, a few tiny holes were made, thin shafts of light and fresh air, but never enough.

I did not move or panic. I was beyond exhaustion, totally drained. I closed my eyes. I heard a scream. One of us had died. A few minutes later, another man died.

The strongest men began to help those who were dying. The weakest were moved toward the air holes, their faces pressed to the shafts of light and air.

A third man died. Our hands and feet were swollen. The smell of urine and vomit filled the truck. The trailer stopped still a couple of times, but the doors remained locked in spite of our screams.

I did not scream because I did not want to weaken my only lung. I did not talk, except for a few whispers to Oscar Rodriguez, next to me. All I did was sit against the wall concentrating on survival, breath by breath. Oscar and others helped me, shielding me so I would not be stepped on, opening a hole near me so I could breathe.

Number four died. The screams continued, intermingled with curses. A fifth man whose face had been pressed against the holes also died.

We all wondered when we would arrive in Havana. We had been riding for hours. Men continued choking on their vomit. Someone screamed that number six had died. Other men began praying. Number seven died. The slime and vomit sloshed the floor of our truck. Then number eight died in the hands of a friend. More screaming, more prayers, and a ninth man died.

The doors opened and the night air came rushing in, cooling us, filling our lungs. Air, pure air. We sucked it in, breath by breath, relishing the moment.

We had reached our destination. As I left the truck I saw nine bodies lying on the ground by the side of the trailer. A tenth man died minutes later, weakened by the ordeal.

After several weeks in a hospital, I rejoined the other members of Brigade 2506, imprisoned at El Principe Castle. After fifteen months of imprisonment, almost 1,100 of us were ransomed off by the U.S. government in exchange for extortion supplies.

It was an honor serving as a member of Assault Brigade 2506. We did our best but were betrayed by the cowardice of politicians in Washington.

I did get to see my children again. After I was freed, my family joined me in Miami.

I can tell you one thing, however. I did not eat crab meat for twenty years after that night at Bay of Pigs.

10

FRANCISCO VERDECIA:
A MEETING WITH GOD

While still a teenager, Francisco Verdecia became involved in the struggle against Fulgencio Batista, joining the ranks of Fidel Castro's 26 of July Movement. Exiled to the United States, he tried to return to Cuba with an armed expedition, being detained by U.S. authorities in Key West. In 1959, after Batista was ousted, Verdecia became an intelligence officer in DIER, the government branch that soon afterwards became the dreaded Department of State Security. Disenchanted with the Castro regime, he joined the resistance network of the 30 of November Movement. On October 13, 1960, Verdecia was arrested on charges of conspiring to assassinate Blas Roca, a top old-line Communist. Condemned to eighteen years of imprisonment, he became a plantado, *one of the stubborn prisoners who refuse to accept Communist indoctrination.*

The following interview, detailing Verdecia's escape from a concentration camp and his flight from Cuba, was conducted in a New York apartment where Verdecia works as superintendent.

Although I had attended Catholic schools as a child, life in the concentration camps turned me into an atheist. Seeing the pain, the cruelty, the senseless suffering of my country, turned me against God . . .

At La Cabana Fortress, I saw friends of mine given quick trials and then sent to face a firing squad. Armando Bernal was one of those friends. His only crime was possession of anti-Communist propaganda. Yet he was given the death penalty. At his trial, the guards did not

95

even allow him to embrace his small son for the last time. It was cruel, senseless. His child attended the trial and yet they did not allow Armando even a few seconds to bid his son farewell. They executed him that night.

Another martyr was Balbino Diaz, a young man in his mid-twenties who slept on the bunk below mine. He was a good-looking man with blondish-brown hair, who died facing a firing squad.

As I lost friends, I lost my faith in God. If there is a God, I asked myself, how can he allow these men to die?

Since I entered prison I wanted to escape. I made dozens of plans which were useless. One of the best was at the Isle of Pines Prison, where a group of us expected to escape in the middle of a hurricane, using a primitive rope which we had manufactured from cloth and rags. An informant spoiled our plans and we were unable to carry out the escape.

In March of 1967 I was transferred to Taco-Taco Prison in Pinar del Rio Province, west of Havana. Together with two trusted friends, Guillermo Fernandez and Felix Hernandez, I began planning an escape. After weeks of scrounging we were able to gather together a few razor blades and five pesos, our meager escape supplies. Every day, when we worked in the fields, we carried our money and razor blades with us, looking for an opportunity to escape.

Early on the morning of June 21, 1967, as we worked in the fields, a fellow prisoner told me that Chao Morales had escaped. Although I was happy that Morales had fled, I realized that security would be tightened for the rest of us. While Guillermo, Felix, and I wondered about our own escape plans, about a hundred of us were taken to an area where we were expected to clear out a jungle of thorny bushes.

As we worked side by side, we began to formulate a plan of escape. On the other side of the thick wall of bushes there was a three-meter slope and a canal with muddy water. Beyond the canal was a cane field about one kilometer long. On the other side of the cane field was a thick forest.

We talked among ourselves. If we could make it to the forest without being seen, we had a good chance of escaping. It was dangerous and foolish, but after seven years of imprisonment I was willing to gamble.

We made a hole through the wall of thorns and branches. When the guards became distracted we slipped through, sliding to the canal below. In a few minutes we found ourselves in the cane field. The field was recently plowed, without cover, so we began to crawl as fast as we could among the furrows, toward the forest ahead.

We crawled for one full kilometer, sweating under the broiling sun, puffing hard. It took a couple of hours. By the time we arrived at the forest we were exhausted, in a stupor. From our new hiding place we could see the guards in the distance, gathering the prisoners for a head count. Our escape had finally been noticed.

Tired and sweaty, we began walking through the forest. Lucky for us, Guillermo was a country boy who knew how to survive in any jungle. A CIA-trained commando, he had been captured in a raid, escaping death by a firing squad by pretending to be insane. He received a thirty-year prison sentence.

As we walked through the forest, Guillermo stopped and bent over looking at the ground.

"Deer tracks," he told us, "we are saved. We follow these tracks and we can slip through holes in the bush that soldiers will be unable to find when they come after us."

He was right. Following those tracks on the ground, we crawled through small cracks in the brush. I had dozens of thorns jabbing at my head, my arms, my legs as I moved under the wall of branches. We felt like human pin cushions, covered by slivers of thorns, our clothing ripping in the branches.

The following days were a nightmare. In the distance we heard the barking of dogs, tracking us. Luckily, the area we were in was full of canals and small riverbeds. We walked for hours on the canals, so the dogs could not follow our scent. Hungry, we ate whatever we could find. One night we ate cauliflowers from a farmer's field. From another farm we stole clothing that was drying on ropes under the hot sun.

After three days on the move, dressed in the clothing we had stolen, cleanly shaved with our razor blades, we decided to try to take a bus to Havana. I walked into the town of San Cristobal and purchased a milk shake and a potato stuffed with meat.

Believing that our chances were good to continue our escape, I was soon joined by Guillermo and Felix. We boarded a bus headed for the town of Artemisa, from where we would transfer to another bus headed for Havana.

A few miles out of San Cristobal, the bus stopped at an army roadblock. Our bus was almost empty. Besides the driver and the three of us, the only other passengers were a couple sitting toward the back of the vehicle.

"They are searching the vehicles," the driver said, looking directly at the three of us. Perhaps he said it as a warning, in case we wanted to get off before the troops boarded us. We did not move.

Two armed soldiers boarded the vehicle.

"Is something wrong?" one of them asked the driver.

"No," the driver answered, "all is well."

Both soldiers looked at us, staring. We stared back. Those few seconds seemed like hours. Without saying another word, both soldiers left. The truck jerked back into motion.

Once we arrived in Havana we hid at a farm in El Cotorro, a place Guillermo knew well. We slept in the bushes, trying to make contacts to help us leave the country. After two weeks, I traveled to La Vibora, a Havana neighborhood where I had lived. Friends helped me out, providing me with money to help us survive and move around.

The three of us decided to travel to Yaguajay, a town in northeastern Cuba. Guillermo grew up in that area and knew many people, including some relatives who would help us out.

One of our contacts took us out of Havana Province to Matanzas, where we took four different bus rides to Yaguajay.

Yaguajay is surrounded by hills. Knowing the area well, Guillermo had us hide in the farms while he made contacts and obtained weapons.

After one week in Yaguajay we decided to make our escape. We had spotted two men who owned a couple of fishing sloops in an isolated beach area. We surprised them, kidnapping them so they could not inform on us. The five of us left Cuba on a flat-bottomed seventeen-foot sailboat with a single mast. Our supplies consisted of one barrel of water, a couple of cans of canned duck meat, and a few tins of condensed milk.

For the first part of the journey, all went well. We dropped the men off at Cayo Langosta key, then proceeded north on our own. The three of us had no knowledge of seamanship, so the journey became more dangerous as we moved alone in the open sea.

That evening at six o'clock the sea became very choppy. Our sailboat began to buck up and down on the waves. Water splashed us. The reflector from a lighthouse lit the sea. Felix later told me that we had been fired upon from the shore at this time, but I really don't remember. At the time I was too busy being terrified by large waves to worry about bullets. It was a long night but we survived the bullets and the weather.

There are moments that I will never forget about those days at sea. One night as Felix and I slept, Guillermo screamed a warning. We woke up to the feeling of a shark ramming against the side of our sailboat. Our vessel tipped over, as we grabbed on in desperation. Our barrel of water and a machete fell overboard. In the pale light of the night I saw a large black shadow moving away swiftly. It was a very frightening moment.

On the third day at sea the sky began to turn dark. A mass of black clouds covered us, encircling the horizon on all sides. There was not a single shaft of light anywhere. The sea was a deep ink color while the sky was slate gray. It felt like a nightmare.

"I think we better do some praying," Guillermo said.

My two friends began to pray. I looked at them. I had my doubts. It had been a long time since I had prayed, since I had felt any faith within me. Reluctantly, I joined them. Without fresh water, dehydrated, broiled by the tropical sun, in a leaky boat, sailing blindly in the middle of the ocean, prayer was the only alternative.

As we finished praying we saw ahead of us a bright light in the distance. The gray blanket of the horizon began to open up. On either side of us the black clouds were rolling away. It was incredible! In a matter of minutes the darkness was behind us and we were sailing on a green ocean with a clear sky above us.

I was stunned. I felt calm. I felt God within me. I was no longer afraid of the ocean, the storm, or the sharks. I did not feel alone anymore.

He does exist after all, I told myself. When I arrive in Miami, I swear, I am going to a church and pray in front of a statue of the Virgin of Charity.

We spent five days at sea. The first ship we saw was a freighter named *Jamaica,* whose captain informed us by screams that we were forty miles southeast of Key West. Ignoring our pleas for help, he left us stranded, almost overturning us in his wake.

The second vessel we saw was a cruise ship. Passengers waved at us, but they also ignored us, and the boat continued on its way.

On the fifth day we saw a third vessel. Much to our dismay, we saw a large red star painted on its chimney. For a few moments we thought that it could be a Soviet vessel, until we saw that it was flying an American flag. It was a Texaco Oil ship.

The ship circled us slowly to prevent capsizing us. Screaming back and forth, they informed us that we were forty miles east of Palm

Beach. Requesting asylum, we were taken aboard. The three of us were tanned as brown leather, emaciated from dehydration, bearded and filthy.

The meal that I ate aboard that ship was the most delicious feast of my life. Slabs of roast beef swimming in hot gravy, mashed potatoes, and ice cold glasses of water. Exactly one month after crawling through the furrows of a canefield to escape from a Communist concentration camp, we arrived to freedom in the United States.

Taken to a refugee processing center in Opa-Locka, I was detained for days while immigration officials prepared our paperwork.

I remember one Sunday in Opa-Locka when a sudden urge made me act irrationally. I jumped out a barracks window, climbed over a fence, and found myself walking the streets of Northwest Miami. Although I knew that I was going to be reprimanded by immigration authorities, there was something that I had to do . . .

I stopped a passing car. A Cuban was driving.

"Where are you headed?" I asked.

"Downtown Miami. And you?"

"To a church. Any church."

"Get in," he said, "there's one near where I'm going."

The Church of Gesu is an old, large building in a street corner of downtown Miami. I walked in. There in a corner stood a plaster figure of Our Lady of Charity, the patron saint of all Cubans. I kneeled on a pew, praying and crying.

A couple of years later, I returned to the Church of Gesu. I had been living in New York, where my family had joined me. On a holiday to Florida, I took them to see the statue of Our Lady of Charity, in front of whom I had cried and thanked God on my arrival to exile. I could not find the image, so I decided to ask a priest.

"Pardon me, father," I said, "but I am looking for the image of Our Lady of Charity which stood over in that corner."

The priest looked puzzled. "My son," he answered me, "we have never had the image of Our Lady of Charity in this church."

11
POLITA GRAU:
A WOMAN IN REBELLION

She is tall, gray-haired, an aristocratic figure of a woman in her early seventies, conservatively dressed and perennially smiling.

Polita Grau lives in a small apartment in Northwest Miami, a complex run by a Catholic Church organization. The modest one-bedroom unit that she shares with her sister is immaculately clean. The walls are covered with photographs and plaques. A large oil painting of her uncle, Dr. Grau San Martin, twice president of Cuba, is in the center of the wall. On a second wall, a bulletin board is filled with snapshots of family and friends. One glossy photograph stands out: it is a picture of Polita at the age of sixty-three, on a beach. She is dressed in a dark blue prison uniform, the trademark of the Cuban women political prisoners in rebellion, those who refused to accept Castro's "rehabilitation program."

Polita Grau is a living legend among Cuban exiles. Working together with her brother, Dr. Ramon "Mongo" Grau Alsina, they established an underground network in Cuba that operated at full capacity for years. Agents of their resistance units played key roles in the investigations of Soviet missiles in Cuba that brought forth the Cuban Missile Crisis. The Graus were involved in two unsuccessful attempts on the life of Fidel Castro, and their huge network helped smuggle thousands of Cuban children out of the island to freedom in the U.S. Captured, they both faced prison as plantados, prisoners in rebellion. Polita Grau's story offers a view of women in Cuba's concentration camps that is both an example of the most horrible of human rights violations and a cou-

101

*rageous tribute to the strength of the human spirit that refuses to bend under tor-
ture and degradation.*

I was never a party-goer or a socialite. I grew up in an environment of politics and conspiracy. When I was barely a teenager, my home in Havana was the center of gathering for many idealistic young students plotting the overthrow of the government of Gerardo Machado.

My uncle, Dr. Ramon Grau San Martin, was a professor at the University of Havana. In 1928, in spite of government censorship and pressure, my uncle sided with the students of the outlawed Revolutionary Student Directorate. By opening his classroom to free debate, my uncle brought upon himself the wrath of the dictatorship and the support of the student rebels. Arrested several times, he became a father figure, a symbol to many of the young people who fought against Machado.

Growing up in the house of Dr. Grau taught me the importance of fighting for one's principles, of struggling to achieve a goal in spite of the odds. As a teenager I helped in any way that I could, in any way that I was allowed.

In September of 1933, as Machado's government toppled in a bloodbath, the Revolutionary Student Directorate appointed my uncle as provisional president of Cuba.

My uncle's government was a reformist, pro-labor movement. In the few brief months that he was in power before being forced to resign by the military power of Fulgencio Batista, my uncle called for a constitutional convention to consolidate democratic principles, clashed openly with U.S. economic interests, and confronted the Communists.

Since the days of the struggle against Machado, I became a political activist. My first husband, Roberto Lago, was a veteran of the Revolutionary Student Directorate, an idealist with deep democratic principles.

I grew up totally immersed in politics. My uncle became president of Cuba for a second time in 1944, when he defeated Batista in an election. His four years in office were followed by the election of his protégé, a former Directorio student, Carlos Prio. Prio never finished his term in office, for on March 10, 1952, Batista again seized power in a *coup d'etat*.

Many different groups conspired to overthrow Batista. One of the half dozen different factions was the Partido Autentico, the political party to which my uncle belonged.

I became very involved in the struggle. I was no longer a teen-ager. I was in my early forties, married, with two children; yet, most of my free time was spent transporting and hiding weapons and explosives, arranging safe hideouts for members of the resistance, collecting funds for the struggle.

One day my mother, Paulina, received a phone call. It was Batista, calling from his office in the Presidential Palace. In a conference with Colonel Esteban Ventura, the police chief requested permission to arrest Pola Grau. Batista, not wanting to arrest the niece of a former president of Cuba, and fearing the publicity that would come from such an arrest, denied permission.

"Get Polita out of the country," Batista told my mother, "or I'll have to have her arrested."

That same afternoon in 1958, my husband, two children, and I left Cuba on a flight bound for Miami. I became an exile for the first time. For the first of many times the prestige of the Grau name had saved my life.

Carlos Prio was planning a coup for the first week in January 1959, but Batista decided to leave the country on New Year's Eve. On the first day of the new year we woke up to the news that the regime had crumbled. While everyone was overjoyed, I felt skeptical. If Fidel Castro was to gain the upper hand, I felt that a new dictatorship would come into being in Cuba. I had never trusted Fidel, considering him a professional agitator that had been involved in too many Latin American revolutions, a political gangster not to be trusted.

I decided to return to Cuba in May of 1959. After observing the Cuban Revolution for five months, I decided that my worst fears had been confirmed — that a new dictatorship was being imposed upon the Cuban people. I returned to Cuba to start, once again, on the road to revolution, to start plotting once more for the rights of my people.

Within days after my arrival I went to visit Dr. Alberto Hernandez, a good friend who had fought against Batista. Hernandez and I had a brief conversation. It took only a few minutes to realize that Alberto felt the same way that I did, that the democratic principles that had fomented the insurrection against Batista were being betrayed and our nation was being sold to the Soviet sphere. I told Alberto that I wanted to become involved in any conspiracy that was being prepared against Castro. Alberto nodded, understandingly. Within a few days I became a member of "Rescate Revolucionario" (Revolutionary Rescue), an organization headed by Tony Varona, a former Directorio student leader who had fought Machado and had later served as prime minister of Cuba under Carlos Prio.

I began working very hard in the newly formed underground network. Our national coordinator was Alberto Cruz, an excellent man, a real patriot. He put me in charge of coordinating the women's section on a national level.

I began structuring an espionage network in the Island utilizing only women. Within a few months, the network was operational in every one of Cuba's six provinces. Each province had an independent network, supervised by a provincial coordinator. The six provincial coordinators reported to Enriqueta Meoqui and Maria Horta, two women who served as my liaison with the regional networks.

We had some very brave women involved in the underground. One that I shall never forget was Maria Dolores Nunez de Beato, an aristocratic widow in her late sixties. In spite of her age, she became the provincial coordinator for Matanzas, where she structured a very efficient group. Her women agents helped hide and feed guerrilla groups operating against Castro in that region. Maria Dolores died of old age years ago, but I still think of her often, as an exemplary woman of tremendous courage.

The women's network was one of the most active units in the Island. One of our most valued agents, Ofelia Miranda, whom I did not know at the time but met later in prison, was directly involved in the investigation of Soviet missile sites in Pinar del Rio Province. The information that she gathered and transmitted through us was later used by the Kennedy administration during the Cuban Missile Crisis.

Another woman who was a key operative in the network was Albertina O'Farrill. Albertina was a very active, dynamic woman. She developed first-rate contacts in many foreign embassies in Havana. Albertina, who appeared to be just a party girl, was really a very valuable agent. Our network had excellent contacts at the embassies of Great Britain, Switzerland, France, the United Arab Republics, Japan, and a dozen Latin American republics. We used these contacts to smuggle information out and to arrange for political asylum for many underground fighters fleeing from Castro's police.

One day I discovered that my brother Mongo was also involved in the resistance movement, at an even deeper level than I was. Mongo and I had a series of long conversations in which we both decided to remain in Cuba fighting against Castro but, in order to save our families, we would send them into exile.

Our uncle, the former president, refused to leave Cuba. Mongo and I sent our families away. My son was almost twenty at the time. I sat down with him and told him that it was important for us that he leave Cuba, to work in the United States. Grudgingly, he accepted, after I promised that I would follow him soon afterwards.

My mother, my husband, my son and daughter, my brother Pancho and his family all left Cuba bound for exile. Only three of us remained: my uncle, my brother Mongo, and myself. I felt saddened because those that I loved dearest had left the country, but glad because I was unencumbered by a family, able to spend all my time conspiring against the system.

My most trusted friend was Nenita Carames, a brave woman who always volunteered for the most dangerous work in our network. I have known her for decades, trusted her completely, and she never let me down. Our friendship still remains.

Late in 1959 my brother Mongo was contacted by a woman working through the British Embassy. In a series of conversations, Mongo was told that the Catholic Bureau in the United States was interested in helping thousands of Cuban children emigrate to the United States. At the time there was much talk in Cuba about the "Patria Potestad," a government edict that would allow the regime to take children away from their parents. Terrified, thousands of Cubans became concerned about the future of their family units. Thousands of Cuban children were already being shipped out of the country, sent to study in the Soviet Union and other satellite countries.

The Catholic Bureau wanted to expedite the exodus of children from Cuba. A coordinator was needed inside the Island to gather the children. My brother Mongo accepted the job.

So began one of the most awesome tasks ever undertaken by a resistance movement. From Miami, Monsignor Bryan Walsh was to send us thousands of false visas, authorizing Cuban children entry into the United States. Inside Cuba, Mongo was to set up a network through parishes and churches, gathering the children, providing them with visas. Once the children had their paperwork ready, our network would have to figure out a way of arranging a seat for them on a flight leaving the county — a tough feat, for seats on airplanes leaving Cuba were in high demand.

We began our task by assembling together a first-rate work team.

Several of the women in my network volunteered to work in the Rescue the Children program. Mongo obtained some excellent contacts, which included several custom inspectors and some key personnel in Pan American and KLM airlines.

My brother then sent trusted contacts to travel throughout Cuba, contacting people he trusted and religious leaders. Although the network was to channel the children through the Catholic Bureau in Miami, the operation encompassed more than a hundred churches and parishes, not only of the Catholic faith but also Baptist and other Protestant churches.

In a few weeks the network was set up. If a parent wanted to leave the country but was bogged down by months of bureaucratic paperwork, he could take out a legal passport for his child, obtain a false visa from us, and send his child ahead in care of the Catholic Bureau. As desperate as the situation was, for many parents who were facing prison because of their political convictions, being able to send the children out of harm's way was a measure of relief impossible to describe, impossible to understand unless one has faced the agony of seeing one's children growing up in a climate of dictatorship and oppression.

Our headquarters for the falsification of the visas was our home, in the Miramar section of Havana. The large house that we shared with Uncle Ramon was located directly across the avenue from the headquarters of the State Security Department. That street in Miramar became a busy place. On one side of the street, Cubans were being arrested, processed, and tortured by Castro's security agents. On the other side of the road, we were busy trying to process as many false visas as we could, running an espionage network and even plotting how to physically eliminate Fidel Castro.

The backyard to our home in Miramar had a large courtyard, with private parking for several vehicles. At times there were traffic jams of cars and people entering and leaving through our back doors, while we tried to do our work as quickly as possible.

With every passing day our task became more monumental. There were times that we would run out of the visas that Monsignor Walsh was sending us, so we would falsify our own. My brother Mongo became an expert at falsifying Bryan Walsh's signature.

Alberto Cruz, who coordinated Rescate's underground units, was living clandestinely, changing hideouts constantly. He was involved in two attempts on the life of Castro in which we participated. One of the attempts was done by introducing poisoned capsules into a milk shake that Castro would drink. Knowing about our activities on behalf of the children's exodus, Cruz left me a small package at Herminia Suarez's house.

To our delight, the package contained the official United States rubber stamps used on adult visas. Mongo was thrilled. Cruz's gift meant that we could reproduce visas in Cuba by the thousands, being able to smuggle out adults as well as children. These visas were directly stamped to the passports.

Israel Padilla, an extraordinary man with excellent forging abilities, Julio Bravo, an executive at Pan American Airlines, and I would meet one night a week. At a single sitting, using the stamps, we produced 300 visas. This went on for months and we received much help from Elvirita Zayas, who worked as a diplomat for the Panamanian Embassy. She allowed us the use of her home, a dangerous proposition with the increased surveillance of State Security.

As time went by, danger increased for Mongo and me. My name began being mentioned in trials of underground freedom fighters. Years later I would find out that a maid that worked in our household for a couple of years was an agent of State Security. Obviously, the regime knew years ahead of our arrest that we were conspiring against the system, yet they probably did not know to what extent our network functioned. We were able to operate for a long time due, no doubt, to our family name. The Grau name still had political clout. Uncle had become president the first time on the wake of a violent revolution; the second time he had swept into office with the widest popular mandate in the political history of the Island. Dr. Ramon Grau San Martin, old and feeble, was still a force to be respected.

I often joked with Mongo that our name was our shield, protecting us from arrest by State Security.

"Yes, Polita," Mongo would say, "but our shield is made of tin. It's a very thin shield indeed."

In 1962, I don't remember exactly when, the flights to the United States stopped. In those last frantic months we had speeded up our operations, trying to move as many kids as we could out of the country. I often went to the airport myself to see the flights leave. On one occasion our contacts at Pan American shifted dozens of regular passengers to another flight to allow children to leave immediately.

When the freedom flights of the early sixties ended, so did our "Save the Children" operation with the Catholic Bureau. I do not really know how many children came with our falsified visas. A conservative estimate has placed the figure at 14,000 children without parents between 1960 and 1962. Several other thousands left with their parents, and hundreds of resistance fighters used our false visas to leave the country. The total number must be over 20,000.

Mongo and I knew that our time of freedom to conspire was coming to an end. The tin shield of the Grau family was beginning to fall apart.

One of the best men in Rescate Revolucionario was Carlos Guerrero, a man in his early fifties who was very dependable. Carlos was arrested by State Security and drugged by his interrogators.

Alberto Cruz, who had spent years living clandestinely, was arrested shortly afterwards. A group of agents from State Security showed up at his meeting place, leading a drugged Carlos Guerrero. Cruz later said that Guerrero looked like a "zombie," staggering as he walked.

I was to be arrested at the house of Herminia Suarez, administrative assistant to my uncle, but I did not show up. State Security did show and arrested Herminia, who said Carlos Guerrero was standing still, leaning over like a drunk trying to regain balance.

One of the saddest memories of my life is that image of a drugged Carlos Guerrero. What sadness must have filled his soul when upon waking up from his drugged stupor he found that he had turned in his good friend, Alberto Cruz. The grief killed him, for he died in prison before his trial.

On the morning of January 21, 1965, hundreds of State Security agents began a series of mass arrests. Key members of our organization began to fall in the dragnet: Alberto Belt, Manolo Companioni, Jose Luis Pelleya. Dozens of men and women were arrested that morning.

At eight in the morning our house was under siege, surrounded by State Security agents. My uncle went to visit the cemetery and my brother Mongo went with him, but State Security watched from a distance without attempting to arrest Mongo. They both returned home without an incident.

I had been resting at home on that day. I was pushing fifty and had been experiencing some menopause problems. With our house surrounded, however, I occupied myself burning any papers, letters, or notes that could be considered incriminatory by the regime. Soon it became obvious that State Security wanted to arrest us when we left the house alone, so as to avoid a scene with our uncle. Inside the house our uncle asked us to remain.

"If they want you," he told Mongo and me, "they'll have to come and get you."

Nenita Carames, my good friend, showed up at our house. She had driven through the ring of secret police in a diplomatic car of the United Arab Republics, driven by a diplomatic contact. The diplomatic car left, but Nenita remained behind. She too was eventually arrested.

Tired of waiting, the State Security agents entered the house. Several of them grabbed Mongo, hitting him. Nenita tried to help my brother, but she was also beaten by the arresting officers. Knowing that to resist would be useless, I walked out of the back door of our home, being escorted by several agents toward a waiting car.

I was to be taken to the new offices of State Security in Marianao; they were no longer on the street opposite our home. As I was being transported, the agents asked me where "the money" was. Apparently, they assumed that since Uncle Ramon had been president of Cuba, he would have millions of pesos stashed away from political days of bribery and graft. I denied any knowledge of hidden treasure.

I was placed in cell number thirty-eight, a small room without toilet facilities. Sharing the cell with me was a woman named Caridad Navarrete. She introduced herself, telling me that she had been accused of belonging to the CIA, a label attached by State Security to any member of the resistance. Caridad motioned me by sign language to remain quiet, for there was a possibility that our cell could be bugged with hidden microphones.

I nodded. I stood next to a wall in the small room. The State Security agents had allowed me to keep my cigarettes. As I lit a match my eyes saw a name scribbled on the wall. By the light of the match I saw the name of Alejandrina Sanchez. Seeing the name made me feel weak and depressed. I had known her. She had been a member of the underground that had attempted suicide when she was captured.

"She tried to kill herself," Caridad said behind me.

"I know her," I answered, sitting down, feeling faint.

At the State Security offices I was interrogated by men. It was a terrible, horrible series of questions, geared to humiliate me, to break my spirit. They threatened me, asked me questions about my family going back thirty years in time, hinted at scandals, even asked about our sexual habits. It was one of the most degrading moments of my life, for I felt defenseless as these totalitarian bureaucrats heaved their personal insults upon me.

Foremost in their minds was the idea that we were millionaires, loaded with graft money.

"Dr. Grau is all alone in that house," they would say to me, "if you give us the money we will allow you freedom. Dr. Grau, your brother, and yourself will be allowed to leave Cuba. Where is it?"

"I am sorry," I kept answering, "I have no idea what you are talking about."

Later, I would find out that they had also tried to extort three million pesos from my uncle in exchange for our freedom.

The harassment did not stop there, however. State Security arranged for a meeting in secret between one of their agents and my brother Pancho, exiled in Miami. In the meeting, which took place in Mexico, my brother told State Security that all members of the Grau family in exile were working fulltime jobs to pay for their room and board, without hidden fortune to back them.

On Mother's Day, 1965, I was allowed a visit by my uncle, who came accompanied by a servant, a faithful employee of many years, Natalia Boulanger. Although visits were usually limited to ten or fifteen minutes, the guards did not seem in a hurry to end the conversation. After a couple of hours, the girl who accompanied my uncle looked at him, her eyes opening in surprise.

"Dr. Grau," she said, "don't you think that this might be a trick, that State Security might be searching our house?"

Uncle hurried home from the visit. When he arrived at our home in Miramar he found the house completely ransacked. The yard had been torn apart by bulldozers, palm trees knocked over, holes broken on the interior plaster walls. It was State Security's last attempt to find the hidden treasure that never existed.

Mongo and I remained seven months at State Security's office in La Vibora. Mongo had it even worse than I did, for he was locked up in a small room where he could hardly walk at all. Later he was transferred to La Cabana Fortress, while I was taken to the women's detention center at Guanajay.

Building a case of conspiracy and treason against Mongo and myself had been easy. Throughout our five years of underground activities, particularly through the activities with the false visas for the children, we had come into contact with so many people that our names had appeared in dozens of interrogations and trials. Only our family name, our "tin shield," had helped us survive conspiring for as long as we had been able to do so.

At the trial, five members of the movement, including Mongo, faced possible death sentences. The "tin shield" of the Grau name would save us one last time, however.

Former Cuban President Carlos Prio, exiled in Miami, traveled to Mexico to meet with the president of that country. Appealing to the Mexican president on the basis of a personal friendship, Prio requested that the Mexican government intercede on our behalf. Since Cuba and Mexico have always had strong economic ties, a request by the Mexican president was not to be taken lightly. The five death sentences were changed to long prison terms. I was given a sentence of thirty years' imprisonment for crimes against the State.

In prison I became a *plantada,* a prisoner in rebellion. I refused to rehabilitate, to receive classes of Marxism, to accept any kind of dictates from the regime that would compromise my political principles. Women prisoners in rebellion dressed in dark blue uniforms of coarse cloth.

I was assigned to a large barracks for women prisoners in Guanajay. When I arrived at Guanajay, in the fall of 1965, the detention center housed over 1,000 women political prisoners.

Our long barracks with double bunk pallets had three large, empty oil drums at one end. The drums were used to warm up food from parcels that relatives of women prisoners would bring when allowed. Anything that would burn, old paper or cardboard, was used to burn and cook. The barracks, which we called the "Heating Stove," had a perennial aroma of burnt paper and refuse.

On a pallet bunk near the three empty cooking drums a lonely figure sat, wrapped in blankets, completely covered, her features hidden by rags. I was told that she was Zoila Aguila, the famous "Girl of the Escambray." A few years before, she had fought alongside her husband in the peasant uprisings of the Escambray Mountains. In the guerrilla war she had lost two infant daughters who died of malnutrition shortly after birth. Zoila became the only woman to lead a band of guerrillas in combat. Captured after months of heavy fighting, she had been beaten and tortured almost to the point of madness. Her husband was shot by a firing squad on June 22, 1964.

"The Girl of the Escambray" was a beautiful woman in her mid-twenties when I first met her. She had long curly hair, covering her shoulders. Mentally burnt-out as she was, she had a sixth sense, picking out infiltrators among our ranks. Once, when a newly arrived prisoner tried to become my friend, the Girl warned me that the new arrival was an infiltrator from State Security. Although I did not pay much attention to her then, time would prove that Zoila was right.

"The Girl of the Escambray" became, in my fourteen years as a prisoner in rebellion, one of my closest, dearest friends.

Prison life was very tough on all of us. The lights inside the barracks were never turned off. We covered our eyes with small pieces of cloth to sleep.

Food was incredibly bad. Boiled macaroni was the staple diet. Dirty rice, badly cooked, and small pieces of canned Soviet meat, which smelled rotted, completed our diet. Finding maggots or small worms in the food was very common. For breakfast we would be given watered, tasteless coffee and hard bread. Sometimes we would take brown sugar that our relatives had brought us and cover the hard bread with it, to make it more edible.

On very rare occasions, when a tour group was visiting the prison, we would be fed chicken. After the maggot-covered noodles and hard bread, a chicken dinner would be an incredible event, a topic of conversation that would last for days.

Once a week we were fed hearts or kidneys. Kidneys have to be washed very well to take away the urine smell, but to me it did not matter how badly they smelled. I had made up my mind that no matter how bad food smelled or how inedible it seemed, I would eat all of it, in order to survive. During my years in prison I saw many women become ill by dehydration and malnutrition. I was determined to survive to avoid the madness that comes with a deficient diet.

Once, when I was at the prison in Guanabacoa, we were fed a ration of fish that smelled foul. The women in our cell block refused to eat. A near riot ensued. The guards argued that the common criminals in the nonpolitical section had eaten the fish without adverse effects. Our women prisoners argued with the guards, accusing them of poisoning us.

I sat down on my bunk and while everyone argued around us, I began to eat the oily, smelly fish.

"Look, girls," one of my bunkmates said, "old lady Pola is eating the fish!"

"We are going to bury her tomorrow," another one said.

But they did not bury me. I survived. Later we found that the fish in question was badly cooked shark meat, which tasted oily and smelled bad but filled an empty stomach.

In the fourteen years that I spent in Castro's jails, I saw scenes of incredible horror. I was lucky that I never received a beating, but I did see many women prisoners beaten often and sometimes severely.

We defended ourselves as best we could against the women guards. Our younger girl prisoners fought very well, shielding the older ones, like myself. When the female guards could not handle us, male guards with rubber hoses came to beat us. I have seen young girls beaten severely, their bones broken, their gums bleeding. One of our women prisoners, Doris Delgado, had her mouth ripped open by a blow from a rubber hose, her salivary gland receiving permanent damage from the beating. Another one of our prisoners, Mercy Pena, received a brutal blow on her chest with a rubber truncheon. Her left breast swelled up, becoming a grotesque ball of black and blue flesh. Mercy was in pain for weeks while the breast healed.

Two of the women, Gloria Gourdin and my friend Nenita Carames, attempted suicide. Many suffered from serious illnesses. In my years as a political prisoner I suffered from dysentery, parasites, skin infections on my feet and under my fingernails. Because of lack of oral hygiene, my teeth rotted, until every tooth in my mouth became a black nub over infected, swollen gums. I lost all my teeth in the prisons of Castro's Cuba.

Worse than the beatings, than the lack of medical care, than the pestilent food, was the humiliating treatment, the constant harassment. On frequent occasions we had *requisas* (searches) where guards would confiscate personal property, ripping through our possessions. One girl whose name I can't remember hid a small burner between her legs during a *requisa*. Since the *requisa* was unexpected and the burner was still warm, the poor girl burned herself seriously.

I did my best to maintain my sanity. I wrote letters to my family as frequently as I was allowed. I took up embroidery as a pastime. From a piece of cloth I made an extra pocket for my uniform in which I embroidered the names of all my family, my husband, children, grandchildren. When the Girl of the Escambray asked me what I had done, I patted the pocket and told her: "I now carry my family in my pocket."

Uncle Ramon also helped me. The old ex-president visited as often as he was allowed, until his death in 1969. I was lucky that he visited me, for he encouraged me to stay a prisoner in rebellion.

"Never bend to the Communists," he would tell me, "all they will do is use you and humiliate you."

Many of our women prisoners were receiving visits from husbands, children, and relatives who pressured them to join the "Reha-bilitation Plan." Many brave ones cracked, hoping for an early release. With no relatives left in Cuba, except for my uncle, who urged me to stay in rebellion, I had an easier time coping mentally than many other women in the rebellion ward.

My fourteen years of incarceration were spent in four different prisons: the women's detention centers at Guanajay and at Guanabacoa and the hypocritically named penal farms "Nuevo Amanecer" (New Dawn) and "America Libre" (Free America), two hellholes of mistreat-ment. I also spent many months at the prison cells of the State Security Headquarters in Havana, becoming the woman prisoner that spent more time than any other being interrogated by State Security.

One of my worst experiences with State Security came while I was at the Guanabacoa Detention Center. A number of our girls had been laid out sick by a chickenpox epidemic, and I had been helping to nurse them when I received notice that I was to be taken to Havana for questioning.

My interrogator was Lieutenant Roldan. He was a pompous man, very vain, forever combing his hair, grooming himself. Short in height but big on ego, Roldan was humorless and mean, one of my worst memories of the years in prison. As I sat down in front of him, Roldan placed a large, glossy photograph in front of me. I looked at the pic-ture. I knew at once what he wanted: only one man in the photograph was still active in Cuba, working as an agent for the Central Intelli-gence Agency.

"Who are these people in the photograph?" he asked.

"I'm this one," I said, "as you see, I am dressed in black, so I as-sume that this picture was taken by your people around the time of my mother's death. This was a condolence call."

"Who are these people?" he repeated.

"This one," I said, pointing to the woman, "is Lidia Rivera, an internationally well-known singer. The man next to her is Fernando Mansera, who is exiled in Mexico."

"And this man?" Roldan asked, pointing at the last man.

"I don't remember who he is," I answered, "he came with Fer-nando."

Roldan looked annoyed.

"Do you expect me to believe this? People come on a condolence call and you don't know who they are?"

"Yes," I answered, "my uncle was a very beloved president. People visited our home constantly that were politically linked to us but that we barely knew."

"Well, Pola," Roldan said, "I'm going to keep you in this building until you talk. I'm going to put you in a cell down in the men's wing and you will rot down there until you decide to talk."

I was placed in a small cell with one bunk and no toilet facilities.

I heard a man crying in a cell nearby. What a terrifying impression the sound of whimpering made! I sat down in my cell, sweating, dressed only in my bra and panties. The whimpering and crying continued.

I began singing in a loud voice. I'm not a singer or composer, but every time that I was taken to State Security I would spend time composing and singing, as a defense mechanism against the fear of the interrogations. I began singing about the women prisoners in Guanajay. The sobbing stopped. On the other side of the wall the male prisoner was quiet, listening. After a few minutes, a male guard came into the cell block, screaming at me to be quiet.

"No," I said very loudly, "you can tell me that I cannot leave because I am your prisoner, but I will not be quiet. I am a woman political prisoner, a *plantada* from Guanabacoa, and I refuse to be quiet."

I continued singing. From that day on, as night began to fall, the prisoner next door would tap on the wall, as a signal for me to begin singing. When I tired of singing, I would tap on the wall as a goodnight signal. One day the tapping stopped. My unknown friend, whom I never saw, had been moved.

That same day I began feeling very sick. I felt alternating chills and hot flashes. I felt very weak. When I slept, I suffered from hallucinations.

It was one of the lowest points in my life. I was half naked in this small cell, without any toilet facilities. I was forced to do my own waste in a corner of the room, squatting on the ground like an animal. Roldan had promised that I would rot here, in this room, but I could not reveal the identity of the man in the photograph. He was still free, still fighting. I was willing to die in my own waste in that small cell rather than surrender to Roldan.

My illness became worse. I was so weak that I could hardly walk. Finally, I was taken to see a medic.

"Have you ever had chicken pox?" the male nurse said.

"No," I answered, "but there was an outbreak at Guanabacoa, where I came from."

"Get this woman out of here," the nurse told an officer, "before we have an epidemic here."

Dressed in my blue uniform, I was taken back to Guanabacoa. Although I was very sick, I felt happy to be out of State Security. God had intervened. The illness had taken me momentarily out of State Security and Lieutenant Roldan's grasp. A young woman prisoner, Alina Hiolt, and I were transferred to the hospital at the military base in Columbia. Placed in a small cell, I began to feel better with each passing day.

Standing by my cell door one morning, I saw a familiar figure strutting in our direction. I recognized the cocky walk, the well-groomed poster boy look. Roldan had come to Columbia looking for me!

"What is wrong, Pola?" Alina said, "You are pale."

"Roldan is coming this way. He has come to Columbia looking for me."

"Lay down on the bed," Alina said, "and cover yourself up. I'll take care of Roldan."

I bundled myself up under some blankets, curling up in bed. Alina stood by the door.

"Are you Roldan?" Alina screamed as the lieutenant approached our cell block.

"Yes, I am Lieutenant Roldan."

"My God, Roldan," Alina said very loudly, "what has happened to you? You look so old, so worn out, and you are losing your hair. You better leave State Security before it kills you. You were a handsome man. Now look at you — you look so old, so wasted. You are an old, balding man, Roldan."

"You are not a raving beauty yourself," the lieutenant answered in a very acid tone, "where is Pola Grau?"

"She is in the bathroom," Alina answered, "would you like to leave a message or would you like to chat a while?"

"Tell Pola Grau that I'll return to see her," the lieutenant said as he walked away with the familiar strut.

"See?" I told Alina. "He has come back for me. He won't leave me alone."

"He will," Alina said, laughing. "He is too much of a prissy, vain man. He will not return. His ego would be crushed. He's probably running to a mirror to check himself for wrinkles."

Amazingly, Alina was right, for Lieutenant Roldan never bothered me again. My friend, the CIA man in the photograph, continued to operate freely until his death, sometime later, of natural causes.

In 1978, Castro needed assistance for his weakening economy. One of the possible sources of revenue was the Cuban exile community in the United States, economically solvent. Considering opening up restricted tourism to Cuba for those exiles he considered to be non-threatening to his system, Castro hoped to pump millions of American dollars into his weakened economy. Furthermore, the issue would be so controversial among exiles that it would split the exile community, weakening the militant groups.

"The Dialogue," as it was referred to by Cubans on both sides of the political spectrum, was inaugurated by a visit of seventy-five exiles to Havana, as guests of the regime. The seventy-five visitors were an odd lot. A few were Castro agents, actively involved in recruiting and promoting the Dialogue under orders from their bosses in Havana. Others were obviously CIA operatives, infiltrated among the Dialogue people to keep tabs for American intelligence. A third group included well-meaning exiles and relatives of political prisoners seeking freedom for friends and relatives who had spent years in Castro's concentration camps.

Although I did not know it, my son, Monchy, had come to Havana with the "Committee of 75," seeking my freedom. In a public meeting, much publicized, in which Fidel Castro met with the committee, my son stood up and addressed the dictator. Saying that he did not care for the political implications of the committee, Monchy said that he had traveled to Havana to plead for freedom for his sixty-three-year-old mother, who had spent the last fourteen years of her life as a political prisoner. Another Cuban in the audience, the mother of a brave male prisoner called Alfredo Izaguirre, chorused my son, requesting the freedom for her son.

Castro promised that he would release many political prisoners as a symbol of good faith toward the Dialogue members of the Cuban community. What would appear to be a public, generous gesture was simply another way of playing politics with the emotions of the Cuban people. Releasing a few thousand political prisoners would be just a way of alleviating the overcrowding in the dozens of concentration camps in Cuba.

The prisoners in rebellion, the *plantados* who had refused Communist indoctrination, were morally opposed to the Dialogue, feeling that it was a betrayal of our convictions. We were willing to walk out of the concentration camps if our iron bars were opened, but we would refuse to join the Dialogue, to endorse in any way a peaceful coexistence with the system that we had fought against for so many years.

At the time of the Dialogue I was imprisoned at "Nuevo Amanecer" (New Dawn), a penal farm in Havana province. A lieutenant named Lester came to see me.

"Has it been a long time," he asked, "since you have had news from your family?"

I felt fists churning inside my chest. Was something wrong? "As often as you allow me to receive letters," I answered. "Is something wrong?"

"No, there is nothing wrong. What if I told you that your son is here, in Cuba?"

"No," I said, feeling my body weakening, "he would not come. He knows better than that. He would not come here."

"I was with your son a few hours ago," he told me, "your son came with the Dialogue people. He has come to intercede on your behalf with the revolutionary government."

I sat down, making an effort not to cry in front of the lieutenant. I felt weak. My son Monchy, whom I had not seen in eighteen years, was in Cuba!

"You will see your son tonight," the lieutenant said. "Dress pretty and look nice."

The next few hours were the longest that I ever spent in all my years of incarceration. For many years I had given up all hope of ever seeing any member of my family again. The agony of separation had been soothed by a few allowed infrequent letters, by a pocket in a uniform with embroidered names, by a few well-thumbed photographs. After all the years of separation, I would see my son in the flesh one more time. It was more than I hoped, more than I ever believed could be possible.

I was transported by car from the penal farm to the offices of State Security, where I was taken to see Lt. Col. Abad Cintas, one of the most powerful men in the repressive force that rules Cuba.

"Pola," he said to me, noticing my nervousness, "would you like a tranquilizer?"

"No, Abad. I don't need one. I would like to use the washroom."

After visiting the restroom, I was taken to a small salon to wait for my son. Abad stood by the door.

"Is there anything that I can do?" he asked.

"When you see my son coming, tell me. I want to be ready."

"I will," he said, "sit down."

"I can't," I answered, "I'm too nervous."

Those few minutes of waiting were agony, pure agony. My whole body felt weak. My hands were wet with cold sweat.

"He is coming," Abad said as I heard noise in the hallway.

My son entered the room. How strange I must have looked to him then, in my blue uniform, a woman in her early sixties without makeup . . . We rushed at each other. His face was covered with tears as he embraced and kissed me.

I began weeping. My arms circled his body. I leaned my face on his shoulder and for the first time in many years I cried freely, without holding back, gasping for breath as I hugged my son.

Over his shoulders, as I cried, I saw a sight that I will never forget. Lt. Col. Abad Cintas, a man known for his cruelty, was looking at us, while tears flowed freely down his face. How brutally moving that scene must have been to inspire a moment of weeping emotion in such a hard, cold man!

I was allowed to spend two hours with Monchy. A few minutes were spent talking about the family while the rest of the time I argued with my son.

"How can you do this?" I said. "You can't trust Communists. They are scum. They might not let you leave now."

"They will, Mother," he said, "a political game is under way. Too much is at stake for them. I'm leaving and I'm taking you with me."

"If I have to compromise my principles," I said, "I'd rather die in jail. Get out now, Monchy, while you still can."

"I'm not leaving without you," he said. "Castro is trying for a propaganda coup. I don't agree with the Dialogue but in order to appear on the level, Castro will have to release many of the best-known political prisoners. Now we have a chance to free some of our people."

For two hours we argued. I hugged him and kissed him as I left, hoping to see him once more before he left Cuba with the Committee of 75.

That night at Nuevo Amanecer, the women gathered around me: the Girl of the Escambray, Maria Amalia, and Araceli Rodriguez. I told them the story of my happiest day of incarceration and they wept with me. Political prisoners are family also. For fourteen years we had shared good times and bad times. We had been joined together by a bond of common suffering that can only be understood by one who has lived and survived fourteen years of rebellion in a Communist concentration camp.

On November 19, 1978, my birthday, I was told that I would be allowed to have dinner with my son. I was thrilled! I assumed that this would be our last visit together before he returned to the United States. I was taken out of Nuevo Amanecer at a time when my friends were at dinner, so I could not see them. At State Security Headquarters I once more saw Lieutenant Colonel Cintas.

"We will allow you to have dinner with your son, Pola," he said, "but you must dress as a civilian."

"For fourteen years I have only worn this," I said, touching my blue uniform that was a symbol of rebellion. "To wear anything else is a capital sin for me, Abad."

"Don't talk to me in religious terms, Pola."

"That is my only way, Abad," I said, "but tonight, for dinner with my son, I'll dress civilian. Only this once, for a special occasion."

A rack of clothing was brought in. The only dress that fit me was a strapless outfit, which made me look like a ridiculous over-the-hill cabaret girl. When Abad saw me, he could not hold back his laughter.

"Do you expect me," I asked, "to see my son dressed like this?"

Abad nodded. He provided a big bandana that, although more ridiculous, took away some of the fleshy gaudiness of the outfit.

I was soon confronted by a man who entered the room, dressed in an ill-fitting bright blue suit. His face seemed familiar.

"Do you recognize him?" I was asked.

"No."

"That's Alfredo Izaguirre."

I embraced Alfredo. He had spent the last eighteen years as a prisoner in rebellion. He looked gaunt. His hair had turned white in his years in prison.

"Alfredo is going to have dinner with his mother and wife," Abad said, "and you with your son."

A vehicle took us out of the building to another side of the State Security complex. We embraced our relatives. My son had brought me a bag with some well-fitting civilian clothing, which made me happy, for I felt very self-conscious with my ridiculous outfit.

All of us were herded into a room full of military personnel. An officer dressed in olive green looked at me and smiled.

"Well, Pola," he asked, "how does it feel to be free?"

I was stunned. Free? I was free? I did not have to return to the penal farm at Nuevo Amanecer? Could it be?

"What do you mean?" I asked.

"You are free, Pola."

"Yes, Mother," my son said, "don't you know?"

"Nobody told me."

"You are free."

Free, after fourteen years. I felt a lump in my chest; tears filled my eyes. I was free to leave with my son, to see my grandchildren, my husband, my daughter.

My son made arrangements to have me housed at the Riviera Hotel for several days, while paperwork was arranged with the American Embassy.

Finally, one morning, in a privately leased small airplane, we left Cuba, bound for Miami. As the little airplane picked up height, I looked at the land below me. For a few brief seconds we flew over Nuevo Amanecer, the penal farm that had until recently been my home. I looked at the buildings and thought about the Girl, Maria Amalia, and Araceli, all those good friends still incarcerated. I would fight for their freedom, even from a foreign country. My son, seeing my tears, realizing that we were flying over Nuevo Amanecer, began singing the Cuban national anthem. I began singing also, as the little airplane headed north.

In 1986 my brother Mongo was released, arriving in Miami — older, his hair white, but his spirit still young, full of fighting spirit. A few months ago he traveled to Geneva to lobby at the United Nations on behalf of human rights of Cuban political prisoners.

Many of my fellow prisoners were eventually released, coming to exile. One was Zoila Aguila, the Girl of the Escambray, one of the two last women from our cell block to be released by the Castro regime.

A few days after her arrival, I took the Girl out for a pleasure ride. We went to the Seaquarium at Key Biscayne, where Zoila was thrilled by the size of the whales and the intelligence of the dolphins. As I took her home, to a house where she was staying with a fellow prisoner, Ela Bravo, the Girl looked at me with a mysterious smile.

"Pola Grau," she said, "I have brought you two gifts from Cuba."

I was curious. What could it be?

"On the day that they took you away for the last time," she said, "I rushed back to the cell block before the guards could come back to confiscate your belongings. I brought you these."

I looked down. In one hand she held a small cardboard fan that my brother had made and painted by hand. In the other hand she held a piece of cloth, an embroidered pocket from a prison uniform.

12

JORGE MONIZ: AIR RAIDS TO CUBA

Fifty-three-year-old Jorge Moniz lives in Coral Gables, Florida. He is em-
ployed as a resettlement case worker in the Dade County administration. Moniz
began his revolutionary activities in the fifties when he joined the DR, a stu-
dent revolutionary movement fighting against Batista's regime. Shortly after
the revolution, he once again conspired, this time to overthrow the new system.

When Batista fled Cuba, I was offered the rank of lieutenant in the
Rebel Army because of my underground activities with DR, the Revolutionary Directorate, which I joined when I was a law student at the
University of Havana. I refused the commission, feeling that the new
head of government, Fidel Castro, was an egocentric personality with
his own power ambitions. I was not aware at the time that Castro was
a Communist, but I did feel a sense of foreboding that in a short time
he would become Cuba's new dictator.

Unfortunately, I was right. Within a few months after Castro
took power, I once again joined the resistance movements that were
forming throughout the Island. Two of my fellow conspirators were
Evelio Duque and Cesar Paez. Duque had been a captain in the guerrilla war against Batista. Against Castro, he became one of the organizers of the guerrilla uprisings in the Escambray during the early sixties. Eventually, he became an exile, and today he is a farmer in
Central America. Paez had also been a captain. For a while he con-

spired in a plan to kill Castro, but it fell through and some of our people were arrested. I left for exile while Paez went to the Escambray, leading a guerrilla force until he was captured. He died a dozen years later of leukemia while still a prisoner of the Castro regime.

When I arrived in Miami in 1962, I met Dr. Orlando Bosch who was, even then, developing a reputation as the most radical of all anti-Castro leaders. Bosch was a pediatrician, a graduate of the University of Havana Medical School who did his internship in Ohio. He fought against Batista then against Castro. In exile, he became one of the co-ordinators of the underground and guerrilla groups in Cuba. Later, when the Escambray efforts crumbled, Bosch merged the splinter groups, becoming the head of MIRR, the Movement for Independence and Revolutionary Rescue.

In the early sixties, Bosch was among the first Cuban leaders to refuse CIA aid. The agency was pumping millions to support the anti-Castro cause, but in turn they demanded total control of the movement and its leadership. Under such circumstances Bosch, and a number of us, could not accept CIA help. To be allies of the U.S. is one thing, to be subservient is another. We were, and still are, fighting for the freedom of our people as patriots, not as employees.

At the time I met Bosch, the doctor was planning a series of daring raids to Cuba. Without CIA aid, with limited resources, we scrapped for donations, supplies, and any equipment that could be adapted to our type of irregular warfare. While other groups were launching commando attacks in speedboats, we decided to bomb coastal refineries and government installations by air.

The idea of flying one- or two-engine planes into Cuban territory through the radar defenses and the air patrols of Castro's air force was a suicidal concept, but we were determined to battle the system at whatever the cost. A small group of volunteers was formed, a squad called "The Suicide Commandos of MIRR."

To determine who would go on the first mission, we decided that two men would accompany the pilot to serve as bombardiers. One, Gervelio Gutierrez (whom we called Mimo), would go on most missions, eventually becoming a pilot himself. To determine who the third man would be, we held a raffle. Pieces of paper were put inside a hat. One piece had the word *sí*, Spanish for "yes." I took my scrap and opened it. It had the word *sí*. I was the chosen one. The honor of being on the first mission was mine.

On the night of August 15, 1963, Mimo Gutierrez and I waited for our airplane and pilot at an abandoned airfield in South Dade County, near the town of Homestead. We had fifteen or twenty sealed jars of *fosforo vivo,* pure phosphorous which ignites on contact with air. We also had half a dozen grenades with pins removed, locked tightly inside glass vases. The idea behind this was that as the glass broke the grenades would explode within seconds of ground impact. We had no other weapons except for individual handguns. In my pocket, I carried a few Cuban pesos, hoping that they would help me in case our mission failed and our plane was shot down.

Mimo Gutierrez, the squad leader, was a wiry little man in his mid-twenties. He had fought in the Escambray Mountains against Batista and had fought against Castro in the resistance. He had served in the U.S. Army with the Cuban units that had trained at Fort Jackson in 1962. Married, with a small son, he was willing to risk his life constantly on behalf of the struggle. Other men would win their assignments by luck of a raffle. Mimo eventually went on almost every mission.

In the darkness of the night we loaded the grenade and chemical explosives on a Beechcraft airplane which had been rented at Fort Lauderdale Airport. The outside lights of the plane were disconnected, for we would fly in total darkness to Cuba and back.

Our plane taxied through the darkness down the abandoned runway. The only light was on the dashboard inside the cabin. Mimo and I squatted, moving the jars into the most comfortable position, hoping that they would not crack inside the cabin.

Within seconds, our plane was flying above the tree tops, heading south beyond Homestead and the Florida Keys to the open waters of the Atlantic Ocean. To avoid being detected by radars from either Cuba or the United States, we flew only 100 feet above the water. In the darkness we could not see anything. Our pilot was flying by his instruments, heading southeast toward Camaguey Province, where our target, the Cunagua Sugar Mill, waited for us. It was an eerie feeling flying through darkness, like moving through a tunnel of black ink. Below we caught glimpses of moonbeams reflecting on the water, so close that they seemed within our grasp. Our pilot had a parachute, but Mimo and I did not, which did not matter, for we were flying so low that use of a parachute would be impossible anyway.

As we flew toward Cuba, I could feel the tension building up inside of me. Three years before, while I was still in Cuba, a CIA plane had been shot down on a similar operation. *Bohemia,* the most popular magazine in the nation, had printed several photographs of the dead American. The poor fellow had smashed through the roof of a house, like a human bomb, splattering on the floor of a bedroom. The photographs had been gruesome, the body lying on the ground, a mass of torn flesh and broken bones. I tried not to think of that image, but it kept coming back. While I sat on the floor of the small cabin, I hoped that I would not end up like the man in the photograph.

After a couple of hours or more, we saw lights in the distance. Cuba was glowing softly in front of us. It was decided that as we flew over the target, I would push the door open against the force of the wind, while Mimo would lob out the grenades and the *fosforo vivo*.

We shifted the jars toward the door. I tied my body to the inside of the plane with a belt as I stood next to the door. The idea of falling with the jars did not appeal to me.

It all happened very fast. The pilot shouted *"Ya!"* and as he let me know that we were over the target, I pushed against the door, against the pressure of the wind. The wind rumbled. The first jar disappeared through the doorway into the darkness below, then another and another. When all of the jars of *fosforo vivo* had been thrown out, Mimo lobbed out the grenades. A few seconds later we saw the flashes of white fire light the ground below us, heard the explosives over the sound of our engine and the wind. As our airplane turned to head north, we saw below us a number of fires burning the canefields.

In a few minutes we were over the water once more, flying through the tunnel of darkness as fast as we could, so close to the water that we seemed to be skimming over the waves. After a few minutes we all began to feel better; the tension began to melt. We had done it! And if we had done it once, we could do it again.

Three days later another one of our planes strafed a Soviet camp in Las Villas Province. I missed that raid, but the following month, on September 8, 1963, I returned to Cuba to firebomb the Jaronu Sugar Mill.

This second trip involved the same crew as my first raid. Knowing that Jaronu had a militia outpost building, we decided to strafe it while using the *fosforo vivo* and the hand grenades. We had obtained a WWII-vintage Johnson machine gun at a very reasonable price. It was a bulky weapon, similar to the Browning automatic rifle, but with a flash suppressor.

This trip was very similar to the first. We took off from our abandoned airstrip near Dixie Highway, flying by instruments only, hugging the water. We came in exactly over our target, dropped the *fosforo vivo* and grenades, then swept back over the mill. I had held the door open as Mimo threw the explosives on the first sweep. Now, on the second ride over the target, I leaned out the door with the Johnson machine gun in my hands. As we flew toward the militia outpost, I pressed back on the trigger, emptying the clip into the building below. To our amazement, the militia never fired back.

One of our bravest men was Luis Diaz, a twenty-three-year-old pilot with ice in his veins. He insisted on carrying out a daytime raid, wanting to film the attack for propaganda purposes. We begged him to desist, but Luis felt that a movie clip would uplift the morale of the exile community. Accompanied by twenty-two-year-old Luis Velarde and twenty-four-year-old Ines Malagon, he set off to attack the Reforma Sugar Mill in June of 1964.

As they attacked the mill, they were intercepted by an airplane which was being flown by Che Guevara's personal bodyguards. In an exchange of machine gun fire, Luis Diaz was killed. Without a pilot, the little plane fell to earth. Malagon and Velarde were captured and executed by a firing squad. The "Suicide Commandos" had its first three martyrs.

My third raid was to the airport at Santa Clara. Once more, I went with Mimo Gutierrez. Our target was well lit as we approached it. We zoomed past the control tower, throwing grenades. The following day, Havana Radio claimed that one militiaman had been killed and three others had been wounded by our attack.

Although our raids were meeting with success, we experienced problems in the United States. The CIA would sponsor exile raids, but the government would not allow us to carry out independent raids. What difference did it make? Whether an attack was being done with the sponsorship of the government or by independents, it was hurting Castro. Yet, the authorities persecuted MIRR activists.

In December of 1963, two boats being prepared for commando raids were seized by authorities. In 1964, Dr. Orlando Bosch was arrested by federal agents for possession of explosives. He was arrested again in 1965 as he prepared an airplane for a raid.

In spite of the odds, we continued to work. Money was collected from sympathizers, weapons were bought, missions were continued. In 1965 infiltration teams were dropped off in Matanzas Province. The Niagara and Bahia Honda sugar mills were attacked by airplane raids, and a team of frogmen damaged a Castro merchant ship on its way to

Vietnam loaded with sugar. A Spanish merchant ship on its way to Cuba was also damaged by a frogman unit of MIRR.

In 1966 one of our airplane raids attacked the thermoelectric plant at Nuevitas, near a missile base. Months later, intelligence sources informed us that Castro had demoted some of the officers at the base because they had not reacted aggressively when our plane struck the Nuevitas plant.

Another air raid, this was back in 1963, targeted a Soviet base at Casilda on the south coast of Las Villas. We converted a large gas container into a crude homemade bomb. The bomb landed dead center on an oil tank, blowing it up, causing a huge fire.

Mimo Gutierrez learned to fly. On November 13, 1966, he attacked the Cepero Bonilla petrochemical plant. His bombs were right on target, causing heavy damages to the center, paralyzing production for two weeks. As he left, it is possible that Mimo's plane was hit by its own shrapnel, for Mimo never returned to Florida. His small plane disappeared over the ocean, never to be found. Somewhere in the depth of the ocean, north of Cuba, his body now rests for eternity. He was a brave man full of love for his country with a spirit of sacrifice and nationalistic ideals. Raul Fantony, another veteran of the Cuban units at Fort Jackson, also disappeared with Mimo. Both in their late twenties, Fantony and Mimo now rest somewhere in the deep blue of the sea, near the coast of the Cuba they fought to free.

In 1966, 1967, and 1968, MIRR commandos attacked British and Japanese merchant vessels on their way to Cuba with cargo. By these attacks we meant to discourage trade with Cuba, damaging the economy.

In October of 1968, Dr. Bosch was arrested once more, accused of firing a recoilless rifle at the *Polanika,* a Warsaw Pact vessel in transit at Dodge Island, Florida. For Bosch it meant the end of the MIRR and his first prison term. Five years later he would be released from a federal penitentiary to resume his activities against Castro as fiercely independent and radical as ever.

There were no more air raids after that. Our old, abandoned airfield was parceled out by some developer who built condo buildings. The war changed. New methods have come into being, but it is all part of one process: the liberation of our people. After twenty-five years in exile, I have not given up. I am still fighting the war.

13

SIXTO NICOT:
GUERRILLA LANDING IN CUBA

Forty-four-year-old Sixto Nicot arrived in Miami on February 18, 1987, after serving sixteen years of a thirty-year prison term at the infamous penitentiary of Boniato, in Cuba's eastern tip. Nicot is only one of three survivors of a series of guerrilla landings sponsored by the anti-Castro group Alfa 66 in 1970. Now residing in Carol City, Nicot works as a stone mason and is still active in Alfa 66.

The first time I left Cuba was in August of 1968. I had been pressured to join the militia unit in Guantanamo, the city where I lived, and I had resisted constantly. I was given the option of joining the militia or being sent to a punishment camp in Camaguey. That's when I decided to leave Cuba.

I joined five other men planning to enter the Guantanamo Naval Base to ask for political asylum. The United States base is surrounded for miles by an assortment of minefields, armed patrols, and fields covered by barbed wire. Most of us, however, knew the area fairly well. Several of the fields that had minefield warning signs were not really mined, the signs being used to intimidate trespassers. In other so-called minefields, we saw cows grazing, so we knew that mines were not planted in that area.

We were lucky. We went through the fields undetected, jumped some wire fences, and found ourselves inside the naval base. A few days later I was on my way to the United States.

I lived in Jersey City for a couple of years. During that time I joined the New York chapter of Alfa 66, a very active anti-Castro group.

In April of 1970, Vicente Mendez, a former guerrilla, landed in Oriente Province with a group of men, planning to start guerrilla operations against the Castro government. I volunteered to go with the second invasion team. Our purpose was to land in northern Oriente Province and make our way to the Sierra Maestra mountains to set up a base for guerrilla operations.

There were nine of us in that second group. Our team leader was Jose Rodriguez Perez, a tall 220-pounder with guerrilla experience. He was a gentle man who lived totally committed to the cause of Cuba's freedom.

In our training camp in the Everglades we trained as a team, practicing guerrilla warfare tactics, learning the use of explosives, building our bodies for the guerrilla mission ahead of us. After several weeks of extremely tough training, we left the United States bound for a landing on Cuba's eastern tip.

On September 14, 1970, we arrived on the northern shores of Oriente Province. When we saw the Cuban coast from our vessel, we were filled with joy. It was one of the happiest moments of my life. We knew very well the hardships and the suffering that awaited us, the knowledge that from the moment that we landed on Cuban soil we would be hunted by thousands of Castro's soldiers, but it did not matter. All nine of us were volunteers and for weeks we had prepared for this day. Now the Cuban shore was in front of us and we were happy, very happy to return once more to fight for freedom in our native soil.

Saying goodbye to our navigator and crew, we boarded Italian-manufactured rafts, moving toward the shore three miles away. I was armed with an AR-15 rifle, an automatic pistol, two grenades, a commando knife, and three knapsacks loaded with ammo, detonating wire, concentrated food tablets, medical supplies, and explosives. Each one of us had about eighty pounds of equipment.

I was the point man, the first one to land. The sun had not come up yet as I moved through the reefs in the darkness. We had landed sixty meters from the entrance to Rio Seco, a small creek near Sama, a coastal town. Hiding the rafts, we began moving inland. After crossing a lemon grove and a canefield, we hid on top of a small hill, an elevated area from which we could see anyone approaching. We spent the whole day there, resting, feeling good because we had not been spotted during the landing.

The following morning, Humberto Ochoa and Jose Barreto left the hill, trying to make contact with someone who could help us. Shortly after noon, they returned in a truck driven by an acquaintance of Humberto. The dilapidated vehicle was a welcome sight. We piled on top of the flatbed, throwing in our knapsacks, jumping up after them.

The broken-down truck moved through country roads. To anyone who saw us, we had to look like soldiers on maneuvers, for our uniforms were identical to those used by Castro's troops. After riding a few miles we switched trucks, when another one of Humberto's contacts gave us a lift until it was almost nighttime.

On a small road on the highway between the town of Banes and the city of Holguin, we stopped a government truck. Manuel Artola and Rodriguez Perez explained to the driver that we were a straggled army unit in need of a lift.

"I can take you for a while," the driver said, "but I'm running low on petrol."

We climbed on top of the vehicle. Amazing as it may sound, we headed for a sugar mill located on the road to Mayari, where we requested a ration of gas from the local political commissar. With a flourish, Artola signed a voucher.

On the outskirts of Holguin, we switched to a fourth truck. This driver was smarter than our previous one. When Artola gave him an order to make a turn in the road, he became suspicious.

"You are not army people, are you?" he asked.

"No," Artola answered him, "we are invaders. If you behave yourself, nothing will happen to you. All of us know how to drive, but you have a license so we need you to cover for us. Do exactly what we say and nothing will happen."

Nervously, the driver nodded.

In the middle of the night we drove past a large army base at Mangos de Baragua. We saluted smartly as we drove past the sentry post.

We felt good. Morale was high among us. We had moved over fifty kilometers inland. After two days in Cuba we had not yet been spotted. In a few hours we would be hiding in the dense brush of the Sierra Maestra mountains, where we planned to organize guerrilla groups to fight the system.

In the early dawn of September 16, we saw a jeep patrolling a road near the town of Contramaestre. We tried to avoid it by taking a roundabout route, but we saw each other again less than a mile down the road.

The soldiers in the jeep signaled us to stop with their lights. We pretended not to see them, moving past them. They maneuvered past us and positioned themselves a mile ahead of us. We decided that we would have to stop this time, but hoped to bluff our way out. Artola volunteered to get off the truck and talk to the soldiers.

"Try to bluff them," Rodriguez Perez told him, "but if they insist on searching the truck, open fire with your pistol and dive off to the side. We'll take care of them."

There were four of them. By coincidence, they were stopping all vehicles on that road because several members of the underground, dressed as soldiers, had killed a lieutenant in Manzanillo a few hours before. Manuel Artola spoke to them very convincingly. One of the four told Artola to go ahead, but another one insisted that they had to search the vehicle.

We knew that as soon as they saw the American weapons, the soldiers would realize that we were invaders. As they approached the vehicle, Artola opened fire on them with his pistol.

I was in the front end of the bed of the truck, behind the cab. I shouldered my AR-15 and emptied the clip. Everyone was firing from our truck. The soldiers were shooting back, but in the darkness we could not see each other. Two of them died in those brief seconds, while the other two retreated into a nearby canefield. Artola climbed back on our vehicle and we sped down the highway. The two soldiers came out of the canefield, turned the jeep around, and sped after us. We continued to exchange gunfire. One of their bullets hit our gas tank. We began losing fuel at an amazing rate.

Ahead of us was the small town of Baire, a village where the first uprising of our War of Independence against Spain had taken place in the nineteenth century. As we approached the town, the sound of gunfire woke up the local militia and police units who began to shoot at our truck. We were caught in a crossfire.

Our team leader, Jose Rodriguez Perez, was the first casualty. A bullet hit him in the forehead, making a long wound on the left side of his skull. He fell down paralyzed and unconscious. Although he would live for almost two more weeks, he never regained full consciousness.

The fire fight was intense. Our men jumped off the truck firing as they ran, trying to reach the hills beyond the town. I covered their retreat from the bed of the truck. Picking up a knapsack full of ammo, I jumped off the vehicle, running behind buildings and through yards of houses toward the grazing fields beyond the village.

As I crossed a street I was hit in the left leg. One bullet hit me above the ankle, while the second round hit my thigh. I continued to fire my weapon as I ran. Humberto Ochoa helped me, covering my retreat, holding me up as we ran.

I knew that I was doomed. My pant leg was covered with blood, and I was weakening. I asked Ochoa to leave me and save himself but he refused, dragging me into a clump of bushes.

Within minutes dozens of soldiers were combing the pasture fields and bushes looking for us. I wanted to open fire, but Humberto talked me out of it. We were surrounded and pinned down.

The man who found us was a young militiaman with a small revolver that shook nervously in his hand. It would have been easy to kill him, but I was weak and Ochoa was tired, exhausted after two days without sleep. The militiaman picked up my pistol, holstered his own, then pointed my handgun toward us.

"You poor fool," I said to him, "that pistol is not even cocked."

In a few seconds we were surrounded by a dozen soldiers. Ochoa was taken away in a jeep, while I was placed in a yellow truck, where I lost consciousness. I was taken to a hospital in Palma Soriano, where I was treated.

While I was in a room, a nurse, seeing my green uniform, thought I was in the army.

"This place is packed with wounded comrades," she said.

"How many?" I asked her.

"There are seventeen or eighteen wounded here," she answered.

I nodded. Our little group had made the enemy pay a heavy price. Seven members of the armed forces had died in combat with us.

More than 5,000 militia and army personnel were deployed to hunt down the half dozen men still loose in the hills. Luis Perez died in combat in a fire fight, while the other five were captured, exhausted. The last one to be captured was Manuel Artola, who hid out for five days while thousands of troops chased him through the hills.

While I was in the hospital I was interrogated constantly. Every time that I fell asleep, an officer would wake me up. The interrogation lasted for hours. When Rodriguez Perez died of wounds, I began using him as an excuse.

"Who recruited you in Alfa 66?"

"Jose Rodriguez Perez," I'd answer.

"How were weapons purchased in the U.S.?"

"Rodriguez Perez bought them."

Eventually, they gave up. I don't know how the others were treated, for I did not see them again until our trial.

Our trial took place at an abandoned farm near the sea, about forty kilometers east of Santiago de Cuba. The trial began at two in the afternoon and it was over by four o'clock.

The prosecutor stood up and announced that the revolutionary government was requesting five death penalties and two thirty-year sentences for us. While he read off the names, we were given small pieces of paper. Mine said that I was to be condemned to thirty years' imprisonment.

The Castro regime seldom executes every member of a resistance unit, even though they may all be equally guilty. I believe that this is done in order to avoid being accused of human rights violations, of genocide. They kill five and let a couple of others rot in jail. It makes them seem more human than if they executed all seven of us. Image is important, even for Communists.

The trial began. The first accused to walk up to the stand was Manuel Artola. The prosecution asked for his death by firing squad.

"Do you have anything to say?"

"No," Artola replied, "you have said it all. You are going to execute me. That has been decided. Nothing I say will change your mind."

"See," the prosecutor said, "he feels no shame for his crimes."

"No, I do not," Artola answered.

Our defense attorney stood up. He was a black man wearing an ill-fitting black suit. "To ask for the execution of this man," he said, "is just. I am a black man of humble background who became a lawyer thanks to this revolution. These men have come to destroy this revolution."

Not one of us was surprised by our defense attorney. Being a defense attorney is the easiest job in Cuba, one that implies agreeing with the prosecution without attempting to help the accused.

Artola was followed by Israel Sosa, a tough twenty-four-year-old from Oriente. The prosecution asked for a death sentence. Sosa repeated Artola's words: "I have nothing to say. Nothing will change your minds."

Jose Amparo Barreto and Humberto Ochoa, my good friend, followed. Both men repeated what Artola and Sosa had said.

The fifth condemned to death was Raymundo Sanchez, a strong black man who fought well. "I am the father of a family," he said, "and I ask for clemency . . ."

"Clemency?" the prosecutor interrupted him. "You are a black man and a laborer. It is inconceivable that you can be against the revolution of the proletariat. You deserve to die."

I was the sixth to take the stand. The prosecutor requested thirty years of incarceration. My statement was the same as that of my first four companions. "I have nothing to say," I repeated.

Alberto Kindelan was the last one to stand up. Thirty years' imprisonment. Kindelan repeated our statement: "I have nothing to say."

The prosecutor looked at Kindelan with anger in his eyes. Kindelan, like Sanchez, was a black man.

"If Lumumba could see you," he said, referring to the slain African Communist leader, "you who are black, like the suffering people of Africa."

Kindelan had dignity. "I don't care about Lumumba," he answered, "or black or white. I came to Cuba to fight the system, not a color."

Our defense attorney merely stated that we were all well condemned, for we were all obviously guilty. In the case of Raymundo Sanchez perhaps the death sentence could be commuted to a stiff jail sentence, he pleaded without effort.

While we sat in silence, the prosecutors, the defense attorney, and the military personnel sat in a corner of the room drinking soft drinks, talking about several subjects, none of which concerned us. After fifteen minutes, our sentence was read.

Manuel Artola, Israel Sosa, Jose Barreto, Humberto Ochoa, and Raymundo Sanchez were condemned to death. Sixto Nicot and Alberto Kindelan were condemned to thirty years. Those receiving death sentences had a right to appeal.

We had a few moments in which to say our goodbyes. An old Ford car waited to take Kindelan and me to jail. I embraced my five friends for the last time.

"If you ever see my son," Artola told me, "tell him that his father did not weaken even in the last hours. Tell him that Cuba will be free because of men like me who died for it."

Kindelan and I sat inside the Ford vehicle, which would take us back to State Security. The car began moving down a badly paved road to the highway. We were only one kilometer away from the house when we heard a salvo of gunfire.

The appeal had been rejected. Cuba had five more martyrs.

TOMAS SAN GIL — *photo from a Cuban government wanted poster. San Gil replaced Osvaldo Ramirez as head of the Escambray guerrillas, until he, too, died in combat.*

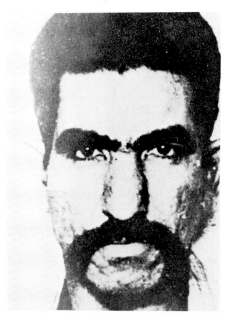

BLAS TARDIO — *guerrilla leader. Of six brothers in his family, only one survived the Escambray war.*

PLINIO PRIETO — *The former schoolteacher was executed for supplying guerrilla forces in the Escambray.*

RAMON DEL SOL — *guerrilla leader. File photo from State Security taken at the time of his capture. Del Sol was executed by firing squad.*

FRANCISCO VERDECIA — *In escaping from a concentration camp, he found God.*

OSVALDO RAMIREZ — *Dressed in the uniform of a captain of the National Revolutionary Police, this photo was taken only weeks before he led the Escambray uprisings.*

Guerrillas in the Escambray, 1960. The man on the left is Diosdado Mesa. The man on the right is guerrilla leader Joaquin Membibre, who met Dr. Armando Zaldivar in the Escambray.

Guerrillas in the Escambray, 1960. The bearded man at center is Sinesio Walsh.

DIOSDADO MESA — *an Escambray guerrilla, 1960.*

Two guerrillas in the Escambray Mountains. At left is Eusebio Penalver; Joaquin Membibre is at right.

Guerrillas in the Escambray, 1960.

Guerrillas in the Escambray. The man at top center is Sinesio Walsh.

Anti-Castro guerrillas in the Escambray Mountains.

JOSE BERBERENA — *with his Thompson tommy gun in the Escambray Mountains of central Cuba.*

JOAQUIN MEMBIBRE — *posing with some of the men in his guerrilla unit (far right). Membibre survived the Escambray and now lives in Miami.*

SINESIO WALSH — *with anti-Castro guerrillas in the Escambray Mountains (top center).*

JOSE PALOMINO COLON — *In this photo taken at the detention center at Topes de Collantes, shortly before he was executed, the man in the background on the right is Dr. Armando Zaldivar.*

TONY SALGADO — *The Bay of Pigs invader was photographed by a Communist journalist moments after his capture. A bandage on his chest covers a wound, and he is wearing pajama bottoms. Only hours after this picture was taken, he rode in the sealed-up truck in which ten of his friends died.*

SINESIO WALSH RIOS — *The brave guerrilla leader was executed by firing squad on October 13, 1960.*

Weapons captured by Castro's forces at La Campana. The shipment never reached the guerrillas.

Castro's militia forces on patrol in the Escambray, 1961.

Explosives captured by Castro's troops at La Campana.

HIRAM GONZALEZ — *the escape artist as he looks today, in his Miami home.*

HIRAM GONZALEZ AND ROBERTO INFANTE — *As a teenager, Roberto was in charge of warning members of the underground of State Security raids. When his brother was executed, Roberto escaped Cuba by seeking asylum in the Costa Rican Embassy.*

MARIO BELLO — *photo taken on a craft during a mission to Cuba.*

ISLE OF PINES PRISON — *one of the circular buildings of Cuba's worst concentration camps of the sixties.*

ELOY GUTIERREZ MENOYO — *former comandante in the war against Batista, founder of Alfa 66 against Castro. Captured during an infiltration raid, he survived twenty-two years of prison, including a beating at Isle of Pines in which all his ribs were broken.*

COMANDANTE FELIX TORRES — *at left. The man on the right is Captain Pardo, one of his assistants. Torres made Dr. Zaldivar strip naked during an interrogation.*

PORFIRIO RAMIREZ — *guerrilla captain and student leader. His execution caused public protests and student strikes in Cuba.*

AURELIO NAZARIO — *one of several members of his family to die in the war against Castro. Nazario was executed in 1970 by firing squad after being captured in an Alfa 66 guerrilla landing.*

31

ERNESTO DIAZ RODRIGUEZ — *A well-known dissident poet, his children's book was smuggled out of a maximum security prison by a guard.*

POLITA GRAU — *in a Cuban prison camp in 1978.*

14

MARIO BELLO:
CLANDESTINE MISSION TO CUBA

Mario Bello is a thirty-four-year-old Cuban exile. Arriving from Cuba at the age of thirteen, he has spent almost twenty years of his life in the struggle against Fidel Castro. Bello is a top man in the military structure of Alfa 66, a well-known anti-Castro group. A veteran of clandestine missions to Cuba, Bello resides in Hialeah, where he owns a retail store. A very popular activist, he has a reputation for being able to produce a punch line under the worst circumstances.

I became a revolutionary at the age of thirteen. I was a very young exile, but I donated my allowance money to anti-Castro organizations. I clipped articles from newspapers and magazines. I had scrapbooks full of clippings on the Cuban struggle for freedom. I was obsessed by this struggle, by the suffering of my country. This faith in the truth of my convictions has sustained me in the struggle all these years.

In 1970 the struggle against Castro was at a very low ebb. Most of the resistance groups had been bled to death or disbanded. Concentration camps and prisons had more than 40,000 inmates. Exile groups were economically bankrupt and mentally fatigued from all the years of fighting. Morale was low.

It was in 1970, as I was graduating from high school, that an event occurred which affected me deeply. Vicente Mendez came along. He was a peasant farmer from Las Villas Province with wide shoulders and an easy smile. He had been a guerrilla captain in the war against Batista. After the country went Communist, he became a guerrilla once more. He was a veteran of the heaviest fighting in the Escambray Mountains in the early sixties. Wounded and sick, Mendez made his way to Miami, where he married and lived quietly enough.

Realizing that nothing much was being done against Castro, Mendez proposed a series of guerrilla landings in Oriente Province to start an uprising. From a military perspective it was suicide. Two teams, totaling less than thirty men, would be persecuted by thousands of well-trained troops from the very second they set foot on Cuban soil.

Vicente Mendez knew the weaknesses of his plan. He knew he was going to die. He saw his mission as a way of lifting the morale of those who opposed the regime inside and outside Cuba. As he traveled the U.S. and Puerto Rico, begging for donations from the Cuban communities, his speeches moved all who heard him. A friend of mine was with him in Michigan during a snow storm. Vicente was wearing a pair of shoes with the sole completely worn out. My friend suggested that they go shopping for a new pair. Mendez just leaned back, puffed on a cigar, and said, "Buy some bullets. The only shoes I need are combat boots waiting for me in Miami. I'll be buried with them on."

The two teams landed and were exterminated. One group made it halfway to the center of Oriente. Mendez died in combat, two bullets in his chest. Three men from the teams survived to tell the story.

There are those critics who will tell you that Mendez died a foolishly suicidal death. I won't be one of them. The man chose his place and time. He sailed to his destiny knowing full well what the result would be. He awoke the exile community, pumping it with pride. I saw men cry from just the thought of the bravery of his deed. Meeting halls became packed once more.

I was moved by Vicente Mendez. In those last few days before graduating from high school, I wrote a letter to Alfa 66 headquarters in Miami. A few days later, I was invited to attend a meeting.

The meeting was on a Friday night. The room was filled with men and women; every social strata was there, from a surgeon to illiterate farmers. They all worked regular jobs and spent their free hours working for the movement. Some worked in fund-raising, while others were active organizing demonstrations, publishing a tabloid newspaper, or programming radio broadcasts.

There has been a lot of propaganda about Cuban anti-Castro groups being financed by the CIA. That was true in the early sixties, but not true at all for the last twenty years.

As a member of the Military Section, I received no reimbursement or pay of any kind. I was expected to buy my own uniform, my own rifle and handgun, my own equipment. I spent weekends at a training camp set up in the Everglades learning basic combat skills. We trained with semiautomatic weapons, so as not to break United States laws. The speedboats we used for missions were purchased piece by piece, as we were able to obtain the funds. Some, who came expecting to be sent into battle at once, spent hours installing motors or applying epoxy to a hull. Revolutionary work can be boring.

There is one mission I'll never forget. It was in October of 1976. Our intelligence department had information about a trip Castro was planning to make to Santiago de Cuba in Oriente. We planned an assassination attempt. Our team had seven men. Two were scheduled to stay, linking up with clandestine contacts. The rest consisted of the team leader, the navigator, and three gunners, of which I was one.

We left Miami on a clear morning. Our twenty-eight-foot boat had a big drive adaptor to increase cruising speed on the Perkins engine. We dressed as typical fishermen on an outing. The following morning, near Bimini, we linked up with another vessel. We transferred the weapons and supplies to our craft. We had one Belgian FN rifle (an excellent weapon), three M-16 rifles, and two M-1 carbines with paratrooper stocks. Each of us had handguns. There were also grenades, packets of plastic explosives, detonating wires, electric timers, walkie-talkie sets, and camera equipment. For those who would stay in Cuba, there were a couple of thousand Cuban pesos, false State Security identity cards, and even ration cards properly stamped. Slowly we plodded on, trying not to attract attention. This is a necessary but often difficult task.

The Caribbean is a gigantic hide-and-seek game. Drug boats headed north with their profitable cargo are hiding from the U.S. Coast Guard. Cubans leaving the island in rafts are hiding out from Castro's navy but seeking asylum from the U.S. Coast Guard, which is in turn seeking the drug smugglers. There are boats full of hungry Haitians headed west, hoping to make it all the way to the U.S. shore. Everyone crisscrosses the path of everyone else in this game of hide-and-seek.

On the fourth day we were approaching Cayo Sal, north of Cuba and south of the Bahamas, when we were spotted. There were two planes, both low-flying observation craft. One was unmarked and painted blue. The second was white and orange, with the U.S. Coast Guard insignia. They passed above us flying low. I could see the faces of the helmeted pilots looking down at us. They photographed us, then swept by again to take more pictures.

I took one of our cameras and began photographing them. The pilot of the blue plane saw it, laughed, and waved at me. I laughed and waved back. All joking aside, we began to worry. The two planes followed us all day. Perhaps they knew who we were. Their constant surveillance indicated that they were tracking us until the Coast Guard cutters could intercept and board us.

In the evening we were left alone. If we stayed in Cayo Sal we would have breakfast with Coast Guard crewmen. We discussed our only option: to escape in the night. The idea of having our weapons and boat confiscated did not appeal to us; that of escaping at night was not appealing either.

There was no moon; the night was black as ink. The sea was choppy and our boat rocked left to right, right to left. Cayo Sal is full of sandbars and coral reefs and we could have smashed the boat, grounded it, or sunk to our deaths. But we wanted to carry out the mission, so we decided to risk the escape.

It was a long night. We moved slowly, without lights. We were dressed in black, and our boat was painted dark blue. If we were out of radar range we had a chance of eluding the interceptors. We lucked out. By some miracle we did not slam into a sandbar. In the morning we turned on some speed, trying to put as much distance as we could between ourselves and the vessels of the U.S. Coast Guard.

From that fourth day on, we moved with care, hiding in the clusters of small keys in the area. We monitored Cuban radio transmissions, keeping track of the movement of their vessels. We always did this, for to approach the Cuban coast it is best to move in slowly when there is a lot of activity in the fishing fleet. Slipping in slowly shows up on their radar as one more bleep. Coming in fast or in a straight line arouses suspicion.

One afternoon we observed a boat moving in the water toward us. Looking through binoculars, we saw that it was a Bahamian Navy patrol boat. It was bad news, for if they boarded us we would find ourselves in a Bahamian prison. They are strict on weapons charges down there. We decided that as long as we were facing the prospect of a twenty-year vacation in the Queen's dungeons, we should try to gamble on another escape. We loaded the weapons and prepared to do battle. The Bahamian boat was much better armed with .50-caliber weapons. They could have had us for lunch. We opened fire when they came close. Little chunks of wood flew in the air. Their crewmen scampered, looking for cover. The patrol boat began to turn in the opposite direction, without firing back a single shot.

Cheering like kids, we sped away, looking for a hideout. We spent the next four days zigzagging the Caribbean. The worst time came at the end of one evening when our overheated engine caught on fire. At the time we were twelve miles away from Cuba. We doused the fire with wet shirts then watched in the distance, in the darkness of the night, the glow of lights on the coast of Camaguey Province. Luckily, the Cuban Komar and Ossa patrol boats do not patrol these waters as well as they should, due to the scarcity of petrol in Cuba.

The hide-and-seek game of the past ten days had depleted our own fuel supply just as we were approaching the eastern tip of Cuba. We were forced to stop at Great Iguana. It was there that our luck ran out. Bahamian authorities arrested us while refueling. That was a frustrating moment. We had spent fourteen days at sea, ten on the run, without showering or shaving and eating canned food. Now, when we were only a few hours from our drop at Baracoa, we were snared.

That first night at Iguana they held us in a small, old jail. We were the only prisoners. The food was catered from a local restaurant. After two weeks of canned food, the hot meal became the high point of our otherwise miserable day. The following day we were transferred to Nassau in a regular tourist flight of Bahamas Air. Handcuffed, bearded, and filthy, wearing black shirts and pants, we looked nasty.

In Nassau we were interrogated. We admitted to being Alfa 66 members on a mission to Cuba. We refused to discuss any more details of the incident. Curiously, no mention was made of the confrontation with the Bahamian Navy patrol boat. Perhaps they believed that it was someone else. We were charged with a number of weapons violations and sent to the Royal Prison. While our trial was pending, we were also interrogated by a member of the U.S. Embassy, to whom we admitted nothing.

At the prison I had an interesting conversation with a trustee named Errol Hayden. It was then that I learned of an incident that had happened while we were at sea. Apparently, the Bahamian authorities had arrested several Cuban fishermen for fishing in Bahamian waters. The Castro government, infuriated, launched a helicopter assault on a small Bahamian prison, rescuing the fishermen. Although no one had been killed, strong negative feelings were being expressed by both parties.

After that event, a few days later, seven exiles get themselves arrested in Iguana! I looked at Hayden and nodded my head. I was not about to be outdone by some Communist. "No doubt," I said, "if we are not liberated at once, my people will also come to free us, armed to the teeth, on speedboats." I made my comment as a bluff and as a joke. Hayden, however, took it seriously. Out of the corner of my eyes I saw that a guard who had been standing down the hall seemed worried.

A few minutes later, the prison warden called for us. He told us that he did not want any problems, that we would be released as soon as a $7,000 fine was received from our organization in Miami. We assured the warden that we did not want to create any problems, that we only wanted to return to Miami. These same feelings were also expressed by a U.S. official that came to see us. Everyone was anxious to see us leave.

We knew that the FBI would be waiting for us in Miami. We decided not to discuss anything with them. If they wanted to press charges against us it would have to be through a grand jury inquest. Thirty days after leaving Miami, we were scheduled to return. We were escorted to the airport by a U.S. government agent and a Bahamian military escort.

We entered the plane bound for Miami as free men, but word had been sent ahead of our arrival. Our plane was taxied to a corner of the runway in Miami. A portable stairway was moved to the door. Six unmarked cars were parked on the grass; a dozen agents stood by the stairs. One agent, a young one, entered the plane. He held up his ID and said aloud, "FBI. Stay where you are." I laughed. Where the hell were we to go? We were inside a plane in a corner of the runway. The FBI cars took us to a federal office, where we were interrogated. An agent sat across from me and I told him my name, my residence, and requested a lawyer.

"We would like to ask you a few questions," he said.

"I would like a lawyer."

"We know everything."

"If you know everything," I said, "then you don't need my answers, do you? Call me a lawyer."

We faced a grand jury a few weeks later. Two of the group, Hugo and Castillo, had to spend a year in a federal penitentiary for neutrality law violations. I received a strong warning to which I never paid any attention. The freedom of Cuba is still the priority in my life.

15
JUAN ROBLES:
COMMANDO RAID TO CUBA

Juan Robles is the nom de guerre *of a Vietnam veteran who resides in South-west Miami. Robles, now a salesman, participated in several commando raids in the early seventies. He is currently active with several exile community and human rights organizations.*

I came to the United States with my parents in 1961, when I was four-teen years old. It was a terrifying day for me, for I was old enough to understand what was happening around me. I was leaving my country, not knowing whether the leaving would be for a few days or a lifetime, to a different country with different language, customs, and culture.

My family settled in Florida. My parents had both been school-teachers in Cuba; both knew a little English, and employment was found for both.

I attended high school, spending those four years growing up as an American with sock-hops, football games, and rock concerts. In those years I began to ask myself questions about my reason for being, my heritage, the politics that had caused the upheaval that brought Castro to power. I read several books on Cuba, becoming more of an anti-Communist than ever before.

In the fall of 1965, I enlisted in the U.S. Army. The Vietnam War was heating up, and I volunteered for overseas duty. At eighteen,

143

with the desire to fight communism, Vietnam seemed the perfect crusade.

I was naive. In South Vietnam we won battles in the field but lost the war in the media, in the politics played in Washington, in the halls of Congress. Vietnam opened my eyes a lot about the weaknesses and inequalities of American politics.

Returning to Florida, I attended college on the G.I. Bill while driving a cab to support myself. At the age of twenty-two, I began to attend meetings of different anti-Castro organizations, wanting to become personally involved in the war against Castro.

In 1973 I was recruited by a friend to join the FLNC, a secret radical organization. Besides the FLNC, there was also Accion Cubana and Joven Cuba, all secret societies sponsoring commando operations and attacks on Cuban embassies and trade offices. The strategy appealed to me, and I volunteered for a mission.

We left Miami by boat in the last days of September, about twenty of us, most with combat experience. We moved slowly in a southeasterly direction, monitoring the radio broadcasts of the Cuban fishing fleet. Our plan was to raid some of the vessels, drop the fishermen off at an island, and sink the ships.

We had an assortment of weapons that included M-16 and M-14 rifles, M-1 carbines, shotguns, and even a recoilless rifle. I had a Remington pump shotgun, a very dependable weapon with solid power.

We spent several days cruising slowly north of Cuba. The fishing fleet travels in clusters. Twenty-one vessels fish in a designated area, hauling their catch to a larger boat, called a factory ship. Once the factory ship is filled to the brim, it returns to Cuba while the other twenty-one boats continue to fish, filling their own supply compartments, returning to Cuba later.

On October 2, 1973, we spotted a factory ship and a Cayo Largo-type fishing vessel. As night was falling, we decided to attack and board both ships. We maintained a safe distance, far enough to see them, but not close enough to be recognized.

We prepared two Zodiac-type gray rafts with motors attached, which we would use for the attack. Those few hours while we waited for night to fall reminded me of Vietnam, of the hours-long waits in the rice paddies, not quite knowing when the fight would start.

About sixteen of us boarded the two rafts. I grabbed a rope in my left hand, holding the shotgun in my right. No one talked as we moved through the water toward the vessels. The only sound was the bubbling of the silenced motors and the slapping of the water against the rubber raft.

Surprisingly, they had no one posted on guard duty. As we boarded, we almost stepped on one of the fishermen sleeping on the deck. The man started to struggle. One of us slit his throat with a knife, wounding him. The struggle woke up the crew. Soon men were running back and forth, screaming. Someone in our group fired two shots and they became subdued, surrendering at once.

We stuffed cotton on the slit throat of the wounded man, then took the crewmen as prisoners toward our own ship. A couple of our men stayed behind, taking over the other fishing boat.

The first stage had been successful. The second stage — the attack and boarding of the factory ship — would be difficult. The ship was over a hundred feet long and twenty feet high off the water, which meant we would need grappling hooks for boarding. Speed and aggressiveness would be essential for a victory.

Our gray rubber rafts bounced on the water as we approached the factory ship. As the ship loomed near, we saw flashes from gunfire and heard explosions. We fired back. The sound was deafening. With one hand I held on to a rope on the raft, bucking on the water like a cowboy on a rodeo horse. With the other hand I fired, tucking the shotgun butt under my armpit. Around me, a dozen men were raking the deck of the factory ship with small weapons fire.

Our rubber raft bumped against the side of the factory ship. El Flaco, who was up front, lost his M-2 rifle, the weapon slipping through his fingers into the dark water. El Flaco was furious. Turning around, he began cursing at our raft pilot, blaming him for losing the weapon by his reckless navigation. Incredible as it may sound, both started to argue and curse while another man threw a grappling hook to board the ship and several of us fired toward the deck.

Boarding the ship was tough. We went up the nylon rope jammed against each other. When we jumped on the deck we spread out, weapons ready. I remember stepping over a body. A weapon was on the deck near him. Later we found out that he was the political commissar of the factory ship. His body was dumped overboard before we set the ship on fire.

The crew had locked themselves inside the lower deck. Two of us fired several shots at the frame and they surrendered at once. Taking them up on deck, we made them huddle in a corner. I told them to kneel with their hands behind their necks. As I moved through the deck, another one of us told the prisoners to stand up. When I returned, I told them to kneel down again.

"Look, son," an old grizzled fisherman told me, "if you are going to shoot me, do it now. My bones are too old for this up-and-down game."

I could not help laughing. "No one is going to shoot you, old man," I told him. "We mean you no harm."

While three of us guarded the crew, the rest of our squad ransacked the factory ship looking for weapons, radio code books, or anything of intelligence value. The radar equipment was smashed with rifle butts. Holes were made in the lower deck to flood the ship. Anything flammable or explosive was spread over the lower deck, and a fire was started.

We took the captured crew back to our mother ship. The factory ship we left behind was a huge mass of wood and steel, burning and sinking slowly in the ocean. Our ship and the captured Cayo Largo began heading north, away from the coast of Cuba.

Of the ten or eleven prisoners, one was a hard-core Communist. He told us flat out that we could kill him, but he would not deny his support for Castro. We answered that we did not kill people for their political beliefs, that we were fighting for a free Cuba, not to become dictators ourselves.

One of us gave a little speech, telling our prisoners that they were welcome to join us if they so wished. We promised that anyone returning with us would be taken to Florida to request political asylum. Anyone not wishing to join would be placed on a small island near the Bahamas. We would notify the Cuban government of the location of the fishermen once we were out of range of a counterattack.

With the exception of one man who was a devoted Communist, the rest of the captives acted friendly toward us. They claimed they could not join us, for their families were back in Cuba. We understood.

We left our captured crewmen at a key north of Cuba. We sank the Cayo Largo fishing vessel with a couple of shells from the recoilless rifle. The fishermen were later picked up by helicopters of Castro's air force.

As we headed back to Florida, I sat on the deck of our vessel. It felt good, really good. We had carried out a good mission, sinking two ships, causing hundreds of thousands of dollars worth of damage to Cuba's economy.

The sun was coming up over the horizon. On our radio we picked up the signals from the gunboats and helicopters moving frantically to the south of us. We were out of harm's way.

I lit a cigarette and looked around. Morale was high. In a couple of days we would be back in Miami, working our jobs, worrying about paying the mortgage and the electric bills. Right now, we were soldiers — fighting for free, buying our own bullets and weapons. I felt a close bond to all those men, a feeling hard to explain, for we were all volunteers united by a common suffering, by a covenant that only we understood.

16
PEDRO SOLARES:
A DAY AT THE UNITED NATIONS

Forty-one-year-old Pedro Solares arrived in the United States at the age of fifteen. A graduate architect from City College of New York, Solares works as a microcomputer manager in Miami. For eleven years he was one of the top echelon of the Abdala Cuban Movement, for which he edited a tabloid publication and formed part of a team broadcasting anti-Castro propaganda to Cuba.

I was a fifth-grade student in 1957 when a coalition of several anti-Batista groups attacked the Presidential Palace in Havana. The raid to kill Batista failed, but its daring caught my imagination. Several dozen revolutionaries, most of them university students, were killed in the operation. The best known among the dead was Jose Antonio Echeverria, an idealistic student who was president of the University Student Federation at the University of Havana. His death affected me; the passion of his convictions impressed me. I did not yet understand why those young men got themselves into such trouble, though I was certain that a climate of agreement and less violence was more desirable.

A few months later we traveled to Spain to visit relatives. We fell in with a lively group of Cubans during the seven-day voyage. They often discussed the problems that affected Cuba. Not only did I get to hear opinions but I noticed something radically new. There were no whispers! It seemed strange that a few miles should make that differ-

148

ence, but it felt good. I was absorbing new ideas, and the way they were expressed, openly and loudly, seemed just about the finest thing that could be — maybe even good enough to justify the risking of life.

I began to find some answers. In the following months, I came to understand the reasons for this struggle. Cuba, I came to believe, needed a change toward what I later identified as democracy and social justice.

Batista's escape delighted me, but my joy was to be brief. Although I was thirteen years old, I was not easily swayed by theatrical politics.

By the middle of 1960, the extent of the Communist takeover was apparent and a sophisticated, repressive apparatus was in place. The opposition was also growing. There were rebellions, conspiracies, guerrilla uprisings. There were daily arrests and executions. The firing squads were working overtime. Of course, we were speaking in whispers again.

There were also student strikes, especially in the private schools. One took place, nationwide, as a result of the execution of the student leader Porfirio Ramirez, a former captain in the Rebel Army, and other guerrilla leaders captured in the Escambray Mountains. At some point, I expressed strong approval of the protest strike and, as a result, a classmate approached me with an offer to join the underground, specifically the DRE (Revolutionary Student Directorate), a very active resistance group.

My job was to distribute *Trinchera* ("Trenches"), the DRE's underground mimeographed publication and pamphlets. Sometimes I would go to a roof and place the pamphlets near the edge with a stone attached to a string on top. I would then go to the door, pull on the string, and rush down the stairs while the wind took care of blowing the papers down to the traffic below.

I expected to receive some urban guerrilla training, but my contact told me that no one under sixteen was allowed to participate. I continued to distribute leaflets and to write political graffiti on the walls, which was done with paint and a brush since spray paint did not exist then.

In the tense days before the Bay of Pigs Invasion, my mother discovered a stack of leaflets at our home. She was horrified. When State Security invaded some homes in the neighborhood, the time seemed ripe to get rid of the pamphlets; we tore, burned, and flushed during an entire afternoon, not an easy task when you live in an apartment. A few days later, the invasion came and failed. When I went to my contact in the DRE, he told me to forget about everything for now. I made other contacts, but to no avail.

Soon thereafter the regime took over all Catholic schools and I did not get to finish my third year in high school. Also, there were rumors that the government intended to take all children away from their parents for indoctrination. Panic had set in. My parents decided that our future in Cuba was bleak and that I was likely to get into more "trouble" and end up in Castro's jails. Their priority was to get me out of Cuba. Later they would see about their own departure.

Through the Marist Brothers, the religious order that ran the school I had attended, my mother was able to obtain a visa for me to enter the United States. The Castro government made sure that the paperwork was as lengthy, tense, and demeaning as possible. My mother and I had to make long lines and endure the standard threats and provocations imposed by very arrogant bureaucrats.

It would be years before I found out that the visas were forged, made by the thousands through an underground network run by Polita and Ramon Grau. I was one of the thousands of children they helped escape from Cuba. They both would endure long years of prison for their noble work. They gave up years of their lives to give us freedom. I pray that my life may someday be worthy of their sacrifice.

On September 28, 1961, I left Cuba. Leaving one's country at the age of fifteen, leaving one's parents and family in a country torn apart by strife and dictatorship, is a traumatic experience. I was leaving without knowing what the future held for me, except a hope that is was better than what awaited me in Cuba. As I embraced my parents at the airport, I wondered if I would see them again. It was the saddest day of my life. We hugged and kissed for a long time. Then they were out of reach, separated from me by a glass partition. As I boarded the plane I could make them out in the crowd and I waved goodbye, pretending to smile. When the plane had taken off and flew past the terminal, I could no longer see my family among the hundreds packed on the roof of the building.

Yet, I was lucky. I was leaving with three close friends from school whom I had known since the first grade. This made leaving less harsh, less terrifying. Other children in that plane had no such luck.

A man working for a Catholic organization headed by Father Bryan Walsh, now a monsignor, received us at the airport. After hours of processing, a group of about ten of us were herded into a large van.

We were rather silent and subdued. We were alone in a foreign country, our lives in the hands of people we never met. Cuba was ninety miles across the sea, yet a whole world away.

Long after, I came to see my life as composed of clearly defined segments. One of those segments was time I spent at the camps for refugee children, even though it lasted only eight months. For me and for thousands of other Cuban children, that period of separation from our family would affect the rest of our lives in ways that we will never understand completely.

Our van drove out of the urban areas and down country roads. Suddenly, it made a right turn where there seemed to be no road, driving between pine trees and a dense wall of bushes. In a clearing we saw a cabin. This was the office of Camp Matecumbe, one of three such refugee centers for children in South Florida. Farther on through the woods there were two large sleeping barracks, a mess hall, and a roofed picnic area. The next morning I would also discover a huge swimming pool. Matecumbe was a summer camp pressed into service for our benefit. Even though dinner was over, some was left since our arrival was expected. Pork chops, mashed potatoes, and milk. The meal was not only filling but also very reassuring.

There were a couple hundred of us at the camp and not enough bunk beds to go around. I was given an army field cot. I met a friend I had not seen since the first grade who let me share his locker. Eventually, the number of children at Matecumbe would nearly triple. The large picnic area was closed off and converted into a dormitory larger than the other two combined, and a third tier was added to all the bunks.

The refugee children centers were to be places of transit. We were to be placed in foster homes or institutions in other states. That meant, however, another break, another step into unknown territory. The youngest of our group was twelve years old and a cousin of one of my friends; he was the mascot of the group. When the news came that he would be sent to Wisconsin with his sister, who was in the camp for girls, he was very scared. Whatever little security he could feel with us was crushed. It was a very hard moment for us, and there was nothing we could do for him. Everything turned out very well for him and his sister, but this new departure was very traumatic.

Most of my stay was at Matecumbe, though I spent some time at another center in Kendall. My friends were sent to different places across the country, and I eventually ended up at Saint Raphael Hall in

Miami, a converted motel with fifty or sixty kids under the direct supervision of Father Walsh. It was a great place made much better by the presence of the good Father. The food was better, and we were in the middle of the city. I spent about six weeks of the eight months between my arrival and that of my parents at Saint Raphael.

The first thing I did upon arrival in the United States was to fill out the necessary papers to have visas given to my parents. It seemed like an eternity, but the day of their arrival finally came. I took a bus to the airport and got lost, walked endless blocks, and was finally given a ride by a kind man who took me directly to the airport. There I met a friend of my family. The plane had already arrived, he told me, and now my parents were going through customs and immigration. I stood waiting impatiently for what seemed like hours.

Finally, the door opened and they came out, looking anxiously for me in the crowd waiting for relatives. I won't even try to describe my feelings. We embraced, we kissed, we cried. The feeling of elation lasted for days, and I can still feel that day as if it happened just yesterday.

Within days my parents made arrangements to move to New York City. There, my father worked as a dishwasher in a hotel, eventually working his way up to pantry chef. My mother worked at several garment manufacturing places. I worked full-time as a busboy during the first difficult months, and on weekends when I went back to school. My life became more settled. I eventually attended the City College of New York.

During this time, I attended many Cuban exile events, such as demonstrations and cultural and patriotic gatherings, but I did not become active in any organization. Then, in September of 1970, a demonstration in front of the United Nations protested the rumored attendance of Fidel Castro to the General Assembly. I did not go. The last few demonstrations had been poorly attended, and I felt disillusioned. As it turned out, there were hundreds of people at the U.N. and even a few arrests. I did not miss the protest called for a few days later when Castro's delegate was to speak. There I found an organization composed of young people about my age.

The Agrupacion Estudiantil Abdala (Abdala Student Movement) was named after a poem written by Jose Marti when he was sixteen years old. In that poem, a young prince dies fighting for his country. Abdala started in 1968 as a study group, but by 1970 it had become an activist student organization with several dozen members in New

York City and northeastern New Jersey. The activism, the similarity in age and backgrounds I shared with most of its members, and the strong feelings of nationalism and willingness to work for Cuba's freedom attracted me to the group.

The first activity in which I participated was the "takeover" of the Security Council at the United Nations building. To the Cuban exiles, the U.N. was a den of hypocrisy. That world body ignored the violations of human rights in Cuba. As a people with a legitimate gripe, we felt neglected. We planned to bring the attention of the world press to the suffering of the Cuban political prisoners, embarrass the U.N., breathe some new life and hope to the disillusioned exile community, and claim the right of our generation to participate in the affairs of our nation. We felt that we had a great deal to offer, given that we knew the language and the culture of the United States, where most exiles live. As college students, we knew the power of the tactics of sit-ins and demonstrations so prevalent at the time.

We picked March 13 for our activity to commemorate the fourteenth anniversary of the attack on the Presidential Palace in 1957, when Jose Antonio Echeverria was killed. Thus, we would express ourselves as revolutionaries continuing the fight for democracy and freedom. We saw ourselves as a generational movement, descendant of the same revolutionary student groups that had battled the dictatorships of Machado in the thirties and Batista in the fifties.

As weeks passed, I became very involved in Abdala. I traveled to Illinois to help a Cuban student association in a confrontation with a pro-Castro group. After my return, I spent most of my time away from school working in the organization of our protest at the U.N.

The final plan included fourteen men and two women. They would join three consecutive tour groups at the U.N. building. Once the first group arrived at the Security Council chamber, we would delay the tour by asking the guide many questions. When all tours were in the chamber, we would rush down the tiers of the visitors seats, jump a railing, and handcuff ourselves to the seats of the delegates. At the same time there would be a public demonstration outside the building. Two other women would be in the tours to give word to the demonstrators of how things went. We expected to be arrested immediately and had plans to call the press with the story, fearing that the U.N. officials would try to hush the whole incident.

Finally, the day arrived. For weeks we had planned our protest, researched our data, made dry runs in small groups, refined details. I was sitting in the Security Council chamber asking stupid questions from the unsuspecting guide. The waiting was over. Then I heard the loud words: "In the name of the Cuban people, we are taking over this building." I jumped from my seat and ran down the steps; I sensed others around me doing the same but I did not look. Behind me one of the guides cried "You can't do that," but we had. In a flash I had the handcuffs around my wrist and attached to the arm of one of the delegate chairs. I looked around. We were all there, handcuffed.

Everything went exactly as planned — not a hitch. Except that we were not ejected immediately. Guards surrounded us. The chief of security came to talk to us. We demanded to see the secretary general, U-Thant.

It turns out that, as our research had shown, nothing like this had ever occurred. Other demonstrations had taken place outside the building, in the jurisdiction of the New York City Police Department. The U.N. guards, under whose jurisdiction we were, were not sure of how to handle the problem. As a result, they even closed down the building. The expected fifteen minutes inside turned into two and a half hours, plenty of time for the press to be alerted and for many Cubans who heard it on the radio to join the demonstration. Among the demonstrators were three students whom I had met in my visit to Illinois and who drove to New York solely on my assurance that the demonstration would be "worth attending." They returned to Chicago as a new chapter of Abdala.

The event received wide publicity, for it was the first time in history that the U.N. was closed down due to a protest. Our protest appeared in a national television news show and in all the local news broadcasts. It was headlined in the papers in New York and Miami and, apparently, by a wire service, since we later found out that it appeared in several newspapers in Europe and Latin America. Of course, it became a topic of conversation for weeks among the Cuban exiles.

Inside the Security Council chamber, the initial excitement gave way to a certain calm as we talked to the guards and to their chief as he kept rushing in and out. One of us lit a cigar and read a paper. I glanced at the clock once in a while. Half hour, one hour — well beyond our most optimistic hopes. I was elated that all was going so well. I had also time to think that a lot of unpleasantness awaited when the legal system took over from U.N. Security; yet, that worry was insignificant, embarrassing, when compared to the sacrifice of those who had died or were suffering in prison camps. At least, I thought, I was doing something useful. We were accomplishing what we set out to do.

The best moment related to this incident came, however, years later. The "grapevine" in Cuba's prisons is amazing. Somehow, the news of our chain-in filtered to the prisoners. A man who had been in a Cuban prison at the time said that the day he found out what we did he felt comforted, as though the world had not forgotten him. This simple fact filled me with satisfaction.

Eventually, the U.N. officials decided that it was time for us to leave. They brought in huge chain clippers and, starting with Rolando Feria and Miriam Alvarez, they moved in, three to hold each one and a fourth to cut the handcuff. Then we were handcuffed again behind our backs and dragged out. There were a few injuries, most of those sustained by Frank Calzon, who hooked his legs to a railing and was pulled and beaten. I was pushed to the floor and choked by one of the guards. My muscles seemed to relax rapidly as soon as air failed to come in.

As I was taken out through a side gate toward a waiting paddy wagon, flashbulbs from photographers' cameras popped in my face. On the other side of the street I saw a group of people and Rafael Rodriguez, one of our youngest members among them, waving excitedly. I knew then that everything had gone better than expected.

We were well treated by the New York police; after all, the problem had not been with them. I suspect that they felt relieved that for once the U.N. security officers had to deal with the messy part of a protest. We were even allowed to watch the news, seeing ourselves being dragged out of the U.N. building and the demonstration still going on, the participants promising that they would stay until our release. We were photographed, fingerprinted, advised by a lawyer. The necessary paperwork was completed, and by midnight we joined the tired demonstrators. Eventually, after many court appearances and many delays, we each paid the $100 fine imposed by a judge. In Cuba we would have been condemned to at least ten years' imprisonment.

Abdala became well known among Cuban exiles. Many Cuban student groups in universities all over the United States, Puerto Rico, and Spain contacted us. Soon we had chapters of Abdala in more than forty universities. Student activism was an important sociological factor in Cuban history. Suddenly, a whole new generation joined the struggle. Many among us had spent half of our lives in the United States, yet we were committed to Cuba's freedom.

Our organizing activities found an unlikely ally. In the late sixties and early seventies, the Castro government capitalized on student dissent in the United States by creating the Venceremos Brigade consisting of American students who, fascinated with the revolutionary myth, were invited to Cuba for a few weeks to "help" harvest one product or another and who were subjected while there to a sophisticated program of propaganda. The radicals would return to propagandize on behalf of the Castro tyranny. Their presence, however, galvanized Cuban students into political action. We confronted the Venceremos Brigade on many occasions. Some of the confrontations were heated radio or television debates, others shout-outs across information booths. A few deteriorated into fistfights.

We planned our strategy according to our resources. We established chapters of Abdala, organized lectures to publicize the reality of the Cuban situation, published a monthly paper and several magazines, and organized innumerable rallies and protest demonstrations.

In May of 1972, Pedro Luis Boitel died during a hunger strike. An engineering student jailed for life by Castro, Boitel became Cuba's best-known symbol of rebellion behind prison walls. His legendary defiance, his idealism, and his strength of character made him a larger than life figure among Cuban exiles. As a jailed student leader, he was specially significant to our movement. For years we had followed his story. And he found out about us.

A few months before his death we received a letter from him. It was a small piece of paper written with the incredibly small yet totally legible handwriting perfected by Cuban prisoners. It had been folded many times to ease smuggling it out. The letter was a message of solidarity with our ideals and encouragement to persevere in the struggle.

Now, Boitel was dead. We felt rage. The symbol of defiance was now a martyr. We could not allow his death to go unnoticed beyond the exile community; we wanted the world to know of his dignity and his suffering. The planning meetings and all other preliminary activities were completed swiftly. We were working with a sense of urgency, but also we were much more experienced at this sort of activity. Fourteen members of Abdala — three women and eleven men — were to chain themselves inside the head of the Statue of Liberty and fly a Cuban flag out of its crown.

The Statue of Liberty, as a symbol of freedom, was the perfect landmark from which to tell the world about the death of a freedom fighter. In a press release we stated that our demonstration was a protest for the generalized apathy toward the plight of Cuban political prisoners in Castro's jails, exemplified by the death of Boitel.

This time I was one of the outside coordinators and among other things was in charge of handing out the handcuffs. Again, everything went exactly as planned, except that the outcome was less complicated than expected. Since the statue is under the jurisdiction of the National Parks, the arrest of the demonstrators was a complicated matter. This time, the only demand was that the demonstrators be allowed to talk to the press. In a compromise, a press conference took place in the head of the statue, and the demonstrators walked out later, surrounded by reporters and photographers. The death of Pedro Luis Boitel, the inhuman conditions in Castro's political jails, and the denial of basic human rights to the Cuban people were featured in broadcasts all over the country and in headlines around the world.

I was a member of Abdala for eleven years. For nearly two years I ran the monthly newspaper, which had a wide circulation among Cuban exiles all over the world. When I moved to Florida in 1973, I joined the team involved in clandestine short-wave transmissions to Cuba.

The broadcasting of thousands of radio shows to Cuba was one of the most important but least publicized activities of Abdala. It was also hard work. About ten of us would spend several hours researching our assigned topics, then meet to write, edit, and type the program which consisted of a mix of news, interviews, commentaries, and an editorial. Then we would rehearse once and do the taping. Three different half-hour weekly programs were assembled from this material, and for a time we were able to add a fourth Sunday transmission, one hour long, which included music and cultural and scientific news.

Then there was the matter of the actual transmissions, for which we had no licence since their character conflicted with all regulations. We figured that the FCC, like most regulatory agencies, was probably understaffed and that if we could avoid actual complaints they would probably leave us alone. The thing to do was to have the transmitter in an isolated area. A very good and patient man let us use his farm, way out in the rural area of Dade County. For years, three or four of us took turns driving to the farm to transmit. Including the drive, it took about four hours to put a half-hour program on the air. It worked, though, for we had no encounters with the FCC.

The radio transmission was not a job for paranoids. For security reasons, only a few knew the location of the transmitter. Only one person would go to air the programs. Most of the time no one lived at the farm and it was pitch dark with all kinds of farm animals roaming around. From inside the hut where the transmitter was, it sounded like a small army was surrounding the place. More than once an inquisitive goat poked its head in the door, startling me.

In time, we even sent some coded messages in our programs. By then, Abdala had managed to structure a few clandestine groups in Cuba to carry out some underground activities on a modest scale.

We had a good, efficient, and dedicated crew in the radio team, and the same goes for the other task forces and for the organization as a whole. I am proud of having been in their company. Even though the organization no longer exists, our influence continues and promises to increase. Among our alumni there are doctors, lawyers, businessmen, school administrators, judges, one elected official, writers, artists, civic leaders. In sum, we are a bright, idealistic generation coming into its own. And let no one be fooled: most of us are still committed to the cause of Cuba's freedom. Our time is yet to come.

17

HUMBERTO LOPEZ: FROM HERO TO OUTLAW

Humberto Lopez is a stocky man in his mid-forties whose body bears the scars of war. Three fingers of his left hand are missing. His left eyeball is made of plastic. In his face and chest there are several small scars made by shrapnel.

A resistance fighter since his teenage years, Lopez is one of the best-known "men of action" in the Cuban exile community. He resides in Miami with his second wife and newborn son.

In the first year of the revolution I became disenchanted with the new system that had seized power. I had been a believer in the Cuban Revolution against Batista, having fought in the underground sabotage teams of the 26 of July Movement while I was still a teenager.

After the triumph, I saw a regime in search of total power, a totalitarian approach to politics beyond the realm of any previous dictatorship ever suffered by the Cuban people. Civil rights vanished and were replaced by the system's total control over the masses. Every cultural and social structure of Cuban society began to crumble under the daily edicts of the new order.

At the age of nineteen I had an office job in the Ministry of Commerce. After working hours I attended clandestine meetings, plotting a new network to oppose Castro. In a short time I was placed in charge of an "action and sabotage" squad.

One of our best sabotages was the destruction of a Commerce

Ministry records warehouse in Old Havana. Three of us went by car to our objective, two entering the building while the driver waited in the vehicle with an M-3 machine gun. Only one guard covered the perimeter of the two-story structure. Timing him, we moved into the building, cracking a glass in an office door. Once inside the warehouse, my companion and I moved quickly from room to room.

We had small vials of *fosforo vivo,* pure phosphorous in water that ignites a few seconds after being exposed to air. We broke the vials on cabinets and boxes of files. Hundreds of boxes jammed together in racks began to ignite. In a couple of minutes, as we left the building undetected, the second-floor fire was already well under way. Within minutes after we left the scene, the whole building was a ball of flame and smoke.

Our driver was inexperienced. Drivers on these type of missions should be men with ice in their veins, but such men are always hard to find. When leaving under such circumstances, the best manner of driving is slowly so as not to be noticed. Our nervous driver, however, took off at bullet speed down those narrow streets of Old Havana. After a couple of blocks we attracted the attention of a militiaman walking a post. As our speeding vehicle moved toward him, the militiaman went down on his knees, raising his snub-nosed machine gun. We opened fire with the M-3 and a handgun. As we passed him he fell under our gunfire.

In April of 1961, the underground in Cuba awaited the invasion from the exile camps of the CIA. The group to which I belonged, the MRR, was ready to spring into action as soon as the landings began. Teams had been assigned to attack all the police stations in Havana, sabotage transportation and communication outlets, and paralyze the city. But the orders never came. By the time that the underground learned of the invasion landing at Bay of Pigs, the assault brigade was pinned down at the beach and State Security was rounding up thousands of suspects. Mass arrests were so huge that jails overflowed and schools and theaters had to be used as improvised detention centers.

My first reaction was: what should I do now? I went to my section leader, telling him that I wanted to start the fighting in support of the invaders, but he just shook his head sadly. The chain of command was frozen, waiting for orders that never came.

Up to the time of the Bay of Pigs, I had continued to work for the Ministry of Commerce. After the invasion failed I went completely underground.

I was burnt-out as far as clandestine activities were concerned. I decided to sneak into one of the embassies in Havana, requesting political asylum.

In 1961 a dozen embassies in Havana were jammed with hundreds of Cubans who had been trying to flee the country. Some, those with diplomatic contacts, entered hidden in the trunks of embassy vehicles. The majority of Cubans, however, sneaked in by jumping the fences or, in some cases, ramming through the gates in vehicles.

My father had left Cuba through the Brazilian Embassy, where I had visited him several times, meeting some of the diplomats. I headed on foot toward the embassy, hoping to talk my way through the gate.

Two militiamen stood by the iron grill gate. I knew one of them from my neighborhood, a young man named Amado. He eyed me suspiciously as I waited for someone from the embassy to come to the gate.

The embassy butler, an elderly gentleman named Rosado, talked to me but did not open the gate to let me in. He looked at me puzzled, not quite knowing what I wanted. I kept talking nonsense. I started rolling my eyes as I tried to signal him to open the gate. A few feet away, on either side of me, the militiamen were fidgety, wondering what I was planning.

Rosado began to open the gate. Both militiamen moved toward me, attempting to block my way. I jumped in, ramming the gate, stumbling through as arms tried to grab me. Rosado fell to the ground, the bottom of the iron gate ripping his shoe, lifting a toenail which began to bleed profusely. I ran over him toward the front door of the building. As I crossed the porch at a sprint, I heard a shot behind me, but kept on running, slamming through the door into the embassy and asylum. Later, when poor Rosado hobbled in on his bleeding foot, I apologized and he cursed me freely.

There were twenty of us in the Brazilian Embassy. The diplomats left in the evening to their individual apartments, but we stayed in the building. I slept in the garage with several dozen others, in mats rolled on the floor. Although we were under the protection of the government of Brazil, the Castro government delayed giving us safepassage permits, making us wait for months before we were allowed to leave Cuba.

I stayed at the embassy from May until December of 1961. On

the day we were to leave, a mob of Castro supporters, sponsored by State Security, stormed the gates, throwing rocks, orange rinds, and garbage at us. From inside the embassy, we returned their stones and garbage. Some of us became so involved that we even threw chairs at the mob. Eventually, we were escorted to waiting vehicles and pushed our way through two thin lines of guards while the mob insulted us, hitting us as we left the embassy.

On the flight out of Cuba, one of our stops was at the island of Curacao, near Venezuela. While we waited for our plane to refuel, a group of us walked over to a hotel where we planned to relax for a couple of hours. To our surprise we found out that a Soviet delegation was staying at the inn. Our two hours of relaxing turned into a massive fistfight in which a couple of Soviets were almost drowned in the swimming pool. We returned to the airplane escorted by several burly policemen.

My father was in Venezuela, where I joined him. He was working at a radio station, broadcasting to Cuba. I wanted to go to the United States, where I had resided as an exile in the days of the struggle against Batista, but the paperwork would take months, a time that I spent working as a broadcaster at the radio station.

In June of 1962 I arrived in Miami, hoping to become involved in the commando raids that were being carried out by the many anti-Castro groups active in the exile community. I was twenty-two, experienced in warfare, and willing to do battle.

I went on several missions to Cuba with various groups. On the most unforgettable trip, three of our vessels were surprised by Hurricane Flora, a full-strength storm which split our little fleet. Huge waves pounded us, a ripping wind almost overturned our boat. Many of the men were seasick as the vessel bucked on the waves. We could not tell where the sea started and the sky ended. We moved, bouncing on the waves, facing a giant wall of water that seemed to stretch into eternity. Somehow, we were lucky enough to return to Florida alive. Some of the men in the other boats were marooned in Cuba, where they died in a gun battle with Castro's army patrols.

At the time, in the early sixties, many exiles believed that the United States would help us liberate Cuba from communism. It was inconceivable to us that the United States would allow a Communist military and subversion base only ninety miles from the shores of Florida. For a time, it seemed as though the U.S. would keep its promise. They sponsored the Bay of Pigs Invasion, trained thousands of Cubans in covert operations, and pumped millions of dollars in equipment and supplies into the struggle.

The problem was that the U.S. helped but never committed itself. They planned and sponsored the Bay of Pigs Invasion, but the operation failed because at the last minute the brigade was stranded and air support never came. They aided underground networks, but some effective anti-Castro groups were never helped because they did not meet the criteria of loyalty the CIA expected. The Communists never seemed to care whether public opinion knew that they supported Castro; the United States admitted helping the exiles, though they only did it halfway, and Castro could not be overthrown with halfway measures.

In the early sixties, the United States sponsored a recruiting campaign among Cuban exiles to join the U.S. Army. A "Cuban Unit" was proposed, with the intent of spearheading the "invasion of Cuba" which, in those days leading to the October Missile Crisis, seemed imminent. I packed a few changes of clothing, signed enlistment papers, and joined the first handful of trainees headed for Fort Knox in Kentucky.

The worst thing about basic training was the time involved. Our morale was high and we wanted to land in Cuba to overthrow the system. New recruits arrived daily until about 2,000 of us were training at Fort Knox in infantry tactics, weapons, and explosives. From Knox we were transferred to Fort Jackson, where more recruits joined the Cuban Units of the U.S. Army until our number reached 5,000 men.

On our graduation day we paraded in front of some generals. As we stood at parade rest, dressed in crisp uniforms, every man wondered when the invasion would take place. We were all volunteers, some as young as seventeen, others in their mid-thirties. Many of us were veterans of the resistance, while others had never held a weapon until their first day at boot camp. But now the training was over and we wanted to fight for the freedom of our country.

Flags furled in the morning air. The anthems of the United States and Cuba were played. It was an emotional moment.

The general that addressed our troops, whose name I do not recall, quickly destroyed our hopes. The timing, he said, was not right for direct U.S. involvement into the affairs of Cuba. Since direct intervention was out of the question, the Cuban Units of the U.S. Army would be deactivated. Those wishing to return to civilian life would be placed on reserve status while those who wished to remain would go to regular army units to serve out their tours of duty.

It was as though a bucket of ice water had been poured on us. Men who had been separated from their families grumbled, feeling as if all the weeks of separation and sacrifice were now being wasted. Worse, the United States was backing out of another commitment to free Cuba.

I was discharged, returning to Miami to rejoin the exile commando organizations. A few hundred remained at Fort Jackson, many later serving in Vietnam.

I worked at a factory where trailers were manufactured. It was tough manual labor, but it paid for the beans.

The MRR, which had been one of the three largest anti-Castro groups in Cuba during the early sixties, was regrouping with Manuel Artime as its leader. Artime was a man in his late thirties, a former lieutenant in Castro's Rebel Army. He became an early opponent of the regime. Later, he was one of the leaders of the ill-fated Bay of Pigs Invasion and as a result, a political prisoner in Cuba for over a year. A favorite of the CIA, he proposed the overthrow of Castro by popular insurrection.

The plan was to carry out hundreds of acts of resistance, coordinated with urban infiltration and guerrilla warfare. Training camps would be set up in Costa Rica and Nicaragua, sponsored on a limited basis by "the Agency." I volunteered to join the infiltration teams. For several weeks, I received intensive training in Miami, provided by American instructors. I learned advanced infiltration tactics, teaching methods, communications, survival, and covert operations procedures.

Four of us left one morning in a plane bound for Costa Rica. There would eventually be a dozen of us, working as instructors in infiltration, training different teams in covert operations. When we arrived in Costa Rica, the camp did not exist. What existed were miles of jungle, thick bush. It was up to us, the dozen instructors, to build our own training base.

I never worked as hard in my life as I did in that Costa Rican jungle. I worked eighteen hours a day, seven days a week for a couple of months. With explosives and a bulldozer, we cleared a twenty-three-mile trail through the bush. Next to the trail we built six small camps, a couple of miles apart from each other. Infiltration teams of five or seven men would live separated from each other, each team being trained individually. Once the camp was operational, we were able to train six teams at the same time — a total of about forty men.

We cut down trees to clear the patches of land and used the logs to build the huts for each camp. Since the ground was swampy, the bulldozer and heavy equipment would become stuck, sinking in the slime. At times of heavy rain the cabins would practically float away.

Mosquitoes, bugs, leeches, snakes. We had every animal in that jungle. The heat was intense. Sweat soaked through our clothing, drenching every garment. Since we had no electric power, we rigged up our own, using small petrol generators to provide lighting.

As soon as the camp was operational we began receiving recruits, most of whom already had some experience in covert activities. There were different types of bases in our operation. Our infiltration base was in Costa Rica, while Nicaragua had a commando base and a guerrilla training camp.

A good friend of mine, Tony Izquierdo, ran the guerrilla center. Tony died a few years ago, fighting against the Sandinistas in Nicaragua.

My work as instructor consisted in training the teams and accompanying them to their infiltration zones. I've lost count of how many times I went on sea missions during this time period. Perhaps a dozen times, perhaps less. On most of these missions, I traveled to the coast of Cuba. Three times I landed with the teams, scouting the beaches.

We had two excellent aluminum torpedo boats, each about 100 feet long. Each boat had a crew of experienced navigators and gunners, all very capable and courageous. Each boat was equipped with a double .50-caliber machine gun, a single .50, four .30-caliber machine guns and a 75mm recoilless rifle. Besides the two gunboats we had a mother ship, used for refueling and supplies, a ponderous vessel that moved at only seven knots per hour. To avoid detection, all our craft were equipped with a variety of registrations, an assortment of flags, signs that could be clipped on in seconds. Not only could our vessels change name and configuration but even colors, for on one occasion the mother ship was spray-painted in the middle of an operation.

The infiltration teams that we dropped off reported back by using first-rate Collins transmitters, so small that they fit in attache cases. Radio operators were taught to alter their codes slightly if captured, to warn us that they had been captured and forced to signal for entrapment.

Nilo Mesa and Elpidio Delgado, two infiltration team members, were captured in Cuba by State Security. Several key words in their messages were missing, while others were out of sequence. We suspected that they had been arrested. When we received a request to pick them up on a desolate beach we felt obliged to go, although we strongly suspected an ambush.

Logic advised us to ignore the message, but our sense of brotherhood pushed us to face the danger of an ambush. A group of us, all volunteers, went on the rescue mission, taking both gunboats. We approached Cuba at night. From the black mass of land a flashlight signaled. We began a slow approach. In the stillness of the night we heard the murmur of voices, saw the red-glowing tips of cigarettes in the darkness.

We turned. It was a trap. From behind a finger of land a frigate appeared, giving chase. They were heavily armed, firing at us with a cannon. Geysers of water spurted up in the ocean near us. Our gunners answered with the recoilless rifle. All three vessels zigzagged in the water, jockeying for firing or evading positions. From the shore, shelling started from some quad 20mm cannons. In seconds we were out of range of the shore batteries, but the shelling exchange and chase by the frigate lasted four hours. Our gunboats were faster than the frigate, but they were persistent in giving chase. We managed to lose them before morning.

The following afternoon one of their planes spotted us. It hovered over our area for a few seconds, dropping a single bomb which missed us, then flew away.

Nilo and Elpidio, we later found out, were sentenced to thirty years' imprisonment.

The CIA was not content with funding us or assisting us politically. They wanted total control, to control every facet of the operation. Artime was willing to accept funding and advice but not sell out the organization. By then many of us distrusted the policy makers. We felt that Bay of Pigs had been lost because our people had been abandoned by the U.S. at the beachhead. To accept help was one thing, but we wanted input and the control of our raids and infiltration planning.

Friction developed between Artime and the CIA. Eventually, in one of our trips to Miami, a group of us met with Artime. He told us that the CIA was going to dismantle the training camps. Without CIA support, the governments of Costa Rica and Nicaragua would not allow us to continue operating within their borders. Because of the CIA's desire for total control, they dismantled an operation that was significantly opposed to Castro. The CIA with one bureaucratic decision accomplished what State Security had not — to fracture the MRR. Without funding to buy weapons, equipment and gunboats, the movement would bleed itself into nonexistence.

With the closing of the training camps, I returned to Miami. A group of the veterans of the camp had a meeting. We needed employment. One man suggested moving to California, another to New York. I decided to toss a coin. New York won, but we decided to move to California anyway. Victor Vidal, whom we called "Watusi," head of security at the base, became my roommate in a modest Los Angeles apartment.

For the first time in my life, I found myself set apart from the Cuban struggle. In my first year in California, I worked three jobs — about eighteen hours a day, six days a week. Watusi worked a similar schedule. Six days of work, and we used Sunday to catch up on our lost sleep.

After a year I had $13,000 in the bank, more money than I had ever seen before. So, on a whim, tired of the working hours, we quit our jobs, jumped in a car, and went on the road to see America. The money lasted three months. I visited forty-seven states. Beaches, mountains and deserts, small towns and big cities. Every day was a new adventure, for we planned as we went along. It was the most carefree, enjoyable time of my life, as though I was able to pack into three months the thrills of being young and irresponsible. Like many other Cubans, my childhood had been lost, dedicated to fighting for my country.

When I returned to California, I married a Cuban girl, worked as a supervisor for an airplane manufacturer, and began attending local meetings of anti-Castro exile groups in the Los Angeles area.

I was earning an honest living, married, with a family; yet, something was missing in my life. I felt bad, guilty that I was not involved enough in the struggle. My nation was suffering, brave men were being executed against firing walls, rotting in prison camps, and I was in California doing nothing much to help them.

In 1970 I left California in a van, accompanied by my wife, stepson, and a dog. I moved back to Miami, the center of exile activities. I was going back to war.

Within a year, I became one of the organizers of the FLNC, Cuba's National Liberation Front. The FLNC was a secret organization, membership by personal reference and invitation. Since all of the exile paramilitary operations now were being done without CIA approval, without the "green light" from the State Department, we were no longer heroes but outlaws. The same government that had trained us in explosives, taught us covert operations, and treated us as heroes, now persecuted us, interrogated us, and raided our homes.

In 1973 I was arrested for the first time. Federal agents raided my home, confiscating about fifty weapons. The charges of possession of weapons and explosives were ironic, for many of those weapons were leftover gifts from the CIA at the time when U.S. policy considered us allies.

The FLNC was a small, very effective organization. From our own resources we scavenged explosives and weapons left over from CIA days. A small network of individuals and organizations helped in the funding of the operation. It was a shoestring operation, but our little group was tightly knit, making it hard for U.S. federal agencies or Cuba's counterintelligence units to infiltrate us.

We began our military operations with three commando raids, sinking and destroying several of the vessels of the Northern Fleet of the Castro government. The purpose behind these attacks on the fishing fleet was to cause damages to the economic structure of the system. We were successful in this, as one of the vessels we sank was a factory ship, loaded with radar equipment worth millions of dollars.

Since our budget was very limited and even a modest raid can cost thousands of dollars to produce, the FLNC began to seek ways of damaging the Castro system at a lower cost. It was then that we began what exile Cubans call "the internationalization of the war," which was aimed at Castro's embassies and government offices throughout the world.

Cuban embassies were bombed in France, Spain, Jamaica, Mexico, and several other countries. The offices in Mexico of the Communist airline, Cubana de Aviacion, were bombed. Between 1972 and 1975 the FLNC carried out a half dozen commando raids into Cuba, as well as more than two dozen bombings and attacks on Cuban installations throughout the world.

Three of our men were briefly held in jail in Mexico after they killed a Castro secret service agent in Merida, in the State of Yucatan, during a gunfight. Gaspar Jimenez escaped a few months later in a daring manner that received much publicity, even on U.S. television.

The FLNC carried out thirty-four operations against the Castro regime without the death of a single one of our men. The Castro regime lost several of its personnel, as well as millions of dollars in damages. The FLNC was one of the most effective of the anti-Castro organizations that ever existed.

One warm night in March of 1974 I was involved in the manufacturing of an explosive device, a small bomb to be placed inside a hollowed-out book. I was with Luis Crespo, a tough veteran of many years of fighting. Our laboratory was the garage of a Southwest Miami residence. Luis and I packed a quarter pound of C-4 plastic explosive into the book. In my hands I held the security system while Luis placed the batteries. It was then that a short circuit triggered the detonator, setting the explosion.

Everything went black. I felt my body being hurled backwards through the air. I did not know what was happening. I did not have time to think. For a few seconds everything was dark. I was sitting on a cement bag. I had lifted my hands in front of my face, to protect myself. Everything in the garage was dark. A small flame burning on the table was being put out by a patting hand.

The side of my face, the left side, felt heavy, as though a weight was pressing against it. Someone took me by the hand and I was moved inside the house. As I staggered in, a woman faced me, looking at me. Her face twisted in horror. She screamed.

I must be in bad shape, I told myself.

"Sit down," the man of the house said.

I was in the living room staring at a couch. No, if I sit down I'll drip blood on it, I thought, so I sat on the floor. I saw that three fingers on my left hand were destroyed, the skin blistered like a cooked sausage, the bone showing white. With my right hand I held my left against my chest. I did not know it yet, but part of the left side of my face was ripped. My left eye was dangling out of its socket, staring down at the floor.

Luis was brought into the living room. His body was covered by black soot. His face was slashed open. I could see teeth and gums right through his cheek. Half of his right arm was gone; all that remained was a bloody stump starting at the elbow. Luis was hallucinating, shaking uncontrollably.

"Luis, are you cold?"

"If I die," he said, "you must continue the struggle."

I nodded. "Are you cold?"

He answered with the same phrase. In those terrible seconds, believing that he was dying, Crespo's greatest preoccupation was concerned not with himself or his loved ones but with the continuation of the struggle for Cuba's freedom.

The owner of the house faced me. "What do I do?" he asked.

"Call an ambulance, but don't make any statements," I told him.

While I waited for the ambulance, I gave the man my address book and told him to hide it, then quietly I asked God for help.

As a result of that explosion, I lost my left eye, three fingers on my left hand, and some of my hearing. Luis lost one-half of his right arm, three fingers of the left hand, some of his hearing, and required extensive plastic surgery.

Beyond the physical problems, the explosion caused enormous legal complications. I woke up from my operation to find myself chained to my hospital bed with a squad of FBI agents waiting to interrogate me. The charges that I faced for possession and use of explosives, possession of automatic weapons, and other violations would mean a maximum penalty of 102 years in a federal penitentiary.

A lot of pressure was put on me to strike a deal by becoming a witness to a grand jury investigation. I refused, for my code of honor did not allow me to become an informant. Crespo also refused to cooperate.

My family life was destroyed. The pressures of the trial brought on a divorce.

I felt anger at the situation. I was being tried for fighting against the same system and even with the same weapons that I had been trained, provided, and encouraged to use by the U.S. government a few years earlier. What I had done in 1964 with government agreement was now a crime in 1974. The dictatorship in Cuba was the same as it had been ten years before, I was the same as I had been ten years before, but the United States policy was not. I had been the expendable pawn.

As a result of the Kennedy-Khrushchev agreement born out of the Cuban Missile Crisis, the Soviets would not build an offensive missile base in Cuba and the U.S. would keep the exiles under control, not helping them or even allowing them to independently liberate the Island. Kennedy and Khrushchev made their agreement, and a few million Cubans were betrayed.

Now the U.S. government accused me of terrorism. But I did not consider myself a terrorist. The FLNC had not engaged in random terror. We had not killed innocent people. Our commando raids had been against military, economic, or political installations. Our bombings of embassies and government properties had been directed at specific targets or individuals which were part of the structure of power or the repressive system. Terrorists kill or maim the innocent, which the FLNC did not. We were a military organization.

In September of 1974, while awaiting sentencing, I left Miami, traveled to Puerto Rico, and from there I left clandestinely for the Dominican Republic, where I had some political contacts that provided me with a false identity. I did not plan on spending my life in a federal penitentiary. I am not a pimp, a bank robber, or a common criminal. I am a Cuban fighting against Castro — and that is what I intend to stay doing.

I lived in Santo Domimgo for over a year until, pressured by the FBI, the government of Dominican Republic arrested me, extraditing me to the U.S. without a trial. In the few days before I was returned to the U.S., the Dominican police tortured me, humiliated me, and beat me with rubber hoses.

In the United States I served seven years before being paroled. I remarried, had a son, and now I live in Miami. Times have changed in many ways, but I still consider myself a freedom fighter and I am still committed to the cause of Cuba's freedom.

18

RAMON CALA:
THE MAN WHO DID NOT QUIT

Ramon Cala in a muscled, beefy man in his late forties. A man with a good sense of humor, Cala is a married businessman residing in Southwest Miami. As can be seen by this interview, he has left the safety of family and the stability of business life more than once in quest of his personal struggle against communism.

I joined the anti-Castro underground in 1960, when I was only twenty years old. I became a member of the urban network of the 30 of November Movement, one of the leading resistance organizations that sprouted in Cuba during the early sixties.

To conspire in Cuba is difficult, very hard. Early in 1959, Castro organized the Committees for the Defense of the Revolution, called CDR. The CDR were, and still are, neighborhood spy committees. In each street Castro supporters joined the CDR units, reporting anything out of the ordinary to the "G-2," the State Security of the Ministry of the Interior. If a man was seen arriving home late, a report would be filed. A woman bringing home a large package would be under suspicion of the CDR. A private party in a home, any unusual gathering of friends, would be a reason for surveillance and searches by the CDR unit.

Conspiracy was difficult. I owned a small restaurant in Havana, across the street from the Jai-Alai building. My little cafeteria became

172

a weapons depot and, occasionally, a safe place to meet and plot the overthrow of the regime.

As time passed the 30 of November Movement began to disintegrate. Courage alone cannot win a war. We had few weapons and a dwindling supply of explosives. Some of the urban underground units were infiltrated by State Security, its members executed or imprisoned. Many of our men, burnt-out by months and years of underground activities, were forced to flee the country one step ahead of the firing squads. Attrition began to destroy the movement.

Realizing that my luck would eventually run out, I decided to leave Cuba. In the United States I could continue the struggle by joining the commando teams that were attacking Cuban government installations in quick, hit-and-run raids.

My luck ran out then, however. I was arrested with six other men in 1965, accused of trying to leave the country illegally. I was taken to La Cabana Fortress, a medieval castle in Havana Harbor, where thousands of Cubans have been imprisoned and thousands others have faced the firing squads.

There are two types of political prisoners in Cuba; those in the "Rehabilitation Plan" and the *plantados,* the stubborn ones. The *plantados,* who refuse to join classes of Marxism, sign confessions of guilt or submit to anything, are tortured and mistreated. Many *plantados* spend years dressed only in their underwear, are caged like animals in rooms without light or toilet facilities, but remain defiant, unbroken.

The prisoners in the Rehabilitation Plan are issued blue uniforms, given slightly better food than the *plantados,* and are often sent to work in penal farms where they are mistreated but not tortured as savagely as the *plantados.*

Plantados are stubborn, brave men and women who would rather sleep in their own filth, spend months locked up in solitary than give their guards the satisfaction of pretending to adapt to communism. At the time I entered prison, all convicts were issued blue uniforms. If a man wanted to join the *plantados* he had to request a transfer to the wing where the "prisoners in rebellion" were held. A request to join the rebellion ward was usually followed by a brutal beating on the spot, to convince other prisoners that rebellion was unhealthy.

In the thirty days I waited for my trial to take place, I decided that I would stay in the Rehabilitation Plan, wearing the blue uniform. I expected to be given five to ten years for my conspiracy charge, and I knew that my chances would be good of being sent to a penal farm. Although I sympathized with the *plantados*, my main objective was to escape, something that would be impossible in a rebellion ward.

While at La Cabana Fortress I saw several men executed by firing squad. One was an exile who had been captured in a boat as he attempted to help some relatives flee the country.

I drew a six-year prison sentence and was sent to Mijar, a penal farm in Oriente Province, on the eastern tip of Cuba. It was a tough place run by a sadist called Chino Mulet.

I began to plot my escape, although I knew that it would be difficult. During my first weeks there a prisoner escaped but was later captured in a dragnet. The guards took him to a small warehouse, where they beat him to death, kicking him and clubbing him for what seemed like hours. I sat in our barracks, unable to help him, hearing him scream time after time . . .

One day my mother came to visit. She was bringing a package for me, some food, whatever she could scrounge up in a country where everything is rationed. I stood helpless while a guard emptied the contents on the ground, stomping on the food, humiliating my mother in front of me, while I was unable to do anything to protect her.

The guards humiliated us constantly as a way of establishing psychological control over us, to break our spirit. Once, during a monthly visit, we were gathered in a large hut with our relatives when it began to rain hard. In the middle of the downpour an officer decided to cancel the visit. Our relatives, women and old men, were forced to walk down a dirt road under a tropical rainstorm, soaked to the bones, while guards laughed and we sat in silent rage.

After Mijar, I was transferred to other farms until, in 1967, I was taken to Limones, a farm where I saw my chances of escaping increase. With Manuel, a friend, I began to plan an escape. We hoarded some food and money and coordinated our escape with friends and relatives.

Our best chance seemed to be to escape while working in the fields. The particular field where we worked was not walled in, although guards patrolled the perimeter area constantly. We arranged for a contact to wait for us in the town of Jatibonico, near our farm at Limones.

God was with us that day. We crawled our way into the sugarcane field, moving slowly, crawling past the armed guards until we were out of their range of vision. Then we walked, trying to stay hidden, toward our destination. The car was waiting and we moved swiftly down Cuba's Central Highway ahead of the roadblocks.

The following day I was in Havana, a free man, looking for a way to escape to the United States. Manuel and I said goodbye to each other. He had his contacts and I had mine. We both realized that on our own, our individual chances of survival were better. For me, it would be the right choice; Manuel was eventually recaptured. He committed suicide by hanging himself in his jail cell.

In Havana I found myself without money, identity, or ration cards. I did, however, have friends — men with whom I had shared years in the resistance. Although the 30 of November Movement had disbanded, other men and other groups were reforming, keeping the flame alive. One of the friends who helped hide me in Havana was Argelio Matos, a young man who had once been my employee in the restaurant I had owned. Matos's father lived in the town of Baracoa in Oriente Province and owned a twelve-foot fishing sloop. Matos suggested we use the sloop to flee the country.

I was ready to try anything. I knew that the longer I stayed in Havana, the more my chances increased of getting caught. I went with Argelio to Baracoa.

We hired a rental car with a driver to take us to Oriente. It was very expensive, but I would have needed proper identification to travel by bus.

On the road from Guantanamo to Baracoa we stopped for a rest. To our left we had the green mountains of the Sierra Maestra, to our right was the sea. In the distance, a few miles away, we could see an American airplane carrier out from Guantanamo Naval Base on maneuvers. I stared at the ship.

"How close it seems," a voice behind me said, "so near and yet so far."

I turned around. It was our driver. He did not know our plan.

"Don't say that, comrade," I answered, "that is no way to talk."

When we arrived at Baracoa, Argelio's father met us with distrust. He knew that I had been jailed and wondered why I was free to roam the country four years ahead of schedule. I told him that I had received an early release and had traveled to Baracoa looking for a rest. He regarded me with suspicion but accepted my answer.

Argelio had a brother-in-law, Ignacio Leyva, who wanted to join us in our escape. Ignacio had a wife and a year-old baby who were going to stay behind. Ignacio promised his wife that he would claim her legally once he reached exile in the United States. I was relieved that she and the baby would stay behind, for I knew that our chances of living through the ordeal would be one in four.

Our provisions consisted of some pork meat, sugar, a few pieces of chocolate, and plastic containers of water. It was decided that Argelio and Ignacio would take the boat out of the dock and meet me at Playa Blanca beach, where they would pick me up.

As I waited with Argelio's sister, I stuffed some religious medals into my shirt. I needed all the protection I could get. Argelio's sister, clutching her baby, told me that she would go with us, that she could not bear to stay behind. I tried to persuade her to stay, but she was stubborn. She had decided that as far as she was concerned they would all be saved or they would all drown, baby included.

At two in the morning we met at the beach in Playa Blanca. When Ignacio saw his wife and baby, he became enraged. He cursed, pleaded, and argued with her. She argued back and won the argument.

We left the shore in that twelve-foot boat, three men, a woman, and a baby. The sea was very choppy, very rough, very dangerous. I was worried about the weather. I knew that in very bad weather the Komar patrol boats would not leave their dock. We could drown, but we were not likely to be machine-gunned in the water.

Our little sloop rocked back and forth in the waves. Being unused to the sea, I began vomiting; I felt dizzy and weak. Around me the sea was moving, splashing us, soaking us.

We did not sleep that night. The sun came up and we realized that the current had been pushing us south at a fast speed. The Island was to the north of us now, and water had begun filling the bottom of our little vessel. A bleak situation began to turn very bad.

I felt guilty, feeling responsible for the life of the woman and the baby. As water was quickly filling the sloop, I knew that we would not see another night before sinking.

At two in the afternoon, with water covering our feet and most of our food spoiled, we saw a ship, a huge carrier, as big as a floating building, moving toward us. I used my underwear, the only white garment we had, to wave at the ship.

I was worried for I could not see the ship's flag. A helicopter flew above us, a voice in Spanish commanding us to move toward the vessel so that they could assist us in boarding. We began maneuvering toward the side of the ship, wondering aloud whether we were being rescued by an American vessel or captured by a Soviet ship. Although we could not control our sloop in the bad weather, the waves moved us toward the hull of the ship, slamming us against its side.

An electric stairway came out from inside the ship. A man

dressed in an olive green uniform stood on the platform, speaking to us in Spanish through a megaphone.

Seeing the man and the uniform, my worst fears seemed to materialize. I believed that I was being captured by a Soviet ship, being addressed by a Cuban army officer.

I began to curse and scream, filled with rage and despair. I threw my religious medals in the water. I felt betrayed by God.

Then I heard laughter. I looked up and saw the man in olive green staring at me. "Cuban," he said in Spanish, "don't you know that the Soviets do not have any carriers yet? We are the United States Navy."

I have never felt such relief, such peace as I felt at that moment. I was saved! I had been rescued by the same ship that I had watched days earlier on the road from Guantanamo.

After a short stay at Guantanamo Naval Base, I arrived in the United States, where I immediately joined Alfa 66, one of the most active anti-Castro groups. I relocated to Chicago, where I worked in the local chapter of Alfa in my spare time. For a living, I worked in a factory.

Every day in Chicago I dreamed of returning to Cuba with commando raids and guerrilla landings. I had come to the United States to carry on the struggle, to continue the war. As much as I love the freedom and opportunities in the United States, I cannot turn my back on my people.

In 1969 I met Vicente Mendez. A former captain in the guerillas of the Escambray, he was traveling throughout the United States recruiting men, begging for financial support, planning a series of guerrilla landings. I joined up.

I left the cold streets of Chicago for the training camps of the Everglades. For better or worse, I was not picked by Mendez for his guerrilla teams, for he was only taking with him men with combat experience in mountain warfare. I was left behind in Miami.

Mendez died in combat in Cuba after several days of fierce fighting near Baracoa, the same area from which I had left Cuba on my way to the United States.

I returned to Chicago briefly, long enough to be arrested at a demonstration during a Soviet Art Exhibit, then returned to Miami to assume the military leadership of Alfa 66.

My dreams of returning to Cuba materialized. Eight times since then I have returned, and luck has always been by my side.

On my second mission I was arrested in the Bahamas and spent two weeks as a guest of the Royal Prison of Her Majesty the Queen, accused of violating weapons laws and of illegal entry.

On my sixth mission I entered Cuba in broad daylight, dropping off an infiltration team at Cardenas Harbor without a hitch. It took Castro's State Security three days before realizing that they had been infiltrated.

Actually, the Cuban organizations have had more problems with U.S. government persecution than with Castro's shore patrols. For every commando raid that is launched from exile, there are two or three that are never carried out. In 1981, at Marathon Key in the southern tip of Florida, the FBI arrested eight of our men as they prepared to leave for Cuba. The bureau confiscated machine guns, hand grenades, and two boats. It had taken hundreds of small donations from Cuban exiles in the United States to buy that equipment. Hundreds of hours of planning and training were wasted. Thousands of dollars more were spent on legal fees.

Because of a State Department policy, we are persecuted here for fighting against communism. But in Cuba, Castro has trained and aided thousands of international terrorists to help destroy democracy. It does not make sense. In the sixties we were heroes, and in the eighties we are treated like criminals. We are the same men with the same principles but American foreign policy changes; it is inconsistent.

The same thing that happened to the Cubans is happening in Nicaragua. I know. I was there in 1983. I thought of Nicaragua as a regional conflict where we could fight communism, but that poor little country has become one more pawn, one more game chip in the international games played between the Soviets and the U.S.

Knowing that Castro had sent hundreds of military advisers to Nicaragua, I volunteered to help the Contras. At first the Contra groups were a little reluctant in accepting my help. They did not want to be accused of using "mercenary troops" in their guerrilla war.

I am not a mercenary, however. A mercenary soldier fights for money; I fight for convictions. In the several months that I was involved with the Nicaraguan Contras I never accepted money nor did I expect to be paid. I even helped to acquire thousands of dollars in equipment and medicines to help the Contras in their war.

I am not at liberty to discuss the arrangements I made to enter Nicaragua. I entered in 1983 accompanied by another Cuban exile and a Nicaraguan Contra that was later killed in action.

I joined a group of guerrillas of the UDN, the Nicaraguan Democratic Union, led by Fernando "El Negro" Chamorro, a former commander in the Sandinista forces who rebelled against the sovietization of Nicaragua. We operated in the southern sector of the country. My first mission with the Contras was a raid on a small village called El Lajero. I volunteered to join the assault team in spite of the fact that I had just arrived at the base camp.

The raid on El Lajero taught me a lesson. Although I had the military knowledge, at the age of forty-three I was no longer a young kid. I was in excellent shape for a commando raid or for running several miles on a Florida beach, but not for the thin mountain air and rough cliffs of Nicaragua. With every passing mile my lungs felt as though they would explode. I began to feel old and tired.

The mission went well and the Contras took control of El Lajero, while two Contras and I set up a roadblock on one of the highways leading to the village. My first guerrilla raid had been a success, but I realized that my capabilities for mountain warfare were limited.

Being a Nicaraguan Contra is not a picnic. The newspapers may at times give the impression that the Contras are a well-trained, well-funded CIA-backed organization. Perhaps it was so with the FDN, the main Contra group, but Chamorro's guerrillas had it tough, very tough. We were poorly equipped and poorly fed. Wild fruits, some rice, and an occasional roasted monkey made up our diet.

One of the most terrifying things I ever saw in Nicaragua was the *lepra de la montana* (mountain leprosy). It consists of tiny worms that eat the skin, making festering holes in a matter of hours. A man would wake up in the morning and find a hole the size of a quarter in his wrist. We would pour gasoline in the holes, hoping to kill the worms and clean the wound. Sometimes it worked and others times it did not. I saw a Contra with holes in his back big enough to put a fist into them. I saw another one whose face was rotting away with mountain leprosy.

I made a couple of trips to Miami, returning with medicine and equipment. It made me feel good to be able to help the Nicaraguans. They are going now through what we Cubans went through twenty-five years ago. They are fighting for their freedom, and they are being stabbed in the back by their allies.

I remember one night in Nicaragua when we expected the Sandinista forces to attack. Twenty-one of us were told to set up an ambush on top of a tall mountain. The clouds were so close that it seemed that we could grab them by just reaching out. If they attacked, they would lose a lot of men, for we were well entrenched and set up for a deadly crossfire. As night began to fall we saw lights in the distance. At first it was just a few lights from trucks and jeeps, but with each passing hour they multiplied until there were hundreds of lights moving in the roads to the north of us. The Sandinistas were grouping thousands of troops for a massive attack.

Every one of us in that mountain was scared. We knew that if the Sandinista battalions came our way we could destroy their point company, killing dozens of them. We also knew that a couple of battalions following them would crush us quickly.

It was a never-ending night. Hour after hour I sat in the bushes, staring at the white beams of light crisscrossing in the darkness below us. The attack never came, but in those few hours all twenty-one of us aged a couple of years.

Eventually I left Nicaragua, returning to Miami where I continued my anti-Castro activities.

I am forty-seven now. For the last twenty-seven years of my life, I have fought against Castro. I am ready to keep on going forever, for as long as it takes until Cuba is free. I will never quit, never give up my dream.

19

RAMON SAUL SANCHEZ:
THE NEW GENERATION

Thirty-two-year-old Ramon Saul Sanchez is the most radical and best known of the second-generation anti-Castro fighters. His story is a poignant tale of a child growing up in a climate of turbulence, change, and growing oppression. His arrival in the United States and his growth as a radical portray the image of a man totally convinced of his mission in life. Recently divorced, he lives in Miami, where he is self-employed in security alarm systems.

I was born in Colon, Matanzas, in 1954. My father was an agricultural engineer. Thinking back on my childhood, I can remember, even though I was very young, the day when Batista fled and Castro took power. In those early years, I was aware of changes occurring around me, changes that were affecting my family and everything in Cuba.

One of my earliest childhood memories was of another child named Tito Sardinas. Tito was about five years older than I was. When I was ten he was about fifteen. We often played together on his small farm when my grandmother went to see his relatives. Then, one day, Tito was not there. I remember my grandmother looking upset, talking to Tito's mother in whispers. I understood that something terrible had happened to my friend. Later I was told that Tito had been arrested by State Security, accused of having served as a messenger taking food to small guerrilla groups hiding out in canefields. Although he was only a boy, he was executed by a firing squad.

I was only a child, not even a teenager, but I began to understand that things were terribly wrong in Cuba, that the government would abuse rather than protect the people. In my town there was a militiaman called "Old Gregorio," whose last name I have forgotten. This man would walk patrols at night, stopping underneath windows to listen in on conversations or to find out if anyone was listening to the radio broadcasts from the exile groups in Miami. If Old Gregorio caught anyone listening to clandestine radio programs, he would report them to the CDR, the local Committee for the Defense of the Revolution, a neighborhood spy group. Even though I was a child, I understood that something was wrong with this system. Why should a man spy on his neighbors, standing at night beneath their windows like a Peeping Tom? What was so bad, so criminal about listening to radio broadcasts?

An old woman in the neighborhood eventually took care of Old Gregorio. As the militiaman stood underneath her window, she threw out a pot of boiling hot water. Old Gregorio was taken to the hospital with serious burns, while the woman proclaimed that the whole incident had been an unfortunate accident.

One of my worst memories of childhood involved my father. Since food was rationed, as were all consumer goods, Cubans have always relied on the black market or a barter system in order to survive. My father did some agricultural engineering work for a farmer, accepting as payment some rice. Arrested by State Security, my father spent several months in a prison in Matanzas Province. Twice I went to see him. I'll never forget those visits. I felt anger and humiliation, a feeling of impotence at not being able to help my father, whose only crime had been to attempt to feed his family.

I left Cuba in May of 1967 through the freedom flights to Miami. My parents were unable to leave, so at the age of thirteen, accompanied by a younger brother, I left Cuba. It was a terrible moment. We were two children alone, on our way to a foreign country, not knowing what awaited us in the United States. As I said goodbye to my father, I wondered if I would ever see him again. As I left Cuba I felt anguish, the sorrow of understanding that my country would continue under a dictatorship, that our family was being split, that our future was uncertain.

In Miami, my only relative was the sister of my stepmother. She waited for us at the airport with a photograph in her hand, to be able to recognize us. When she saw us, two scared children, she kissed us, hugged us, and took us to her home. For two years we lived with her. Her love and understanding helped me survive the anguish of being separated from my father.

When my father was finally allowed to leave Cuba, I had already started high school in Miami, working at a grocery store to earn some money. On one particular day, a man entered the store. As I helped him with his groceries, I noticed a religious image of Saint Barbara, a gold medal hanging from a chain around his neck. Curiously, I noticed that the image was broken, having a piece missing. I made a remark about it and the man smiled. He answered by telling me that he would not fix the medal because it had a sentimental value. As it turned out, he told me the story of how the medal had been damaged when he escaped from Cuba.

I had heard the story before. One of the most daring escapes from the Island in 1969 was accomplished by several dozen people jammed into a trailer truck, speeding down the highway to Guantanamo Naval Base, ramming through roadblocks and militia outposts, seeking asylum under a rain of bullets. The escape, suicidal and daring, had made front-page news in many newspapers in the United States.

As I talked to the man, I realized that he was involved in the revolutionary groups attempting to overthrow Castro. I told him that I, too, wanted to join the groups, although I was not yet sixteen years old.

A few days later I joined my first anti-Castro group. My first task was learning how to clean weapons and ammunition. A few weeks later I was allowed to train with adults in the weekend training camps set up to teach commando tactics to exiles.

By the age of seventeen I was involved in the commando raids to Cuba being carried out by several groups against the Castro regime.

That Cuban exiles have managed to carry out several dozen commando raids over the last two decades is a credit to the tenacity of the revolutionary groups. Without support from the CIA, persecuted by the U.S. Coast Guard and the FBI, financing operations out of small donations and from our pockets, buying weapons illegally, providing our own intelligence and logistic support — all these have made a normally difficult task almost impossible.

Those Cuban exiles who have participated over the years in commando raids deserve special recognition. These men, who work forty-hour jobs, who have families and responsibilities, have left the safety of the United States time after time to risk death in Cuba, storms at sea,

the wrath of the U.S. authorities and the dangers of attacking installations with inadequate intelligence and logistics. Yet, in spite of it all,
they continue to go. Their love of freedom and their sense of responsibility to the cause of Cuba is worthy of admiration.

I was a member of the FLNC, one of the most efficient of all exile
groups, which carried out more than thirty operations in a five-year period during the early to mid-seventies. Later, I started my own group,
the OPLC, the Organization for the Liberation of Cuba. It was an organization geared to the new breed of Cuban exiles, some as young as
high school age, others being seasoned veterans of years of revolutionary activity, although chronologically young.

One of the best men in the OPLC was Lino Gonzalez. Lino had
started fighting against Castro while still a teenager in his native Oriente Province. Arrested for committing acts of sabotage, Lino served
two years in Castro's concentration camps. He arrived in the U.S. in
his early twenties. A thin, little man who always had health problems,
he was fierce, determined, with an iron will. Arrested by U.S. authorities during a demonstration to protest the deportation to Cuba of
Andres Rodriguez, a stowaway who was denied asylum by the Immigration and Naturalization Service, Lino spent sixty days in jail in
Miami. Although he should have been in a hospital, he served his time
without complaint. After being released, his health worsened. Sadly,
Lino Gonzalez, who would have preferred to die on a Cuban beach
fighting for Cuba's freedom, died in a Miami hospital of a blood disease at the age of thirty-two.

In 1981 a grand jury was convened in New York City with the
purpose of investigating anti-Castro activities in the United States.
Dozens of exiles were subpoenaed to testify, as the FBI sought to crush
many organizations still active in the war against Castro.

As I received a subpoena, I believed that I was being harassed illegally, in order to protect United States interests. I knew that I would
be asked by the grand jury about a failed attempt on the life of Fidel
Castro when the Cuban dictator visited the United Nations in 1979. I
found it hypocritical that the U.S. government would try to prosecute
me when this same government, by their own admission, had attempted to eliminate Castro on two dozen occasions, even asking the
help of organized crime in one instance.

In 1963, when the Cuban Missile Crisis occurred, the Kennedy
administration, by presidential choice, without the approval of Congress, had sealed an agreement known to all exiles as the Kennedy-

Khrushchev Pact. In this betrayal to Cubans, the Soviets agreed to limit offensive armament in Cuba if the Kennedy administration agreed to stop support of exile activities, and indeed, to persecute those exiles that refused to give up the struggle.

The Kennedy-Khrushchev Pact was immoral. It said, in effect, that the U.S. would police the Cuban exile community on behalf of Castro. Kennedy betrayed the Cuban people twice. The first time at the Bay of Pigs, when he refused to provide the promised air cover. The second time during the Missile Crisis, when he sold out to Khrushchev in an immoral treaty.

For years, the exiles had been trained and helped by the U.S. Suddenly, without having any input, our fate had been sealed by the superpowers. Were we supposed to turn our backs on our people because the United States had decided to renege on its promises? Could we turn off our feelings like one turns off the water on a spigot? No, of course not. As Cubans it is our duty and our sacred right to fight for our freedom. That right, the right of the people, is above the policy made by any nation to protect its interests. Would George Washington have quit if the French had denied him support in the war against Britain? Of course not.

As exiles, we have been persecuted in the United States for trying to liberate our country from communism. Dozens of exiles have been arrested on weapons charges, on charges of violating the Neutrality Act. Hundreds of weapons and dozens of boats have been confiscated by federal authorities over the years. The FBI has been more effective against Cubans in the U.S. than Castro's navy has been in stopping commando raids.

I went to the grand jury and refused to testify. In my case, the Fifth Amendment was waived and I was granted immunity from prosecution. I still refused to testify, however, for I would not then — and never will — testify on behalf of any government against the cause of Cuba's freedom. In contempt of court, I was placed under arrest, being sent to a federal penitentiary.

For not testifying, I served eighteen months in jail. Later, still refusing to testify, I was condemned to nine years' imprisonment — the longest sentence imposed on anyone in the United States for refusing to testify in front of a grand jury. I drew a stiffer sentence for my political stand than the worst members of organized crime ever did.

During my incarceration, frustrated that no sentence was being imposed, I went on a hunger strike. I wanted either to be charged with a crime or released.

Hunger strikes are tough. During the first three of four days I felt intense hunger, short dizzy spells, and strong headaches. The prison guards brought food into the cell, letting me smell the meat, the mashed potatoes. It took all my willpower to stay away from the tray. On the fourth day I began to feel stomach cramps. It felt as though a fist was closing around my gut.

After seven or eight days I felt at peace, in a stupor. After ten days, strange reactions began to happen. My body was feeding on itself. I could feel a horrible smell coming out of every pore of my skin.

After twenty-one days I began to pass out, twice cutting my head on the ground as I fell. By court order I was transferred from a federal penitentiary in New York to a federal hospital in Springfield, Missouri. For days I was tied to my bed and fed intravenously. Tubes were shoved up my nose and down my throat, sometimes so roughly that my nose would bleed.

One night, when I refused to drink water, I was placed in a punishment cell. Outside, it was freezing cold, the ground covered with snow. Inside my small room it felt like a meat freezer. I was not given a blanket or a cot to sleep on. I curled up in a fetal position. I was freezing to death, weak from the strike, without even body fat to protect me. My nose and mouth were bleeding from the cold. I was dressed only in my underwear. I shivered without control as though I were suffering from an epileptic fit. It was the longest night of my life, the most cruel moment of suffering that I have ever endured. I was sure I was going to die. I was also angry, upset that in a democracy my civil rights were being violated. I was receiving treatment worthy of a Castro detention center, not a U.S. penitentiary.

The warden came to see me. I told him why I was on a hunger strike. I demanded better treatment, for I was not a pimp, a drug dealer or a mass murderer, but a man who had been jailed due to political circumstances. I was transferred from the punishment room.

Most of my time in federal penitentiaries was served in an old, cream-colored building in Terre Haute, Indiana, a maximum security center that once housed Al Capone. Ironically, on the day I arrived, a common criminal, a Cuban from the Mariel Boatlift, greeted me. He seemed to know who I was. I asked him how he knew me. He showed me a clipping on his bulletin board. It was an article that I had written for a Miami newspaper, with a sketch of me. The prisoner had been so impressed that he had cut out the clipping and tacked it to the board. It made me feel useful. Even jailed, I could, in a modest way, do something to fill my people with hope.

I was released in November of 1986, after serving four and a half years. Now, as my parole time is ending, I am, once more, ready to return to the struggle. My life, by my own choice, is committed to the cause of Cuba's freedom. Until my country is free, I will continue doing whatever I feel is right on its behalf. While Cuba suffers, I will not rest.

20

GILBERTO CANTO:
THE MAN WHO TALKED TOO MUCH

Seventy-two-year-old Gilberto Canto is now retired and living in Miami Beach. Although not a member of the resistance, he dared step beyond the boundaries of political propriety in Castro's Cuba. This is his story of the consequences of talking to a foreigner at a tourist resort.

I was sixty years old when I was arrested for the crime of talking to a tourist.

On vacation from my work as translator for a government office, I traveled to the town of Soroa with my sister and brother-in-law, planning to spend a week's vacation in the town resort.

Soroa is in a very pretty valley with green rolling hills and tall palm trees. The resort was a small inn with a restaurant and a swimming pool that had a patio bar and deck overlooking the valley.

The first night was uneventful. The second day the tourists came. It was a tour group from France. I watched them as they came in, with their European clothing and cameras. Their visit did not surprise me, for the Castro government promotes tourism as one of the main sources of national revenue. Tourists, however, are not allowed much free time. Their tours are programed so that they are herded together constantly, keeping them from straying among the people. Tourists only see what the government wants them to see.

At night, in the restaurant, little French flags adorned several tables. To the tourists it must have seemed a quaint little gesture on the part of their guides. To the Cubans, it meant that the tables with the flags were reserved for the tour.

After dinner I walked to the patio deck. A group of young Cubans were attempting to talk to several of the tourists. Bored, with little to do, I agreed to serve as their translator.

As I began translating, several waiters and resort employees stood close to us. Hotel employees in resorts catering to tourists are screened for their loyalty, being expected to serve as informants for State Security.

The questions I translated were innocent in nature. One young Cuban asked about the currency, another asked questions about geography and art. Although young, they knew their limits, asking only the safe questions that would keep them out of harm's way with State Security.

After the group broke up, I continued talking for several minutes with one of the tourists. He was from Switzerland, in his late twenties or early thirties. A confirmed Communist, he told me that he had recently visited both East and West Germany. He said that he had read about the Paris-to-Cuba tour in a Communist trade journal in Europe, where weeklong tours to the Island were offered at very reasonable rates.

I told him that I found it ironic that as a Communist he was allowed to visit both East and West Germany, since the East Germans were not allowed to visit the other half of their divided nation. He did not like my answer and began to argue my point. I told him that the Berlin Wall was built by the East German government to keep their own people from leaving for the west.

A few moments later, when he took out a pack of cigarettes, I said: "Do you realize that in Cuba cigarettes are rationed to two packs a week? I know Cubans who will pay twenty pesos for a pack of cigarettes."

He looked stunned, for he knew that Cuba was a tobacco producer. He said he did not believe that statement. I answered him by saying: "Look, this is not a secret. This is something that even Cuban newspapers publish. This is something that every Cuban knows."

My brief assertion had been an understatement. It is impossible for those living in Western consumer societies to understand the rigors of Communist rationing. There are two reasons for rationing. The first, because the economy is so badly managed, consumer goods are scarce. The second is that a citizen who is too busy standing in line to procure a piece of meat will be more concerned with eating than with demanding human rights.

To illustrate the extremes of this rationing system, I will tell you about a neighbor I had in Havana. This man had a pet canary, which, of course, needed birdseed to eat and survive. My neighbor had to apply for a ration card on behalf of the canary in order to obtain some feed for the bird. The idea of a ration card for a canary does not seem preposterous to the Castro government.

The Swiss tourist walked away from me after I made the statement about the cigarette rationing. As he walked away, he shook his head from side to side, seeming upset. Our conversation had lasted no more than five minutes.

Several hotel employees huddled together and stared at me, but I was not worried, for they had been too far from us to listen to our conversation.

I quickly forgot about the little discussion with the Swiss tourist. All I had done was make some statements about East Germany and rationing in Cuba. I was critical of the system, but it was far from sedition or open rebellion.

I spent some time in the lobby talking to some other guests, one of whom was an army captain. We discussed art and other safe topics, steering away from politics.

I realize now that State Security waited for the right time to arrest me. Several hours later, when I was ready to retire for the night, two men dressed in civilian clothes requested to talk to me in private. The men identified themselves as members of State Security. I was told that I was under arrest and was expected to leave with them immediately. Seeing that I was a small, sixty-year-old man, incapable of fleeing or fighting back, they allowed me to go to our room and inform my sister that I was under arrest. Needless to say, the scene was unsavory and the look of anguish on her face is something I don't wish to remember but I'll never forget.

I was taken by jeep to the local jail at a small town named Candelaria, near the resort hotel. The stucco jail had only two cells facing an open courtyard. I was placed in one. My neighbor was a black man in laborer's clothes who kept begging the guard to release him. Apparently, the poor fellow had misplaced the identification card that all Cubans must carry. Although he was well known in the village, he was still being detained.

On that first night there were no interrogations. They did not process me, only wrote my name down on a ledger, confiscated my valuables, my pipe and my tobacco, and then locked me in the courtyard cell.

The following morning I was taken by car to the city of Pinar del Rio, the provincial capital. In the outskirts of the city, our car drove past an open iron gate toward a big, old Spanish manor. There was no sign, nothing to indicate that the building housed the regional headquarters of the feared State Security police.

That first morning I was fingerprinted and photographed. I was made to stand facing the walls at all times that I was not being processed. I was later placed in a large cell with four sleeping mats and a small toilet. High up on the wall, a small window provided some light and ventilation. One single electric light bulb shone day and night. Although there was room to house four prisoners, I was the only one.

That morning I was interrogated for the first time. A young lieutenant questioned me in his office. He sat behind a metal desk, dressed in a green fatigue uniform, without a name tag or regimental insignia, and talked sternly. He informed me that he knew about my conversation with the tourist, but demanded to know my explanation of the events.

Having had time to think about my predicament, I believed that the State Security agents would not have interrogated the tourist. Cuba is very dependent on tourism, very aware of the importance of projecting a proper international image. To question a tourist in any obvious way would be unthinkable. If they had not questioned the tourist and if no one had overheard our conversation, the agents could only imagine what was said but could not be sure unless I confessed.

I decided not to admit guilt. I protested, trying to sound convincing. I even told the lieutenant that he should seek the tourist and question him at once. The lieutenant nodded his head, but I knew it would not happen, for Cuba's image must remain untarnished. After the interrogation I was returned to the cell with the high window.

Every morning for four mornings, the interrogation was repeated. The lieutenant would warn me that he knew and was certain that I was guilty of having criticized the government. Every morning for four mornings I pleaded my innocence as convincingly as I could.

Every day was spent in solitary confinement, designed, I'm sure, to intimidate me, to bore me to the point of confession. It did not bother me, however. As a young man I had spent twelve years living in the United States, where I served as an ensign in the Merchant Marine during the Second World War. I had learned to fight boredom aboard ships, so sitting by myself for four days was not intolerable. On the contrary, sitting alone allowed me to relax and I was able to think, to fortify and adapt to my new circumstances.

After four days, State Security decided that further interrogations were pointless. I was sent to Havana one morning. There I was told that I would be transferred to the regional prison in the city of Pinar del Rio to await trial.

I arrived at the prison in the evening. It is a large, functional structure with five wings, two of which are used exclusively for political prisoners. In my wing we had 240 men with 220 beds. Almost two dozen men slept on the floor, bundled as well as they could. The 240 men in my wing shared three toilets and four shower stalls. The smell of human waste was strong and stagnant. The showers had only cold water.

Food at the prison was doled in small amounts, without variety. For breakfast we received a small piece of bread and watered coffee. Lunch consisted of a few forkfuls of rice and peas. Dinner was a handful of rice with a small slice of fish or dry tinned meat. I lost eight pounds in one month.

My 239 roommates were a cultured, intelligent group. In my wing we had among the prisoners several doctors, architects, and engineers, all of whom had been captured in a dragnet of a clandestine network. While I stayed in that wing I was never bored. To fight boredom, prisoners organized study groups, played chess, or read whatever materials were not confiscated by our censors. I volunteered to teach languages for my stay, which I hoped would be brief.

After a week in Pinar del Rio, I was scheduled for trial. My relatives traveled from Havana to Pinar del Rio, a distance of about a hundred miles. Almost two weeks had passed since my short conversation with the Swiss tourist at the patio bar in Soroa. On the day of my trial, nothing happened. At the end of the day I was told that other trials had backlogged mine. My trial would be rescheduled for a later date.

It depressed me to think that my sisters had traveled so far through second-rate roads in lousy buses to attend a trial postponement. They had left Havana in the middle of the night in order to arrive at Pinar del Rio by early morning. My two poor sisters sat through hours of courtroom babble without seeing my trial, then returned to

Havana in another four-hour ride. Twenty-nine days after my arrest, I went to trial once again. I had a government-appointed lawyer to plead my case. The only time that I saw this attorney was for a brief conversation before the trial. While waiting for my case to come to docket, I witnessed the trial of a young man being accused of conspiracy to leave Cuba. Unlike some who had been arrested because they had attempted to leave the country in makeshift rafts, this youth had been arrested for possession of an outboard motor. It sounds absurd, but mere possession of an outboard motor was considered tangible evidence that the owner was planning on leaving the country, a crime punishable by three years in prison. I did not find out what happened to him, but I suspect that, like many others, he received a three-year sentence for attempting to leave "our socialist paradise."

My own trial lasted a few minutes. I was accused of besmirching the government in a conversation with a tourist. The prosecutor launched into a tirade in which I was accused of being an antisocial element, a dangerous enemy of the system. My defense attorney, in keeping with the charade, admitted that I was guilty and a danger to society, but pleaded for parole so that I could continue serving the country as a translator for the Cuba Tobacco government office. That night I returned to the Pinar del Rio prison. I knew that it would take three or four days for notification of sentence; therefore, I resigned myself to another wait.

The days went by fast and I was finally released after thirty-two days of confinement. A small piece of paper informed me that I was judged guilty and sentenced to a year's parole.

That's my story. A five-minute conversation with a tourist earned me thirty-two days in prison, a year's parole, an eight-pound weight loss, and a lot of aggravation. Such is life in Cuba today.

21

ANDRES NAZARIO SARGEN: THE STRUGGLE CONTINUES

Seventy-year-old Andres Nazario Sargen is the head of Alfa 66, the longest lived anti-Castro movement, active since 1962. Nazario Sargen, a farmer and agrarian labor leader, was a comandante of the II Front of Escambray in the war against Batista. A veteran of commando raids, Nazario Sargen is, despite his age, a very agressive, hard-working individual with the health of a man thirty years younger.

I was born seventy years ago in Zaza del Medio, a small village in Central Cuba, a tobacco-growing farming community. I was one of a dozen brothers and sisters on a small farm equipped with the luxury of an outhouse.

While still a teenager, I became an organizer of agricultural workers' unions. I taught peasant farmers basic rules of hygiene, showed them how they could improve crop production, created farm purchasing groups to obtain new equipment, and lobbied for agricultural reforms. As a political reformer I did not advocate only protesting but I believed in self-improvement, in knowledge, in technology.

As I matured, I developed a personal political philosophy. I do not like labels but consider myself a progressive humanist. I believe in free enterprise, in a system that helps human beings not only from an economic or legal viewpoint but also from a more human perspective. As technology increases, we will have five-hour workdays, more people employed, and increased production. I believe that it is vital for a society to provide cultural and educational outlets to improve the quality of life of its people. To provide five-hour workdays is only half of the story: the other half is that we must provide channels for self-expression, educational development, and cultural enrichment to fulfill the human needs of the people.

When Batista took power in 1952, I was in my mid-thirties, with children. I owned a rice mill, spending much of my time working with cooperative farm groups and tobacco agricultural workers. From the time that Batista took control, I opposed him. Although Batista had enacted some positive laws, such as the provision of rural teachers for the peasant farmers, his government was unconstitutional, full of political favoritism and economic corruption. A dictatorship, whether of the right or the left, is still a dictatorship.

Many members of my family fought in the struggle against Batista. I was one of the founders of the II Front of Escambray, the movement led by Eloy Gutierrez Menoyo. I began in the urban underground, obtaining and sending weapons and medicines to the mountains where uprisings were being prepared. Under police persecution, I eventually joined the guerrilla forces and I became a comandante, the highest rank in the Rebel Army. I worked in logistics and supplies, survived several airplane strafings and skirmishes, as well as the battle in which we took the town of Manicaragua.

When the Cuban Revolution came to power in 1959, I soon realized that a new uprising was inevitable. Castro, in quest for power, sold out the democratic principles of our revolution, turning our nation into a Soviet satellite. In January of 1962, with comandantes Eloy Gutierrez Menoyo, Lazaro Ascencio, and Armando Fleites, as well as a group of officers and civilians, I arrived in the United States by boat. Four comandantes arriving together produced a stir in the growing exile community.

In October of 1962, Alfa 66 was born. It was a revolutionary movement made up for the most part of veterans of the II Front of Escambray, men who had once fought together against Batista. Alfa meant the beginning, and sixty-six, the number of its charter members.

Today, twenty-five years later, Alfa 66 is the oldest and largest of all anti-Castro organizations. In retrospect, I believe that our organization has grown and survived in spite of the odds because we defined our struggle, created a mystique, and developed and retained our leadership while identifying ourselves with the people.

Let me explain this: we defined our struggle as a struggle of the Cuban people. Other groups have lived and died by CIA aid or lack of it, but Alfa 66 has always been independent in thought and action. We have bought our own equipment, our own weapons, our own boats. When we had three speedboats, we used all three. When we did not have any, we dipped into our own pockets and bought some more boats. This political and economic independence has helped us to survive, for we have been accountable only to ourselves and to no one else.

For twenty-five years we have created a mystique based on our actions: twenty commando raids; the infiltration of more than a dozen teams of men into the Island; hundreds of sabotages; the structuring of an underground resistance movement; conspiracies started even from inside concentration camps; radio transmissions; the creation of an exile structure with dozens of chapters on three continents, with thousands of active members and supporters; the creation of a feeling in the national consciousness that we are the antithesis of Castroism. The legend of Alfa 66 is real, based on sacrifice. Our support base has grown through the years, and even our enemies acknowledge our existence.

Our leadership has been of high quality and willing to confront extreme hardships. Eloy Gutierrez Menoyo was captured in Cuba and spent twenty-two years in Castro's concentration camps. He faced hunger strikes, lost his hearing in one ear from a beating, had all his ribs broken and, in 1972, was accused by the regime of having conspired to kill Castro even from within his prison cell. Vicente Mendez and Jose Rodriguez Perez landed in Cuba and died in combat. Much of our actual leadership is composed of men and women who have been with our organization for twenty years or more.

During all this time we have identified ourselves with the Cuban people. Ours has been a grass-roots movement. Our leadership has come from the most humble class of the Cuban people. Vicente Mendez was a peasant farmer and Ernesto Diaz, the prison poet, was a fisherman.

My family has paid a heavy price in the war against Castro. One of my nephews, Adolfo Sargen, a guerrilla leader in the Escambray, was executed in 1963. Another nephew, Aurelio Nazario, was captured in a guerrilla infiltration and executed in 1970. A third nephew, Emilio Nazario, spent twelve years in a Castro concentration camp. My sister Ofelia, my brother Jorge, and my son were arrested and jailed by State Security. I have survived two attempts on my life and I have been arrested in the United States for violation of the Neutrality Act and possession of weapons.

For the last twenty-five years I have worked for Alfa 66 seven days a week, sixteen hours a day. I have never received a salary; every single hour was given of my own free will. My wife and my children have worked to support me, for they understand how important it is for me to work full-time. Both my children paid for their college education with scholarships and loans. I do not consider myself unemployed; my job is the cause of Cuba's freedom.

To understand our history, one has only to see what the enemy prints about us. In 1972 *Moncada,* the magazine of the Revolutionary Armed Forces, printed an article detailing how Gutierrez Menoyo, who was serving time in a maximum security prison, had organized a secret network of Alfa 66 cells. The resistance units stretched beyond the prison walls to cities in Cuba. Menoyo led these units from inside prison walls, using coded messages smuggled out by friends and visitors. What did this article mean? It showed that in spite of the repression, Cubans have managed to fight even from inside jail.

Before that, in 1970, we landed guerrilla infiltration teams in Oriente Province, in eastern Cuba, led by Vicente Mendez and Jose Rodriguez Perez. Both teams were captured or killed; but before they fell, Castro had to mobilize 10,000 soldiers. At the same time, a commando operation sank two fishing vessels, holding eleven prisoners for a week. Castro was in an uproar. For two weeks all economic activities ceased in Cuba while Castro mobilized hundreds of thousands in programmed political rallies. As his sugar cane harvest failed, as the nation sank into greater economic distress, Castro accused us of being his most powerful enemy.

In 1980 the incidents at the Peruvian Embassy in Havana — the mass request for political asylum — formed an uprising, a revolution within the revolution. Castro tried to defuse the political bomb by allowing a mass exodus, by deporting a few hundred criminals among the thousands who left the country. But, in reality, the events at the Peruvian Embassy were an internal coup from the people to the system.

As thousands of Cubans arrived in the Mariel Boatlift, Alfa 66 set up a refugee help center which assisted hundreds of new arrivals in becoming a vital part of the Cuban exile community. Many of the new arrivals were anxious to join the struggle, seeking training, wishing to return to the Island equipped to battle the system.

In 1981 the "Plan Maximo Gomez," named for the hero of our War of Independence in the 1890s, became operational. The strategy of the plan was to train several dozen new arrivals in techniques of urban guerrilla warfare, explosives, and communications, and dropping them off to organize clandestine groups inside the Island. The new arrivals were, of course, extremely knowledgeable about the way to survive inside Cuba, having left just a few months before. Many of them had clandestine contacts inside the Island, people that they trusted to organize small units.

Between 1981 and 1984, we carried out a dozen infiltrations into Cuba, dropping off fifty urban team leaders. From a strategic point of view, these operations were the most successful ever achieved by us. In spite of the myth of invincibility of the system, every team landed in Cuba undetected. As a matter of fact, some of the infiltrations were undetected for days, the regime becoming aware only after waves of sabotages started in the region.

Each infiltrator carried a handgun, ammunition, several hand grenades, some explosives, packets of small anti-Castro stickers, communication codes, false identification cards, and Cuban money. They hid out in cities they knew, where they had friends and relatives, where they dressed in civilian clothing, mingling with the population.

They were a brave group, ranging in age from the very young, like Tony Becil, who was a teenager, to Luis Yanes, a very brave man in his forties. Becil, a sensitive kid who wrote poetry, was captured and executed in 1981. Yanes landed, formed an effective group, attacked an army outpost in Las Villas Province, killing three soldiers, was wounded, captured and executed in 1984.

One of the most impressive clandestine operations of the Maximo Gomez Plan was the 170 sabotages carried out by Grupo Zapata, which began operations in Matanzas and Havana provinces in 1978.

The Zapata Group established contact with us through one of their members who was able to leave the country at the time of the boatlift. Through our clandestine network, we established a link-up, being able to coordinate some activities. The Zapata Group continued to operate intact for three more years, after which thirty-five of their members were arrested and convicted to prison. Yet, the group, linked to Alfa 66, survived and is still operating in 1987.

To understand the actual conditions of the resistance movements in Cuba today, one must study Sentencing Cause Number Nine of the Havana Tribunal, April 6, 1983, involving the Zapata Group. Fifteen members of the group were given prison sentences of twenty or thirty years. Fourteen others were given sentences of two to ten years, while five others were placed under parole terms. One woman, Caridad Pavon, committed suicide before the trial.

By the State Security report on Sentencing Cause Number Nine, the Zapata Group was accused of carrying out 170 different acts of sabotage between 1978 and 1983. In twenty-eight different acts of arson the group burned down 135,000 tons of sugar cane at fields in a dozen different locations. The group was also accused of destruction by fire of more than a dozen vehicles, as well as several government buildings and warehouses. By spreading hundreds of homemade spikes on highways, they punctured dozens of tires, an expensive commodity in the Island. The Zapata Group also destroyed telephone and power lines, distributed anti-Castro leaflets, and carried out industrial sabotages in several factories.

What does this all mean? In the words of their own prosecutors, the regime admits vulnerability. It took the powerful State Security five years to break to some extent the Zapata Group. With limited resources, like the homemade spikes, Molotov cocktails, bombs made of plastic bags and candles, these freedom fighters carried out at least 170 different operations, caused the government millions of dollars in damage, and created a spirit of rebellion throughout Havana and Matanzas provinces.

We are now in the fall of 1987. For twenty-eight years, Castro has ruled Cuba like a medieval feudal landlord; yet, what has he accomplished? In the past few months, air force general Rafael del Pino and Maj. Julio Azpillaga Lombard have asked for asylum. General del Pino, a decorated pilot who fought against our side at the Bay of Pigs, who was Cuban Air Force chief in Angola, where he flew war missions, has painted a pathetic picture of life in Cuba under Castro.

Castro has proclaimed his regime a workers' dictatorship, yet workers are forced to labor long hours while consumer goods are rationed. General del Pino has stated that high-ranking military officers and selected members of the Communist aristocracy are provided with special stores to shop, with restaurants for their private use, with special privileges denied to the Cuban proletariat. Del Pino has told in his Radio Marti interviews how some high-ranking men in the Castro inner circle have several homes and automobiles, while there is a shortage of housing in Cuba. The general, who for almost three decades was a trusted part of the inner circle, has spoken of a nation plagued by poor economic planning, of a people oppressed by a repressive apparatus, of a nation that is repaying its debt to the Soviet Union by sending its young to die as mercenary soldiers in Angola and other Soviet colonialist wars.

That is why, after twenty-five years, Alfa 66 still exists. Our group and other groups like ours exist because we are an expression of the will of the people, of the desire of the Cuban nation to be free. Until the ultimate goal of freedom is met, canefields will continue to burn and the war will continue to rage.

22

ANGEL CUADRA:
POETS BEHIND STONE WALLS

Fifty-year-old Angel Cuadra, one of Cuba's best-known poets, arrived in exile in 1985. A lawyer, actor, and author, Cuadra spent fifteen years of his life as a political prisoner in Castro's concentration camps. He is presently active with cultural and political exile groups in the Miami area, where he is employed by a bank.

I was one of the organizers of the First Congress of Writers and Intellectuals which took place in Havana in 1960. Although I served as secretary to the Congress, I was upset by the political opportunism displayed by some writers, most of whom had not even had the courage to oppose the Batista government.

At the time, I was a practicing attorney, an actor, and a poet. I had been active with Grupo Renuevo, a cultural organization. As a writer, I had won several awards, one of them from the Circle of Iberoamerican Poets. Some of my poems had been translated into Russian and published in the Soviet Union. Yet, in spite of all the achievements, I refused to join the Writer's Union, feeling opposed to the political censoring being imposed on Cuban intellectuals by the regime.

Rebelling against the oppression and totalitarian actions of the new system ruling Cuba, I became a conspirator. In 1962 I became the publisher of *Cuba Democratica,* an underground publication, a true *samizdat* aimed at battling against the system on an ideological level.

The publishing of resistance leaflets is, in totalitarian societies, not only an act of defiance but also a difficult challenge. Printing equipment, supplies, and even paper are extremely difficult to obtain. From a print shop that was being taken over by the revolutionary government, I stole a mimeograph machine. The requisitions for ink and paper were obtained through falsified purchase orders that I obtained while working as a government attorney. In spite of the repression, we overcame the obstacles.

The activities of my resistance unit were not limited to preparing leaflets. With the help of a chemistry teacher we manufactured crude but effective incendiary devices for urban sabotages. We also stockpiled whatever weapons we could find, preparing a guerrilla uprising.

In the early sixties, guerrilla activity was rampant throughout Cuba, particularly in the Escambray Mountains, the Sierra de los Organos, and the Sierra Maestra Mountains, where Castro had fought against Batista. Our military group leader, Roberto Arias, favored the Sierra Maestra in eastern Cuba. A thirty-four-year-old man, Arias was a dedicated patriot who was willing to leave his pregnant wife to face the perils of life as a partisan. I prepared small leaflets for him to take on his trip, being aware that our war was not only military but also ideological. Arias was very enthused with the propaganda.

"Angel," he told me, "I am going to the mountains with a rifle in one hand and a leaflet in the other."

Arias led an uprising in the Baracoa area of Oriente, where he was hunted by hundreds of militiamen. Captured, he spent his final hours telling other prisoners that they should continue the resistance at whatever the cost. With three other guerrillas, he faced the firing squad bravely. A few months later his wife gave birth to a daughter.

Enrique Abreu was another exceptional friend from my days with the resistance. He was captured in an attempt to assassinate Fidel Castro. A man of incredible courage, he dared to tell his captors at his trial that, if freed, he would gladly make an attempt once more on Castro's life. The following evening he was executed by firing squad.

Together with four other writers, I began a clandestine publication named *Trinchera Literaria* (Literary Trenches). Two of those men, Carlos Casanova and Luis Angel Casa, are exiled today. Of the other two, one remains in Cuba and the other committed suicide.

In 1967 my life as a conspirator ended as I was arrested by State Security. I was taken to a torture chamber, where the interrogators threatened to pluck out my eyes if I did not inform on fellow conspirators. It was one of the hardest moments of my life, but I knew that I would rather die than spend the rest of my life living in the shame of having betrayed those who were risking their own lives for the cause of Cuba's freedom. I refused to talk. Luck being on my side, I was not tortured.

I remember one conversation that I had with my interrogators. As one of the men babbled out the merits of collective property versus private property, I reflected on what people would think of these concepts six centuries from now. In a few hundred years, men might reflect that we had killed each other over outdated concepts, as the religious wars of six centuries back often appear ridiculous to us now. Still, as the Spanish philosopher Ortega y Gasset said, we are all victims of our circumstances. Although there are no eternal truths in politics, each man must live by his feelings, by his convictions in his designated time in history.

In April of 1967, I entered La Cabana Fortress, sentenced to fifteen years' imprisonment. In the following years, I would live in most of the worst detention centers on the Island: El Principe Castle, Melena, and the horrible Boniato Prison in Oriente Province. Although I was a witness to many horrors during my years of incarceration, I also developed friendships with some of our nation's finest human beings.

Even in the most horrible concentration camps, under the worst conditions imaginable, culture has flourished within the prison walls. Faced with the anguish of imprisonment, political prisoners have used their lives within the wall to enrich themselves. At times, when repression diminished, we were sometimes allowed to receive books or painting materials from visitors. Even when we were not allowed books or gifts, we organized our own literary contests, poetry readings. Those who had education or knowledge became teachers to those who did not. Illiterate men learned to read and write, studied foreign languages and philosophy. I taught literature and often served as judge in the literary contests.

One of the best artists among political prisoners was Julio Hernandez Rojo, a one-time architecture student who had been a member of DRE, the Revolutionary Student Directorate. He is a gifted painter, now exiled in Miami.

There are men still in Cuba's concentration camps who deserve recognition for their writing talent; I am speaking of Guillermo Rivas and Ernesto Diaz Rodriguez.

Guillermo Rivas is a gifted poet, a journalist who once worked for the Cuban government in Brazil. He was also one of the main organizers of the Cuban Pavillion at Expo 67 in Canada. Now imprisoned, he has produced excellent poetry, very genuine, with a baroque style.

Ernesto Diaz Rodriguez is an amazing man. He is forty-eight years old, a humble fisherman from the town of Cojimar, near Havana, the same place that served as setting for Hemingway's "Old Man and the Sea." He left Cuba in 1961, becoming one of the most daring navigators and seaborne commandos of Alfa 66, the well-known anti-Castro movement. He had led the commando attack at the naval station at Tarara Beach in 1963. In 1964 he piloted the craft that dropped Eloy Gutierrez Menoyo and his infiltration squad in Oriente Province. In 1966 he dropped off Panchito Avila and an infiltration team in Pinar del Rio Province. On December 4, 1968, after dozens of daring trips, he was captured in Bahia Honda, near the port of Mariel.

I met Ernesto in the detention centers of Cuba. For years, I shared hundreds of hours with him, seeing him suffer beatings and long hunger strikes. During our years together I also saw him develop into a true intellectual, one of the finest poets that Cuba has produced this century.

Ernesto Diaz Rodriguez is a miracle product, a sensitive man who has spent his almost two decades in jail studying, learning every minute, developing his inner self. In 1976 some of his poetry was smuggled out of Cuba, published in a book called *Un Testimonio Urgente* (An Urgent Testimony). Acclaimed as a first-rate poet, this sensitive fisherman has produced quality literature under the most adverse circumstances.

It is common for political prisoners to write protest poetry, but it is unusual for a political prisoner in a concentration camp to write poetry aimed at children. Ernesto Diaz's latest book, *Campana del Alba* (Bell of Dawn), published in Miami in 1987, is a book of poetry for children. This work says much about the man. What a gentle soul, what human sensibility beats within his breast! To be able to write for children while being surrounded by hunger, disease, and oppression, to be able to show tenderness and love under the stress of totalitarian repression is the mark of a true poet. I sincerely believe that in time Ernesto Diaz's work will come to be regarded as the finest work in children's poetry in twentieth-century Hispanic literature.

Art, when it has quality, when it is genuine, transcends time. I believe that much of the literature of men like Guillermo Rivas, Ernesto Diaz and myself, as well as many others, will be studied in years to come by historians. Although Castro has intended to show us as right-wing reactionaries, our work, our art will prove that is not so, that we who have suffered his slavery were humanists, men of convictions, of principles, nationalists who stood up and suffered for our ideals.

In 1977, after ten years, I was released, allowed to work as a construction worker while serving out a five-year parole. But I would only spend three months outside the detention centers. In my brief period of time in the streets of Havana, I sent to friends in Miami a collection of poems, many of them critical of the regime. Published in Miami, *Impromtus* was well received by the exiles, but it did not gain me any friends among the members of State Security in Havana. Arrested once again, I was sent to Boniato Prison to serve the last five years of my original sentence.

I did not mind. The mission of a writer is to be true to his work and to be willing to suffer, if need be, to carry out his work. I knew that publishing the book would create personal problems, would send me back to confinement, but it was something that had to be done. I was willing to pay the price of defiance, to suffer for my work without regrets.

Inside the walls of Boniato, I continued to write, continued to teach, continued to spend time with friends like Ernesto Diaz. Although we were in a maximum security center, we still managed to smuggle out our writings. Some was done in the traditional manner of scribbling on little pieces of paper, passing notes to our relatives or friends in those rare times when visits were allowed. In some circumstances, however, we managed to gain the trust of guards — amazing as it may sound, impossible as it may seem.

One of the great weaknesses of totalitarian regimes is that the repressive force must be made up of men of flesh and blood rather than robots. Many of the guards of the Ministry of the Interior were sadists, but others were real human beings who in time came to realize that we were men of principle. One such guard, ashamed of wearing his uniform, helped us smuggle our work out of prison. Indeed, it was this guard, who still today wears the uniform, who risked his life in order to smuggle out of a maximum security center Ernesto Diaz's beautiful book of poetry for children.

This is the flaw in the system. Structures can be created to oppress, but the oppressors will feel guilt and eventually turn against the master who created the structure.

Before eventually coming to exile after my release from jail, I was able to spend almost three years in Havana. One incident particularly comes to mind from this period of time. I was introduced, through a friend, to a man who was and still is a high-ranking military officer of the regime. This officer was part of the "new breed," one who was too young to remember the struggle against Batista, the Bay of Pigs, or the Missile Crisis, having been a small child at the time. Curious when he found out that I had been a political prisoner, the officer asked me some questions. Obviously, he wanted to understand what had motivated me to conspire against the system. In the next few weeks we met several times and I saw a change in his attitude. I created doubts in his mind that had not existed there before. Eventually, he came to realize that his vision of what he wished Cuba to be was not very different from that of another Cuban who had spent fifteen years of his life imprisoned for his beliefs.

I have now spent over two years in the United States; yet, although I live in freedom, I miss Cuba. I wish I was back on the Island, still conspiring against the system, being useful to the struggle, even if it is only convincing an officer that there are other alternatives in life than living under the heel of oppression.

23
JORGE VALLS:
THE DEATH OF PEDRO LUIS BOITEL

A wiry man in his early fifties, Jorge Valls is one of Cuba's most brilliant and controversial intellects. A charter member of the Revolutionary Directorate that fought against Batista during the fifties, Valls was exiled in Mexico at the time of the triumph of the Cuban Revolution.

In 1964, Valls dared to defend Marcos Rodriguez, a friend from his DR days then being accused of having been an informant for Batista's police. Feeling that Rodriguez was being used as a scapegoat in a power struggle between Fidel Castro and the old Communists of the PSP, the Popular Socialist Party, Valls stood up in court for his friend, although he knew that this moral stand would not save Rodriguez, whose fate had been cast by the purging powers. Rodriguez was executed and Valls went on to serve twenty years and forty days as a plantado *a prisoner in rebellion.*

Currently living in New York, where he earns a modest living as a writer, Valls tells in his interview of his perspective of the Cuban Revolution and of the last days of Pedro Luis Boitel, the engineering student who died on May 24, 1972, after a hunger strike. Boitel, Cuba's best-known martyr in the present struggle, was a cellmate of Valls for several years.

First of all, we must understand, we must admit to ourselves, that history is irreversible and that the Cuban Revolution is irreversible. The Cuban Revolution, whether we like it or not, has left its imprint on our culture, on our society, on the ten million souls that together form our nation. We can change the future, but we cannot change the past.

The sun rises and sets every day. Yesterday's sun does not return. It belongs to the past. Everything in life has a mathematical progression. After number one comes two, and after two comes three. After Monday comes Tuesday and then Wednesday. What we do on one day we can change on another, but we cannot erase it or pretend it never existed.

What we are living now in Cuba is similar to the time that Europe faced from 1922 to 1945. The present government of Cuba is a synthesis of Stalin, Mussolini, and Hitler, a totalitarian phenomenon, a fascism-communism blend.

From the times of the struggle against Batista, I could see that these totalitarian attitudes were being formed. Fidel Castro at that time was a budding *caudillo* with militarist-fascist tendencies. His group of followers during his university days moved around him with the trappings and discipline of a fascist organization.

After Batista fled to Europe, I returned to Cuba from exile in Mexico. Several of my professors had lived in Europe during the time of the rise of fascism. I had studied the process, and then I saw this process in the flesh in 1959 Cuba. The uniforms, the berets, the flags, collective hysteria, speeches and rallies. The revolution proclaimed itself democratic, but democratic principles were violated from the first day with mass executions, with sham trials. No attempt was made to help the situation. When a group of air force pilots were acquitted by a revolutionary tribunal, Castro himself ordered them retried and found guilty.

Fidel Castro became one of the great emperors of the twentieth century. With personal appeal, he substituted a structured, collective conscience with an emotional, collective hysteria. Castro demanded executions in public, and the masses chorused his cries. Castro admitted that he had lied to the people, cynically telling them that he had done so for their own welfare, and the masses cheered him. The whole nation became shrouded in a collective shame.

It was a bad time in my life. The problem with being sane at the time of collective insanity meant that either I was the one insane or I possessed the truth. In time, as hysteria began to decline, came the division of factions. The minority, led by Castro, controlled the structures of power, reorganizing the fiber of society at their whim. As rebellion grew, the Cuban nation was plunged into a collective genocide which has cost the lives of thousands throughout the last three decades.

I went to prison, as thousands of others also did, and I do not believe that I deserve to be considered a hero for my stand. I simply did what I felt appropriate, acted as I felt I should, and paid the price accordingly.

Among the political prisoners that I knew, Pedro Luis Boitel was most unique. A young university student who had publicly opposed the takeover of the Student Federation by the regime, he was eventually arrested, being condemned to forty-two years' imprisonment. Through his hunger strikes he became the best known of all prisoners in rebellion serving time in Castro's detention centers. Boitel was a living symbol. He reminded me of a character in one of Andre Malraux's works, a man who saw war as his individual quest. Boitel would fit into the metaphysical scope of anarchism, although he never defined himself as such. The struggle against the system was a very personal thing for him.

I remember after his next to the last hunger strike, as he explained to me what his intentions were, he blurted out: "Because a man alone can do no more."

That phrase defined him. Boitel saw himself as a man alone, as a single entity opposing this system, all alone. He had the pessimistic existentialism of Camus. War was a personal, individual process. He fought without worrying about strategic considerations. He saw himself as part of the struggle, as a symbol of the struggle.

When he entered his last hunger strike, he simply gave me a small piece of paper, a note declaring that he was entering a hunger strike, that I should not interfere. We had adjoining beds. I sat on my cot, looked at him, and saw in Boitel a death wish.

He refused to eat. After fifteen days, officers of the Ministry of the Interior came to see him, asked him if he wanted anything. But Boitel did not answer. After thirty days they returned, but Boitel still did not answer.

I wanted to communicate with him, but after he entered his last hunger strike Pedro Luis only talked to two prisoners, Osvaldo Figueroa and Rafael Gonzalez.

I saw him die minute by minute, week by week. And I could not do anything, only sit on my cot and pray. After a certain amount of time he was in a state of stupor, as though he was dozing.

We asked the penal authorities to feed Boitel intravenously, but they ignored our request. After the body had fed upon fat and muscles, it attacked the central nervous system. After fifty days Boitel did not sleep; he only laid on his cot unmoving, staring, without uttering a sound.

A few hours before he died, the prison authorities took him away on a stretcher. He was a shrunken shell of bones and dried skin. The color of his skin was the color of wax on a candle. From my neck I took a religious medal of the Sacred Heart, which I placed under his pillow. He died stoically.

This was the worst time of my life. The only thing that sustained me were my religious convictions, my faith in God. I have always had this faith, this belief.

The saddest thing about our struggle has been the cost in human life on both sides. Man is unique, immortal, unsubstitutable. There was only one Pedro Luis Boitel. There is only one Jorge Valls. Procreation can create new beings, but it cannot duplicate existing ones nor can it bring back to life those who have died. The biggest failure of the system has been this, not to understand that man is unique and cannot be substituted.

Who confronts the forces of totalitarianism? Armies? No, for armies become defenders of political structures. What opposes the machinery, the oppressive structure, is the concept of individual man, unique and absolute — the human person in the absolute affirmation of his conviction, the living confession of his faith, of truth, beyond pain or death.

Index

211